IT'S YOUR WORLD— IF YOU DON'T LIKE IT, CHANGE IT

Activism for Teenagers

Mikki Halpin

SIMON PULSE

New York London Toronto Sydney

For Ruby, who has already changed the world

 SIMON PULSE

An imprint of Simon & Schuster Children's Publishing Division

1230 Avenue of the Americas, New York, NY 10020

Copyright © 2004 by Mikki Halpin

All rights reserved, including the right of reproduction in whole or in part in any form.

SIMON PULSE, Series logo, and colophon are registered trademarks of Simon & Schuster, Inc.

Designed by Greg Stadnyk

The text of this book was set in Apollo and Swiss.

Manufactured in the United States of America

First Simon Pulse edition September 2004

2 4 6 8 10 9 7 5 3 1

Library of Congress Control Number 2004109045

ISBN 0-689-87448-0

The issues • put up a peace poster • interview a veteran of war • organize a teach-in at your school • start a faith-based peace coalition • go to a big protest • Ana's story • Hannah's story • the 5-minute activist • resources

Fighting the Spread of HIV/AIDS .133

The issues • get tested • fight for comprehensive sex education • get local businesses to sign an anti-discrimination pledge • other activism ideas • Laura's story • Henry's story • the 5-minute activist • resources

Stopping School Violence and Bullying 166

The issues • make an anti-violence contract with your parents • distribute a flyer about the warning signs of possible school violence • create a bully box • connect with an at-risk youth • Britt's story • Missy's story • resources

Defending Women's Rights 189

The issues • learn about feminist history • discuss feminism with someone from another generation • speak out about dating violence • find out if your school is Title IX compliant • have a letter-writing party to fight for women's reproductive rights • Sara's story • Erica's story • the 5-minute activist • resources

Protecting Civil Rights and Civil Liberty .230

The issues • find out what data the government has on file about you • start an alternative school paper • do an art project about surveillance in your community • host

a video screening about the Fourth Amendment •
Ashley's story • Alan's story • resources

Promoting Tolerance Toward Lesbian, Gay, Bisexual, Transgender, and Questioning Youth 259

The issues • talk to your parents about an lgbtq issue in the news • start a gay/straight alliance at your school • assess whether your school is safe for lgbtq youth • make a voter guide • Sarah's story • Stacey's story • resources

You Can So Change the World

There's more to being a teenager than dating drama, shopping, and video games. You know this, but it probably seems like the rest of the world doesn't. There are things you care about and things that you want to change. There are things that *have* to change. You have the power to change them.

Right now in the United States, twenty-six percent of the population is under eighteen. That's more than seventy million people. Imagine what it would be like if you and everyone around you got to tell the world what you think. Don't wait until you're old enough to vote to take action. Starting today, starting right now, you can make your voice heard on the issues that matter to you.

This book is about activism, a word that is intimidating to a lot of people. When they hear about an "activist," they imagine some crazy guy with a picket sign on the evening news, protesting something they've never even heard about. Well, that's one kind of activist. I like to think of an activist as someone who acts on his or her beliefs and values.

Acting on your beliefs can happen in a lot of ways. You might buy only organic food, or you might circulate a petition to ask for organic food in your school cafeteria. Some activists are agitators; some aren't. Some are connected to larger organizations, and others do things solo. Activism is a continuum, and you have to tailor your actions in a way that's comfortable for you. But I bet that once you get going and see the changes you can make, you'll find yourself becoming more and more outspoken and committed.

Here's a good example of activism. Kayla Gernrich and Sara Stowell are sixteen-year-olds who live in Milton, Vermont. Their best friend, Allison Barkyoumb, had a heart condition that was life threatening—getting a heart transplant was her only option. Allison was on the transplant list for more than three weeks, and died while still waiting for a heart. Kayla and Sara, while grieving for their friend, learned that it's often difficult for teenagers to get transplants because other teens don't know that they can arrange to be donors.

In March 2003 Kayla and Sara started EarthAngels, a grassroots group that educates teenagers about organ donation and explains how to become a donor. Kayla and Sara could have done other things; they could have hooked up with a larger, national group and lobbied Congress to promote education about organ donation; they could have set up a scholarship in Allison's name to give to heart transplant survivors; they could have done a fundraiser car wash and given the money to the American Heart Association. They are doing what feels right to them, and they know that they are making a difference. (The EarthAngels Web site is www.earthangelsorg.com.)

Why People Become Activists

People become activists for all sorts of reasons. Some people choose to speak out on an issue after losing a loved one, like Kayla and Sara did. Others might be dealing with injustice in their own lives, or seeing it around them, and decide to fight. Many activists feel a moral or religious obligation to help others and work toward the greater good. You might become an activist for what seem like purely selfish reasons—you don't want to drink tap water with pollutants in it; that's valid too.

But the reason that most people *stay* activists is this: It feels good. It feels right to give back and to be a part of something bigger than yourself. No matter how big of an individualist you are, you aren't alone in this world, and helping others will also benefit you. Besides that, activism can be a lot of fun—you can meet others who share your beliefs, learn more about the world around you, and do things you never thought you'd do.

One Person *Can* Make a Difference

You might be thinking, *Well, I'm just one person. How big of a difference can I make?* There are two answers to that question. First, one person can totally make a difference. You are a citizen of the world, and what you do matters. Whether you are sitting at your computer writing letters, challenging a racist remark, or putting an anti-war sign in your window for the whole neighborhood to see, your actions are affecting people and making change. Second, you don't have to go it alone. You can get your friends to do activist stuff with you, or you can hook up with people who are already working on the issue you are interested in.

Choosing Your Cause

It might be totally obvious to you what your cause is—

you know already that you want to be an animal welfare activist or that you want to get involved in the fight against HIV/AIDS. If you know already, that's great. Some people have a harder time figuring out exactly where they want to put their energies—there are a lot of issues out there. It's worth taking a little time to figure out what you really want to do—if you try to do too much, you run the risk of burning out.

Think about what really bugs you. Is there one issue that seems to come up over and over in different ways? Try going through a week of your life writing down all of the things that strike you as wrong. (Okay, it might be a long list, but try it anyway.) Look down your list and see if there is a common theme. If your list contains a lot of things like "The girls at my school get hassled by the guys in the hallways," "Our science teacher always calls on guys first," and "My female friends all seem to think that having unsafe sex is okay," then doing some women's rights activism might be a good fit for you.

Here are some other things to keep in mind when choosing your cause:

- There is no perfect, ideal issue. It would be nice if the sun came out and trumpets played when you hit on the right one, but that's not going to happen.
- Remember that everything is interrelated. If you choose to work on environmental issues, you are also indirectly helping animals. If you are active in promoting free speech, then your work might enable an anti-war activist to be heard.
- Choosing a cause that benefits you directly is okay, and even desirable! If you and your brothers and sisters all have asthma, and you decide to

work on getting better health services in your community, that's just fine.

- Along those lines, think about choosing a cause that you know your friends will be interested in also. It's fun to do things in groups and they might have ideas you haven't thought of yet.

- It's not unusual to be active in several causes, or to sometimes switch your focus. You might do a lot of animal welfare activism but also be on some civil rights mailing lists. Or maybe you start off working to change your school's sex ed curriculum, and then become involved in volunteering at your local free clinic.

Do Your Research

Research your cause and arm yourself with facts. Online is a great place to research . . . up to a point. Google is your friend, but you can't trust everything that comes up in a search engine. It's good to verify things for yourself as much as possible. If a Web site claims that there is a superfund (that means extremely toxic) site in your neighborhood, cross-check it with the EPA site or www.scorecard.org, where you can enter your zip code and get environmental information back. Try not to go into an online trance, where you just keep clicking on more and more Web sites. Take notes and keep track of where you learn what.

Libraries are another good place to research. Not only do they have, well, books, but they also have tons of reference materials and librarians who can help you. Use reference material like old newspapers and magazines to learn about your cause and gather information you can use, like speeches your principal has made to the school board. The library is also a great place to get names and addresses you might need. The librarians can help you with your work and point you to things you wouldn't find on your own. (Plus, librarians are often activists themselves! They work to prevent books and Web sites from being banned, to stop the government from looking at your private records, and to promote public access to information.)

Find out who the major activist groups are that work on your issue. You could go to a few of their meetings, or check out some newsletters to see what specific kinds of activism are happening in your area—marches, letter-writing campaigns, or whatever. Maybe you'll join a campaign already in progress, or your research will spark an idea no one has thought of yet.

This book has chapters on many of the major issues that teenagers say they care about: racism, animal welfare, the environment, women's rights, war, HIV/AIDS, civil rights, school violence, and the rights of gay, lesbian, bisexual, transgender, and questioning youth. If you want to get going on one of these issues, then head right for that chapter. But you don't need to limit yourself to the causes in this book. You might choose to become active in suicide prevention, domestic violence awareness, or anti-globalization—there are a million issues and sub-issues out there, and one of them is right for you. No matter what your cause, this book can help you choose the level of activism you are comfortable with and guide you on your way to becoming an activist.

How This Book Works

This book is organized into broad topical chapters. Each chapter begins with an introduction to the issue: who it affects, who is involved, what's at stake, and what's happening right now. The issues section also talks about what different activist groups are doing in relation to that topic.

Running down the side of the main chapter text are profiles of teenagers who are activists working on the chapter topic. The profiles are intentionally diverse; reading through them you can see that there is a level of commitment and engagement that suits every individual.

The main part of every chapter is suggestions for activism projects, divided into four sections: The At-Home Activist, The Campus Activist, The Community Activist, and The 5-Minute Activist. You should probably read through all of the project ideas before you decide which one you want to do—or you might end up doing more than one of them. If you don't see a project that appeals to you, try reading the other chapters—many of the projects in the book can be adapted to other issues. You can also look through the resources at the end of each chapter—the Web sites that are listed will have even more ideas.

The At-Home Activist section has projects that you can do without even leaving your house. They might involve your family or be something that you do on your own. These projects are also good ones to start off with if you are new to activism. Don't discount home-based activism—it can be very powerful. It's not like you are an activist out in the world, and then you go home and stop being one. Your at-home work could lead to some big changes in your own personal behaviors and habits, or the behaviors of your entire household, and it can also help you reinforce values that led to your activism.

The project ideas for the Campus Activists tend to be a bit more elaborate and require a bit more time than the at-home activist projects do. (But they are still totally doable.) Being an activist at school is natural—you spend most of your time at school, so it's a great place to speak your mind and try to change things. Activism at school also offers a lot of ways to involve your friends in what you are doing.

School offers a great place to reach your peers, and there are certainly a lot of things that need to change at most schools. But it can also be a little intimidating to think about being the person who initiates the change. That's why most of the campus projects suggest you enlist others. Most teenagers who take a deep breath and are willing to stand up for what they think is right discover that there are a lot of other students who feel the same way they do. Planning your project carefully and getting others involved at the organizing level can ensure that your efforts are successful.

Community activism is probably the closest thing to what most people think of when they think of activism. A community activist project will involve your community—it will educate them, help them, or allow them to express their feelings on an important topic. Examples of community activism include an AIDS awareness campaign, fighting to get your state or city to recognize domestic partnerships, or a peace rally in the park. A community project generally offers everyone, even total strangers, the opportunity to be involved.

A community project requires that you reach out beyond your own circle of friends and family and make some new connections. This is called organizing—getting a community together to make change. That way you can split up tasks and get more done, as each of you develops areas of expertise. If you are planning to put AIDS awareness ads in your local paper, one person could work on getting the paper to donate the space, one could design the ads, while another one researches the best information to put in the ads.

In most of the chapters you'll see a section called the 5-Minute Activist. The action projects in this section are super quick and easy things you can do on the Internet to benefit the cause(s) you care about. Basically these projects involve visiting one of two types of Web sites: "click to e-mail" and "click to donate."

A "click to e-mail" Web site is a site with an interface that lets you quickly and easily send e-mails to select people (usually United States Senators and Representatives). Most sites have a boilerplate text written—you just add your name and click. Sometimes they ask you to enter your zip code so that they can send the e-mail to the congressperson who represents your area. The sites are updated often with new e-mails focused on recent events or pending legislation.

Letter writing can be an effective way to work within the system to effect change. You should know, though, that e-mails are not generally considered as effective as regular mail—senators and representatives know how easy it is to send an e-mail, so they pay more attention when someone takes the time to sit down and write a letter on paper. That said, collective e-mail campaigns have been known to raise awareness and draw attention to particular issues.

This book only recommends "click to e-mail" Web sites when "click to donate" sites for the chapter topic aren't available. A "click to donate" site is set up in order to let anyone, anywhere, with a Net connection contribute to the charity of his or her choice. The way "click to donate" sites work is that the group who runs the site asks companies to be sponsors. Usually they ask companies whose products are related to the cause, like asking a pet food company to sponsor an animal rescue site. The company agrees to donate a certain amount of money to the charity for every click made to the donation button.

Why do companies do this? Well, it's corporate philanthropy, which does exist (really!), but it's also a form of advertising. There's nothing wrong with that, but you should be aware. The corporation knows that when people go to the charity site to click, they will see the company's logo, and perhaps associate that company with the good work the site is doing.

What a lot of people don't realize about "click to donate" sites is that you can usually only click once per day. That sounds simple, but it's not. The programs that tabulate the clicks calculate them on a twenty-four-hour cycle. That means that if you click one day at three p.m. and the next day at noon, your second click won't be counted because twenty-four hours have not gone by.

There are ways to deal with this. You might want to download a little reminder program, such as the one at www.easydonations.net/clicktodonate.htm. It will alert you when it's time to click. Setting a reminder up on your cell phone is a good idea too.

Efforts have been made to vet the Web sites listed

in the 5-Minute Activist sections and throughout the book to make sure they are legit. They are sites that have been around for a while, and ones that are associated with reputable charities and organizations. Any specifics mentioned about a site were current as of this writing in June 2004. Feel free to do your own investigating too, of course. Exercise the same care you do elsewhere on the Internet—don't give out personal information like your phone number, social security number, or address; don't give out credit card information except on secure sites; and never agree to meet alone with someone you don't know. For more information on Internet safety, check out www.safekids.com/safeteens/safeteens.htm.

The last section in every chapter is the resource section. This section lists Web sites and books that may be helpful to you as an activist. The materials have been chosen because they are informative, and also because they are specifically activist in nature—they have ideas for projects you can do and ways for you to connect with other activists, or they will otherwise help you in the projects you choose to do. At the very end of the book, the General Activism Resources section lists books and Web sites that are applicable to all areas of activism, like handbooks and organizing manuals.

A Few More Things

As you move forward, remember that the things that make you a good person also make you a good activist. Being kind and respectful to others, even if you disagree with them, will help every project you undertake go more smoothly. Sometimes it's hard not to get caught up in a conflict with a person or a group and lose yourself in hating, but when you sense that happening, take a step back. Focus on the injustice you are fighting or the good you are doing. Use your anger to do what you can, and don't waste it on people who aren't open to change. Figure out a way to go around them.

Sometimes you might also need to go around people who are on the same side of the issues that you are. Some older activists and established activist groups aren't as welcoming to young people as they could be. They might point you to a youth chapter that's aimed at college and graduate students, or they might think you'd be a great office assistant until you're old enough to be a real activist.

If this happens to you, you can stick around and try to change the group from within, or bail on them and find a place that's a better fit—or you could start your own group. When New York City's high school activists ran up against resistance from older activists, they formed Youth Bloc (www.youthbloc.org), which has now become a respected organization in its own right. (Youth Bloc members must be under eighteen or still in high school.)

Your parents or guardians might also express some skepticism when you start speaking out about the issues that are important to you. It's possible they are also buying into that stereotype of the shallow teenager. But talking to your parents about your values—values you probably got from them—and why you want to act on them might convince them that this isn't just an adolescent phase. It's who you are.

Good luck with whatever you do!

Helping Animals

Every year in America, more than four million companion animals are needlessly put to death in shelters. Countless more are living on the streets, sick and hungry. Others are abused or neglected. Twenty million are being used in laboratories. Pro-animal activists work to save and care for these animals, and to be their advocates because they can't speak for themselves. They set up no-kill shelters, rescue feral animals, and educate people about responsible pet ownership. Some activists work to discourage or end animal testing and the use of animals in research or education. They may also seek to ensure that any animal used in research does not suffer needlessly. Other animal welfare activists work toward preserving habitats for wild animals, ending sport hunting, and creating refuges for those whose habitat has been lost.

You are probably already familiar with some of the major animal activist organizations: the World Wildlife Fund, the American Society for the Prevention of Cruelty to Animals (ASPCA), the Humane Society of the United States, the Philippe Cousteau Foundation, and People for the Ethical Treatment of Animals (PETA). Many people who care deeply about animals generously give money to support these institutions and their work.

You don't need cash to donate if you want to contribute to animal welfare. One approach is to change your own behavior. Going vegetarian and seeking out cruelty-free products to use in your home are easy steps that anyone can take. You can take your activism further with some of the action projects in this chapter. Volunteering or working at shelters, reporting cases of abuse and neglect, and being a responsible pet owner are also ethical choices that promote animal welfare. Helping animals has the potential to become your life's work, since there are many career choices that can promote animal welfare. This is a movement that, like environmentalism, touches almost every aspect of life on earth.

You may have heard of a branch of animal activism known as the animal rights movement. Broadly speaking, the people in the animal rights movement believe that animals should have the same rights as humans. They often take hard-line positions on issues and may use extreme tactics to reach their goals. For example, rather than working to make research using animals more humane, and to reduce the number of animals used, animal rights activists believe that all animal testing and research should be eliminated immediately. The majority of animal rights activists work to achieve their goals in traditional ways like boycotting. But there are others who do or condone unlawful acts such as breaking into research laboratories and freeing the animals. Don't get involved with anyone who is breaking the law. Stick with well-established groups like the ones mentioned in this chapter and channel your love of animals into legal and positive change.

Helping animals is an area of activism that emphasizes compassion. You are advocating for those who truly cannot speak for themselves. It can be especially rewarding because the results are often more immediate and less abstract. You can see with your eyes when you've helped a dog or a cat get adopted into a good home, or when you've worked to prevent a habitat from being destroyed. And best of all, you get to spend a lot of time with the creatures that inspired you to become an activist in the first place—the animals themselves.

THE AT-HOME ACTIVIST

Be a Responsible Pet Owner

If you or your family have a pet, or are thinking about getting one, make sure that you are doing everything you can to keep it healthy and safe.

Adopt your pet from a shelter. Some shelter animals have been rescued or abandoned; others had to be given up when their owners moved or died. These are animals who need and deserve a loving home. They usually have been spayed or neutered (or it is a condition of adoption) and have all their shots. Although many shelters are no-kill—which means that they will take care of every animal they have,

SHAKIRA'S STORY

Shakira Croce is seventeen years old and she is a junior at Gainesville High in Gainesville, Georgia.

I think the first time my love of animals led me to make a stand about something was when I was about twelve. I became a vegetarian. Some of my parents' friends were vegetarians and that was a new concept to me. Before that I hadn't really thought about what I was eating. They told me about how most of the animals that [become] food come from factory farms where they're kept in small cages. They go to slaughter with no painkillers or anything. I did some more research and I was horrified. I thought of my pet cat who I love. It was like, "What's the difference between Smokey and the animals that I'm eating?" That's when it clicked. This cat is an animal who gives me love and affection and I wouldn't want to eat my cat or anything.

So I got into being a vegetarian. I was in seventh grade, and at my middle school there wasn't anything

whether or not it finds a home—some are not. About half of the animals in shelters across America every year are euthanized because they have nowhere to go.

Most shelters will ask you some questions and want to know about your home situation before they let you adopt a pet. They want to make sure that it will be a good fit, and that both you and the animal will be happy. In many cases the shelter will promise to take the pet back if it doesn't work out for any reason. It's tempting to get your pet from the pet store, but pet store animals cost more and often come from inhumane puppy mills or other unethical sources. If you or your family have your heart set on a certain breed of animal, you can ask a local shelter to keep on the lookout for you, or you can contact a rescue group particularly for that breed.

Spay, neuter, and vaccinate your pet. Spaying and neutering is the only way to stop or slow the animal over-population in this country. Thousands of animals are in shelters and on the streets because of this growing problem. Just one unneutered cat and her young can be responsible for 420,000 kittens in seven years. Even if you think you will find a home for all the kittens or puppies your pet has, every one of them will be taking the place that could have gone to an animal in a shelter waiting to be adopted. Vaccinating your pets and keeping up with their booster shots will keep them healthy and prevent them from catching any diseases if they come into contact with other animals. It doesn't cost much: The Humane Society estimates that the average cat owner will spend about a hundred dollars on veterinary care every year; dog owners can expect to spend about twice that.

Get your pet an ID tag with your name and phone number on it. Some vets and shelters now offer to implant a microchip, which is painless for your pet, has all your information, and will never get lost. If you do get a microchip you should still get a collar and tag—if your neighbor finds your dog, he or she might not have a scanner!

One important thing that even the most responsible pet owners can forget is to prepare for your pet's welfare in case of a disaster. Whether it's a blackout, storm, earthquake, or other emergency, you and your family should have a plan that ensures that you and your pets will get through it safely.

One way to do this is to create a "go bag" with everything your pet might need for a few days and keep it with your other emergency supplies. Things to include are any medicine your pet requires, portable water and food bowls, some water and some food, a litter box, a leash, and a carrying bag. If for any reason you need to evacuate quickly, you can grab your pet and the bag and be ready to go. You might even want to have some fam-

vegetarian to eat at lunch except maybe once a week. Not even like a little bit of lettuce. So I went up to the head of the cafeteria and asked her, "Are there any vegetarian options or can you improvise any?" She said, "Well, we have cooked vegetables like once a week." And I said, "Yeah, having a cooked vegetable side isn't the same as having a vegetarian meal."

She said that there were no other kids who wanted a vegetarian option so that's where I came up with the idea of circulating a petition amongst my classmates and some teachers. It said that we wanted vegetarian options in the cafeteria, and I got about two hundred signatures in a week or two. Then I went back to her with it and she said that she'd had no idea that so many people were open to this and that she would see what she could do.

The experience of getting the signatures was really positive. I liked going around to people and meeting new people and talking to them about my own beliefs and ideas. A lot of the people were really open to the idea, and the ones who weren't could usually be persuaded. I

ily safety drills, including the pets, to make sure everyone knows what to do.

You could also connect with your neighbors who also have pets. In the event of a disaster, you can agree to look out for one another and each other's animals. Pledge that if for some reason your neighbors can't get home during an emergency, after making sure your own family is safe you will check on their pets, and they will do the same for you. (Make sure you know where one another's "go bags" are stored.)

If you can't commit to a pet, or are nervous about pet ownership, consider fostering. Fostering means that you take care of an animal until a home is found for it. Contact your local animal adoption centers to inquire about this—but be aware that the guidelines can be quite stringent (and you might end up falling in love with and keeping the pet).

Make Your Home a Cruelty-Free Zone

More and more cosmetic and home product companies are phasing out animal testing or rejecting it outright. Support these companies by buying and using their products. Write them letters to tell them you applaud their stance on animal testing. Look for the Coalition for Consumer Information on Cosmetics (CCIC) logo 🐇 on packages—this indicates that the company has adopted the coalition's no-animal-testing policy. You can also call the CCIC hotline at 1-888-546-CCIC for a list of companies that adhere to this standard. The CCIC Web site is www.leapingbunny.org.

Try checking the Web sites of your favorite products to see if they have taken a no-animal-testing position. Make sure not only that they don't conduct tests on their own, but also that they don't use in their products ingredients that have been tested on animals. If they don't have a position posted, write to them and ask what it is. Tell them you want to use their product but you can't if they are harming animals to create it.

THE CAMPUS ACTIVIST

Refuse Dissection

If you are dreading your science class requirement to dissect a frog or a fetal pig, there is something you can do about it. Some states (California, Florida, Illinois, Louisiana, Maine, Maryland, New York, Pennsylvania, and Rhode Island) and many local school boards will allow you to choose an alternative to dissection. You should do some research and see what the situation is for your school by calling the school district or school board and asking.

Start with your science teacher. Meet with him or her outside of classroom hours and explain why

would tell them why I'd become a vegetarian and what I'd learned in my research. Then we'd talk about why having a vegetarian option was a good idea. I told them that vegetarians shouldn't be discriminated against, and that even if you aren't a vegetarian, this is a great opportunity to get some better food.

We ended up getting a full salad bar with baked potatoes and everything like that, which was really nice. Not all the kids in the middle school were vegetarians. I knew of maybe a handful really, but all the kids really wanted a salad bar so that was really nice, a good alternative to the daily mystery meat.

Then in high school, my freshman year, I founded SPAAR, Students Promoting Awareness of Animal Rights. I was getting more involved in these types of issues and I thought, "Oh, it'd be so cool if we had a club for animal rights," but we didn't have one. I tried to found one, but it took almost the whole year to do.

I started out with a group of friends who were also interested in animal rights. There were about twenty-five

you don't want to participate in the dissection. You can say things like, "I fundamentally believe that harming animals just so I can learn anatomy or whatever is wrong." Be clear that this is about your core values, and not just because of the ickiness factor. If you found that your school district or state allows students to use alternative programs, point this out (and be able to prove it). Have an alternative idea ready to suggest. The Humane Society has materials such as a Digital Frog CD-ROM available for loan that can help you to avoid taking part in activities that go against your beliefs. Visit www.hsus.programs/research/alt_dissection.html for a list of the available materials. You can look for other ideas in the NORINA database (Norwegian Inventory of Audiovisuals) at oslovet.veths.no/NORINA.

If your science teacher says no, the next step is to go to the principal or vice principal. In this situation, it's best to have a bit more backup. You could ask your parents to write a letter supporting your decision, and bring some literature (also available at the humane society Web site) explaining that you would learn just as much with your alternative as with a dead animal. Point out that your alternative probably costs a lot less than buying the fetal pigs or frogs or whatever. If your principal isn't going for it, ask when the next school board meeting is and how you can get this matter put on the agenda.

Preparing for the school board meeting means getting the word out and having all your materials in order. Make a petition saying that you want to have dissection alternatives in your science class. Put up flyers around school and send e-mails asking your fellow students if they want to join you in asking for dissection alternatives. Have any interested parties sign your petition and ask them to come to the school board meeting with their parents. You should also ask any local animal welfare groups, shelters, or education reform organizations to come to the school board meeting. If they are willing to write a letter of support or even speak on your behalf, that's great.

Finally, you should contact your local media. You probably know who that is, but if you want some names and addresses, there is a tool on the Human Rights Campaign Web site (www.hrc.org) that lets you enter your zip code and get local media listings. Go to the site and click on "Take Action Resources." It's on the menu to the left. There's another one on the Congress.org site (www.congress.org)—click on "Media Guide" on the home page.

Now that you have the contact info for local media, make a press release to send out to them. You can do it in any word processing program. Always put your current contact information at the top of a press release. Give it a good headline, something like "Local Student to Challenge School Board's Dissection

of us, and we went to the principal's office. The reason I think it's a good idea to do things like have petitions or bring students with you is so you can show that you have a following, it's not just you. It's nice for you to have the ideas and be like the nucleus, but then you need to show that you have a following and more kids are interested in what you are interested in.

We all filed in and he was like, whoa. But then he really resisted the club. He never came out and actually said no for the first six months. He would just say things like, "You need a mission statement." I'd get that to him and then he'd say, "Well, you need to have a sponsor. . . ."

Finally after six months he said, "We live in the poultry capital of the world and I'm really not sure what the community's response is going to be to this. I don't think you can start your club." That didn't sound right. So that weekend I went on the Internet and I looked on a site that lists federal laws affecting students. I found Equal Access Law Title 20, Chapter 52, Section 4071, which says that if you have any clubs in your school, you have to allow students who

Policy." Put where and when the meeting is going to take place right underneath that. The body of your press release should be structured like a news story, with the most important facts first. It should also be written in the third person. In this case the important facts are:

- Your name, what school you go to, what year you are in school
- Why you refuse to participate in dissection
- The fact that you went to your teacher and your principal before deciding to go to the school board (give their names)
- The reasons they gave for turning you down
- The fact that you have proposed an alternative, and what that alternative is
- Who your supporters are (parents, fellow students, organizations)

Less important but still useful facts include:

- The other states and districts that allow alternatives to animal testing
- That science is a requirement for graduation so you have to take this class (if true)
- That dissection alternatives such as the Digital Frog CD-ROM are often cheaper than dissection

Make it look good by centering the headline and using a readable font like Palatino or Courier. Run the spell check and have someone else review your press release before you send it out. Faxing and mailing hard copies are still the best ways to distribute press releases. You can also e-mail it to the reporters you've chosen if you have their e-mail addresses, but many of them might not accept e-mail with attachments, so put it in the body of the e-mail as well.

Send your press release about a week before the board meeting and send another one that has "Reminder!" on it the day before. Having press at your event means that your issue will get as much attention as possible.

Your own prep for the school board meeting includes getting your materials together. Write a statement about why you do not want to participate in dissection. Be passionate, but be as clear as possible. Stay focused on your beliefs and why they mean you can't do the experiment. Explain that you think the school board should change its policy—don't complain about the unresponsiveness of your school administration. Tell them about your proposed alternative. Mention your supporters and the fact that you appreciate the chance to speak.

You should also make an information packet for everyone on the board, plus a few extra for the press and other people at the meeting. Each packet should have a copy of your statement with your contact information. You can make a fact sheet with some of the facts on your press release

want to start more clubs to start them.

I printed out the text of the law and I gave it to the principal's secretary to give to him. I guess it was pretty good follow-up, because a day or two later he called me down to his office and said, "Well, you need to find a time and a place for your club." That was the best feeling. So we started and we kind of advertised and told other people about how we'd gotten it started. We had about ten kids at the end of the year, and now we have about twenty; this is our second year.

We hold events for World Farm Animals Day and National Meat-Out Day to raise awareness. We hand out samples of vegetarian food and distribute leaflets. We also got CD-ROMs donated to our school to use as an alternative to dissection. We gave the CDs to our science department and now they aren't having any animal dissections at all this year. The program is just so great and less expensive and everything like that, so that was really good.

We also have seasonal campaigns. We just got finished with an anti-fur

and a timeline of when you began this process, when you met with the principal, etc. Put in copies of any letters of support and your petition if you have one. Include information about your proposed alternative.

Before the meeting, greet everyone who has come to support you and thank them for coming. Give members of the press or people who don't know about the issue copies of your information packet, and give one to each board member. If members of the press want to interview you, get their business cards first. You might want to ask one of your parents to be with you when you talk to the press. Answer their questions clearly and honestly, and take advantage of the opportunity to present your case. Repeat your core points: You are acting on deeply held beliefs, and you have an alternative that others have found educationally acceptable.

When the meeting begins, wait until your agenda item is called and walk up to the microphone or podium. You'll probably be nervous, but try to make eye contact with each board member as you give your presentation. Don't look down at your statement too much if you can help it. Different school boards have different rules of order, but they might ask you a few questions after you speak. Answer them as best you can, and refer them to your information packet when appropriate. If you get asked something you don't know, say something like, "I don't have that information at this moment but I can certainly get it to you." (Then actually do that after the meeting.) The "other side," if there is one, will probably also get to speak, and possibly your supporters.

If the school board votes right then and there, you'll have your answer. Often you have to wait a week or two. If you win, congratulations! Send out thank-you notes to everyone who helped you out and go off to your new, improved science class.

If you don't win, you have a few choices. You could suck it up and do the dissection. You could go to class every day but still refuse to take part in the experiment—the consequences for this might be that you get an F or a zero for that part of the class, depending on your school and how harsh the policies are. You can contact the American Civil Liberties Union and the Humane Society to see if they are willing to help you file a lawsuit to take further legal action.

Whatever happens, you've stood up for what you believe in, and you've possibly made it easier for the *next* student at your school who wants to refuse dissection.

Make An Animal Research College Guide

If you are a junior or a senior, you are probably gearing up for college—taking a lot of tests and try-

campaign where we put a display in our school media center with leaflets and stuff. We held a special meeting where the whole school is invited to come and watch, and we showed this video called *The Witness*. It's a really good documentary about the fur industry. We do stuff outside of school, like we volunteer at the Humane Society. Whenever there's some kind of animal rights legislation going through, we always call our senator and representatives.

SPAAR members, especially me, write letters to the editor rather frequently. We write them to the school paper but also to the local paper, which is a really good thing that gets the whole community involved. We usually write a response to something we see in the paper. Like if they cover hunting or something, then we'll write a series of letters that show an opposite point of view, like "Don't call it sportsmanship, it's not quite a sport." We've written about circuses and hunting, and a lot about the poultry industry, which is a big thing around here.

There are some things to do to make sure your letter

ing to decide where to apply. You and your classmates can make more informed decisions if you know what kind of research is happening at the schools you are considering. Making an animal research college guide is a great way to educate people about what goes on in laboratories, and it's useful, too.

It takes just a little digging to get the information about animal research on any given campus. A good way to start is to write a letter to the head of the science faculty or any on-campus research labs, asking them what types of animal research takes place there. Make your questions as specific as possible. Ask how the animals are housed, where they come from, what types of experiments are being conducted, what types of animals are being used, etc. Ask who is funding the research and what it is for.

The United States Department of Agriculture's Animal and Plant Health Inspection Service has two Web sites that can also help you find out about the policies at your potential colleges: www.aphis.usda.gov/ac and http://foia.aphis.usda.gov. It's probably easier to get information from state-funded schools—but private schools often are participating in federally funded programs that require them to disclose information.

After you've compiled information about your colleges of choice, make it available to other students. One good way is to create a little brochure or a flyer that gives the names of schools and what's going on where. Tell your classmates that you aren't telling them where to go to school—you are just giving them information that might help them make that choice. Make sure to include how and where you got your information.

THE COMMUNITY ACTIVIST

Volunteer at a Shelter

Your local animal shelter or rescue organization can always use a helping hand. If you have the time to commit to volunteering, you'll get to work hands-on every day with animals who need love and attention. But make sure that you are ready to deal with all aspects of animal care: You may have to clean cages or help with sick animals. Make sure you know what you are getting into before you promise to show up on a regular basis. Some shelters, such as the Brooklyn Animal Resource Coalition (www.barcshelter.org) in New York City, have walking programs. If you pass the screening to be a dog walker, you can show up whenever you have some free time and "check out" a dog to walk. The dog will get some exercise and companionship, and you will too. Make sure to investigate any shelter you get involved with. Ask if it's a no-kill shelter—that means that they will never euthanize animals.

gets published. Don't be too emotional. Try and stick with the facts and don't let it get too long—keep it to the point. I think the most important thing is to make sure you've checked and double-checked the sources of every fact you put in there. If you have just one sentence that might be kind of wrong in the whole letter, that's the only thing they're gonna pay attention to, so be very cautious of that.

When I first started writing I would always follow up like a week later. I'd call or e-mail to see if they were printing my letter. Now I've written so many I don't have to do that. The responses to my letters can get pretty lively. I remember once there were like four letters all responding to this letter that I had written a few days before. I'd written a letter that asked questions like, "Was Jesus a hunter?" "Are his teachings of mercy and compassion in line with shooting a deer with a semiautomatic rifle?" People were pretty upset about that.

Sometimes it's kind of hard seeing so much negative feedback. But the people who come up and say, "Wow, I really liked that last letter, I'm so glad someone's speaking

Be an Active Citizen for Local Animals

If you see an animal being abused or neglected, report it. This includes dogs being chained or tethered for long periods of time, or circus or other show animals that show signs of neglect. Stray dogs and cats need your help—call an animal rescue organization associated with a no-kill shelter that can come and get the animal. They will attempt to find the owner, and if the animal is lost (or feral), they will spay or neuter it and make sure that it goes to a good home or is otherwise cared for. In time you may learn enough to attempt to trap strays or ferals yourself—but don't do this until you are confident you can do it safely. You can get special safe traps from your Humane Society. If an animal seems sick, aggressive, or injured, don't attempt to touch it—it will react instinctively and you could get hurt. Call the appropriate authorities and keep an eye on the animal until they arrive.

Start a "Pets Are Wonderful Support" Chapter in Your Town

Pets Are Wonderful Support, also known as PAWS*, is a group that helps people who are homebound due to illness care for their pets. PAWS volunteers go into their clients' homes in order to clean, feed, and walk the animal, and basically do whatever it needs. That way, the pet doesn't need to be removed from the home and both the animal and its owner benefit. Studies show that living with their beloved pets can aid people's recovery and relieve the suffering of even the sickest patients. By working with PAWS, you are helping both animals and people.

*Unsurprisingly, there are many pro-animal organizations that use the acronym "PAWS." In addition to Pets Are Wonderful Support, there's the Performing Animal Welfare Society, the Progressive Animal Welfare Society, and Paws for Life, to name a few. It can be hard to keep them straight. The Progressive Animal Welfare Society maintains a pretty good list of all the PAWS: www.paws.org/about/wrongpaws/. By working for PAWS you are helping both animals and people.

PAWS was originally started to help people with HIV/AIDS but now helps many other types of people. It is based in San Francisco and only serves that community, but its Web site has a great section explaining how you can start your own PAWS chapter. Download it here: www.pawssf.org. The tool kit is a little bureaucratic—it goes on about how to get a board of directors and apply for nonprofit status. If you don't want to deal with all that, you might want to see if you can partner with a group that is already helping those who are homebound.

up" make it all worth it. I just don't really listen or take to heart any of the criticism. My parents are really supportive of me. Whenever I write a letter, they're always really excited when it's printed. I know my mom especially might be a little defensive when negative responses appear because she feels like they are talking about her baby, but I think my parents realize that the people who are writing these letters aren't worth it. They don't let it bother them because I refuse to let it bother me.

I will always be an activist. I can't see myself not being involved in something. When you know something's wrong you have to do something about it, you can't just sit there and not do anything. I would tell anyone who wants to be an activist to never underestimate his or her own power. When someone says, "You can't do it," make it your goal to prove them wrong. Persistence really does pay off. I've really learned that through activism everyone can make a difference. It's all about being a compassionate person, being comfortable with your beliefs, and wanting other people to be aware of different views.

THE 5-MINUTE ACTIVIST

The Animal Rescue Site

Launched in 2002 by two environmental activists, the Animal Rescue Site is one of the best-known "click to donate" sites. Every click provides a bowl of food to an animal in need. The program is sponsor-supported and the food is distributed by the site's charity partners, which include the North Shore Animal League America and some wildlife sanctuaries. You can visit every day and click.

www.theanimalrescuesite.com

Care2

This is an environmental directory site, but their action center includes several ways to "click to donate" for animals. They have an option for primates that flows money to the Jane Goodall Institute, one for big cats that operates through the Wildlife Conservation Society, and one that will allow you to help provide veterinary care for animals in need through the Humane Society. One visit a day.

www.care2.com

RESOURCES

Web Sites

The American Society for the Prevention of Cruelty to Animals

Founded in 1866, the ASPCA is the nation's oldest

humane society. It does do a vast amount of work—everything from animal poison control and local shelter outreach to recommending books for kids. It publishes *Animal Watch* magazine and produces *Animal Precinct*, a TV show on Animal Planet about New York City's Humane Law Enforcement agents. The site is full of information (the FAQs alone are worth a visit) and the Fight Animal Cruelty page has a lot of ideas and resources for actions. Check out the lobbying section too.

www.aspca.org

The Animal Concerns Community

The main feature here is an online forum where you can connect with other people who care about animals. The daily newsfeed is really useful as well, and there is a comprehensive database of resources for information on over a dozen animal-related topics, including animal rescue, breeding, violence, neglect, and animals being used as food and clothing.

www.animalconcerns.org

You can read more about SPAAR on the Web site, www.geocities.com/spaarclub /SPAAR.html. The full text of the Equal Access Law is here: www4.law.cornell.edu/uscode /20/4071.html.

EMMA'S STORY

Emma Barnett is fifteen and a sophomore at Bard High School Early College in New York City.

When I was twelve, I was in PETCO, which is a big pet store in Union Square in Manhattan. Inside PETCO they have this area with a lot of cats for adoption. I was looking at the cats, and Marlene, the woman who runs the adoption center, came up to me and asked me what I thought of maybe wanting to volunteer there.

I've always liked animals but I'd never pursued [anything in that field], so when she offered I was really excited about it. I came in the next day. At first I wasn't really sure what to do so I just asked and they gave me stuff to do. I was really enthusiastic. I started off cleaning cages and things like that, just taking care of the

Farm Animal Reform Movement

FARM is a nationwide group whose aim is to reform people's eating practices and the treatment of farm animals. The group advocates a plant-based diet while agitating for better monitoring of farm animals and more stringent laws to prevent abuse. FARM also works to bring animal and vegetarian issues into our national political discussion by raising them with candidates during primaries and at conventions.

www.farmusa.org

The Humane Society of the United States

The Humane Society works to create a world where human and animal interaction is guided by compassion. The site offers information on pets, wildlife, farm animals, marine mammals, and animals in research. It gives suggestions for pet adoption and offers guidelines for making your pet feel comfortable in his or her new home. You can also watch videos on topics ranging from the treatment of exotic pets to choosing the right veterinarian. Want to do more? Visit Animal Sheltering Online (www.hsus2.org/sheltering) for volunteer and job opportunities.

www.hsus.org

HumaneTeen

This is an offshoot of the Humane Society. The site encourages visitors to start pro-animal clubs, and offers a lot of support material. The stories of what some of these groups have done are inspiring. The site is super useful even if you don't go the club route, though, with ideas for animal-oriented term papers and projects to do (like teaching younger kids about humane treatment of animals). It's a great starting point for any animal activist.

www.humaneteen.org

Kids for Animal Rights in Education

Founded by fifteen-year-old Brittney Buckley, KARE's mission is to reach out to others and educate them about animal welfare in the hopes that suffering can be reduced. Most of the members are also teenagers. There is an area where you can interact with other activists, and a lot of cruelty-free resources. The site's a little wonky, but if you poke around you can find everything.

www.kare.homestead.com

People for the Ethical Treatment of Animals and PETA2

There's a lot of misinformation out there about PETA, so it's

cats. Then as time went by I had more responsibilities. I was able to answer people's questions, and I was able to train new volunteers.

KittyKind is the name of the organization that runs the adoption program in PETCO. It is a nonprofit, no-kill cat rescue and adoption group in NYC. They've saved thousands of cats. These cats come from everywhere. People find them on the streets and in abandoned buildings. We get some from animal hospitals and shelters. Sometimes people just drop them off. We've had tons of times when people just left cats in boxes in the store and snuck out.

When a cat comes in, we take it to the vet and have it tested. We have some vets we work with who give us discounts. If the cat is very sick or needs to be socialized, usually we have a volunteer or someone foster it until it's ready to go up for adoption. Then we put it in one of the cages at KittyKind and keep taking care of it until someone takes it home.

If someone comes in and wants a cat, we have them talk to one of the adoption representatives. The representative asks them

worth looking to see how the organization describes itself. Its home page says, "PETA believes that animals deserve the most basic rights—consideration of their own best interests regardless of whether they are useful to humans. Like you, they are capable of suffering and have interests in leading their own lives; therefore, they are not ours to use—for food, clothing, entertainment, or experimentation, or for any other reason." This fairly simple statement is the cornerstone of one of the most powerful animal activist groups around today. PETA distributes educational literature, creates slick promotional videos, does outreach to seemingly everyone, has a zillion campaigns, and yes, protests at fashion shows and makes posters with naked actresses on them. Its main Web site has fair-minded FAQs explaining its positions, action alerts, and a variety of projects you can get involved with, most of which are noncontroversial. PETA2.org is the teen site, and PETA also operates www.college-activist.com and www.animalactivist.com.
www.peta.org

Scientists Center for Animal Welfare

SCAW is a twenty-five-year-old educational association concerned with the treatment of animals in institutional research. It seeks to reform research and provide ethical guidelines, not to stop research. It has a few publications, has an oversight committee, and provides workshops on the subject. The site is worth checking out to see how those on the "inside" are dealing with the laboratory animal issue.
www.scaw.com

The Vegetarian Resource Group

The VRG has more than just a zillion recipes and ideas for vegan and vegetarian meals. It also has information on sports nutrition, a vegetarian FAQ, tips on travel (weirdly, there are several vegan dude ranches), and a vegetarian game to test your animal-free prowess—a good-spirited and comprehensive site.

www.vrg.org

World Wildlife Fund

This well-established conservation fund has alerts and information about habitat and wildlife issues around the globe. The Conservation Action Network lets you send faxes and letters for regional, national, and international alerts. You can create an account and track your successes. This takes a bit more time than just clicking (see the 5-Minute Activist section), but it's well worth the time. Most recently the Conservation Action Network has successfully campaigned to restore funding that will preserve wetlands in Tennessee, and to pass legislation to keep marine

different kinds of questions, like if they've had a cat before, was it declawed? We don't support declawing at KittyKind. It's very bad for cats. We ask them what happened to their old cat— did they put it to sleep, did they give it away? You know, things like that, and several other interview questions. Then if the adoption representative decides that the person is a good person to have a cat, they are able to adopt.

The cat that was there the longest without getting adopted was Shana. She was there for six months or so. She became like the mascot. I was like, "I am going to find this cat a home!" Everyone wanted a kitten or a young cat, not a little fat, chubby calico cat. She was a little ornery, but she would always sit on this pillow and she was the most adorable thing. Eventually she was adopted and I was so happy.

My cat is from KittyKind. His name is Sammy and he is orange and white. My mom didn't really want a cat, but after 9/11 she let me start fostering. I guess she thought it would make me feel better. I brought him home and he drove my mom crazy, but

turtles from being caught in fishing nets in Mozambique, and raised $19,000 to help stop gorillas from being hunted in Africa.
www.worldwildlife.org

Books

Animal Liberation
By Peter Singer
Published in 1975 and inspired by the deplorable conditions of animals used for laboratory testing, this is the book that launched the modern animal rights movement. It's full of polemic arguing that animals must be freed from their second-rate status and accorded the same rights as humans. Whether you agree or disagree, it's worth reading to see the words that have inspired so many activists.

Dominion: The Power of Man, the Suffering of Animals, and the Call to Mercy
By Matthew Scully
Scully, a former speechwriter for President George W. Bush, places himself between the animal rights and the animal welfare camps—he doesn't think animals should have status equal to humans, but he makes a compelling case that they ought to be afforded more rights, respect, and dignity than they currently enjoy. He addresses various reprehensible industries, such as whaling and factory farming, exposes them for what they are, and rebuts the arguments made in their defense. He's very sarcastic, but it's a lively read.

One at a Time: A Week in an American Animal Shelter

By Diane Leigh and
Marilee Geyer

This is a true account of seven days in a Northern California animal shelter. The stories of the seventy-five animals who pass through the shelter during that week are told via excerpts from shelter records and interviews with volunteers, employees, and visitors. It also follows each animal to the end of its interaction with the shelter. Some endings are happy; others are not. Good to read if you are thinking of volunteering.

Shadow Cats: Tales from New York City's Animal Underground

By Janet Jensen

This is a fascinating look at the lives of feral cats in New York City. Some have been abandoned; others are the latest in a line of ferals. Jensen tells of her efforts to rescue feral cats, which results in some unexpected adventures.

then she and my dad both fell absolutely in love with him. He is so spoiled, he acts like he owns the house.

I've learned so much about cats through volunteering. I know how to take care of them. I know what they should eat, what they shouldn't eat, how you should treat them with different kinds of medicine, different things like that. I was interested in becoming a vet when I was a little younger, but now I don't really know. I definitely want to work with animals for the rest of my life.

This has been a wonderful experience. When a kitten comes in from outside and it has no home and it's so skinny, and you see it get better and then go to someone who's going to give it a home, that's awesome.

For more information about KittyKind, and for advice on what to do if you find an abandoned animal, check out www.kittykind.org.

The Student's Vegetarian Cookbook, Revised: Quick, Easy, Cheap, and Tasty Vegetarian Recipes

By Carole Raymond

Whether you are a newly minted vegetarian wondering how to begin or an old hand who is tired of eating the same things all the time, this cookbook can be of help. All of the recipes can be prepared in twenty minutes or less, and it's comprehensive, including desserts, snacks, and breakfasts. Vegan recipes are also included.

We the Creatures: Fifty-One Contemporary American Poets on Animal Rights and Appreciation

Edited by C. J. Sage

Every movement has its artists, and the animal rights movement is no different. This book isn't about radical steps taken in order to liberate animals—it's a lyrical appreciation of their existence. Pulitzer Prize winner Stephen Dunn is among the contributors.

Fighting Racism

Racism is a problem throughout our

society. African Americans, Asian Americans, Native Americans, and Irish Americans are among the many groups who have suffered from racist discrimination in the United States. Most recently, since the terror attacks of September 11, 2001, Arab Americans and other people of Middle Eastern descent have come under attack. Racism may also be a factor in some forms of religious intolerance, such as hate crimes committed against Muslims and Jews. Although great strides have been made, we still have a long way to go before we live in a society of mutual respect and understanding.

Let's start with a basic working definition of racism.

Racism is the belief that different races have different characters and abilities. Extending from that is the belief that one race is superior to others because of these characteristics. Racism is also discrimination or persecution based on these beliefs.

Even with a clear definition, it is still sometimes hard to pin racism down. Many of us are in denial about our own internalized racism. For as long as there has been racism, there have been arguments over what it is—slave owners used to insist they loved their slaves, for example. Fortunately, you don't need to assume the role of judge in order to be an anti-racism activist. Try to take people as they are, and don't assume anything.

Is "nigger" a bad word?

There's no easy answer to this. To many people it's the ultimate bad word and should never, ever be uttered. To others it's a term of friendship or endearment—this also goes for terms like "Heeb" or "Injun." Those who use it may say that they are "reclaiming" the term and turning it into something positive. Some feel that only members of a group can use one of these terms negatively or positively, and that those outside the group should avoid it. However, others argue that using it within a group may reflect the self-hate that the group has learned in a racist society.

Context is everything, so think before you speak. If you feel comfortable using "nigger" or words like it, it's your choice, but be aware that others may not feel the same way you do.

And if you are in a situation where you think the word is being used in a negative way by someone else, try asking the person why he or she said it. Speak up if it's being used as a racial epithet or a term of hate. You might not change the other person's mind immediately, but you could plant a seed that leads to a change someday.

Racism and intolerance can take many forms, and so can anti-racism activism. Some activists promote tolerance and acceptance of others (including those of different religions) on an interpersonal level. Some work to protect the civil rights of those who have been discriminated against because of their race. Others work for institutional change, attempting to improve access for minorities to things like health care, education, and elected office.

In many towns there are white high schools and black high schools, or an Asian and white high school, and a Hispanic and black school. As a result, many young people are rarely exposed to teenagers of other ethnicities—even in mixed high schools, students often separate themselves. Only one in every eight teenagers reports having a friend of another race. Racial separation breeds misinformation and intolerance.

Racism is a factor in many issues affecting minority youth of color. Hispanic and African-American teenagers are more likely to drop out of school than other teenagers. Youth of color are less likely to have access to health care and education about safer sex and birth control, and they account for a majority of HIV/AIDS cases in young women age thirteen to eighteen—the fastest growing population of those infected with HIV/AIDS. Black youth are more likely to be convicted of a crime as adults than white youth, even when facing the same charges. Black youth are also locked up for longer than white youth convicted of the same crimes.

If you choose to become an activist working on this issue, you will be joining many others who also fight racism. In the resource guide you will find organizations and Web sites that can help you with whatever you choose to do. Take advantage of them. And remember that every victory counts—even small ones. When you stand up to someone who tells a racist joke or makes a racial slur, you are making a powerful statement. You are being an activist.

THE AT-HOME ACTIVIST

Test Yourself for Bias

You may think of yourself as completely open-minded about race, but even the most tolerant of us can have hidden biases that we aren't aware of. And if you think that because you are, say, a Native American that you can't be racist, think again. You live in the same society we all do, and some racist beliefs may have crept into your thinking.

There is a good tolerance test at www.tolerance.org/hidden_bias/. It's completely private and provides information after you take it to help you understand your results. There are several tests on the page covering black vs. white bias, anti-Arab bias, and more. Take as many as you feel like taking. It's not a regular, boring test—it's more like a video game and tests your responses to different stimuli.

Try and get your whole family to take the test and discuss the results at dinner or after religious services—whenever you can get them all together. You may find that even in the same house, individuals can have widely divergent responses. Talking to your family about race can help you understand where each person is coming from, and let you know if you might need to do some more at-home activism on this issue.

Plan a "Race Matters" Movie Night

Watching a movie that has a racial theme can be a great to launch a conversation about with your family. Suggest a movie night at your house. Tell everyone that it's important to you that they come. Make some good snacks and get a movie.

Rent a movie that touches on the subject of race or racism. It could be a documentary or a Hollywood movie. Choose a movie that's appropriate for your family (if you have young siblings, something that's PG-13 might be too much). If you have trouble finding the movie you want, try your local library—sometimes they can be ordered. Also try a small, arty video store instead of a big chain because they often have a better selection.

Suggested Titles (Listed Alphabetically)

Do the Right Thing (1989)

In Brooklyn's Bed-Stuy neighborhood, racial tensions erupt on a hot summer day. A local Italian-owned pizza place that's been around forever and a newly opened Korean deli become the focus of long-running resentments and ethnic clashes. The movie's ending is quite violent—only rent this if no young kids will be there.

CHIKA'S STORY

Chika Oduah is eighteen and a senior at Chamblee Charter High School. She lives in Lihtonia, Georgia.

I am strong in my beliefs. If I think that my beliefs are being violated, I speak up.

My parents sometimes make racial slurs, and I always argue with them. It's hard to challenge them because we're Nigerian. Nigerian children are not supposed to talk back to their parents at all, but I don't want my parents to remain ignorant. I don't want them to say, "Japanese people can't drive," because that's not true. They are trying to pass on that ignorance to me, and I won't let them. It is kind of hard. Sometimes they think I'm being disrespectful. But I think it's good if I get it in their heads and get them thinking about it.

I'm a member of Amnesty International and an antislavery human rights organization called iAbolish. I found these groups by typing "human rights groups" on Google, but I did research them before I joined them. I signed up for iAbolish's

Forgotten Fires (1998) (Documentary)

This movie looks at the aftermath of the burning of two black churches by the Ku Klux Klan in a small town in South Carolina in 1995. Among those interviewed are the church's leaders, who discuss how their community coped with the tragedy, and several Klansmen, who discuss why they felt driven to commit these crimes.

Guess Who's Coming to Dinner (1967)

A white couple is surprised when their daughter brings her fiancé to meet them—he's black. They are forced to examine their own perspectives on race in a time when interracial marriage was newly legal and not very common. This movie was considered quite shocking when it came out.

In the Heat of the Night (1967)

A black detective from Philadelphia is home visiting his mother in a small Southern town when a wealthy white man is murdered. The detective is arrested but eventually helps the town detective solve the murder. *In the Heat of the Night* won five Academy Awards, including Best Picture.

In the Name of the Father (1993)

Based on a true story, this movie highlights the Irish antagonism toward the British presence in Northern Ireland, and the reciprocal persecution of the Irish by the British. A young Irishman visiting London is falsely accused and convicted of planting an IRA bomb. The British government goes so far as to frame his father as well, and the two fight to clear their names while behind bars. A compelling film that shows prejudice and intolerance can exist even between groups of the same color. (The British call the Irish "white niggers.")

Mississippi Burning (1988)

In 1964 in the midst of the civil rights movement, two white activists disappear while working to register black voters. The FBI is called in to investigate. The locals, including the sheriff's department, are resentful and possibly involved in the disappearance.

Mississippi Masala (1992)

An Indian family escapes the political tensions in Uganda and moves to Mississippi. They make a home for themselves and a living running a small hotel. But when their daughter begins dating a black man, they forbid her to see him. Denzel Washington plays the boyfriend.

weekly e-mail alert; they call it the Freedom Action Network. They tell you what's going on, like, "Australia is bringing in children from Vietnam to work as sex slaves." They will suggest you write a personalized letter to the president of Australia or Vietnam, or to [our president], and they will give you addresses, fax numbers, phone numbers, all the contact information.

After I get the alert, I usually research a little more. I read newspapers and check on the Internet. I use the site Indymedia.org for international news. I've written letters to the president of Kenya and the president of Ghana asking them to take action about things like the slavery in their country, sex slaves, slavery because of skin color, and child labor laws. Usually in return I get form letters. Once, I think it was in Kenya, they wrote back and said, "We are currently in the process of changing the law because so many people petitioned and wrote us letters." I really felt like I did something.

I talk about this stuff at school all the time. I get mixed reactions. Sometimes it's, "Oh, really? That's

Salt of the Earth (1954)

Based on a true story set in a zinc mine in New Mexico. The Mexican workers go on strike to protest unfair wages (they are paid less than their Anglo counterparts in other mines). When the white-owned company cracks down on the strike, the wives of the workers carry on the fight. This film wasn't widely released for years because its creators were suspected of being communists and were blacklisted in Hollywood.

School Ties (1992)

Set in the 1950s, a Jewish football player goes to a fancy prep school on a scholarship but hides his religion to try and fit in. When he is exposed, he faces losing his friends and his popularity. It stars Ben Affleck, Chris O'Donnell, Matt Damon, and Brendan Fraser in the days before they were big stars.

Suture (1993)

At his father's funeral, a white man meets his black half brother for the first time. They lead very different lives—one is rich and successful and the other is nearly homeless. While race is never explicitly discussed, this very arty movie raises interesting questions about racial identity.

To Kill a Mockingbird (1962)

When a black man is unjustly accused of rape, a white lawyer fights for his client's freedom. At the same time, the lawyer attempts to educate his children about race and the insidious traps of racism. The story is told from the perspective of the lawyer's young daughter.

Trading Places (1983)

A white banker and a black street hustler are forced to live each other's lives as a result of a bet between two millionaires. Starring Dan Aykroyd and Eddie Murphy, this comedy is hilarious but still touches on racial issues and stereotypes.

Who Killed Vincent Chin? (1988) (Documentary)

Vincent Chin was a Chinese automobile engineer who was killed by another auto worker who thought Chin was Japanese and blamed him for the Japanese auto industry that was threatening American jobs. Chin's murderer got off with three years' probation.

(There are more movie ideas at www.viewingrace.org.)

After the movie have a family discussion. Ask everyone what

great!" and then they forget about it. People talk a lot, they get excited, and they get the information, and then they don't do it. That's the difference between activists and the regular population.

At my school I'm part of a group called Nia Umoja. It's a multicultural unity and awareness group. Nia Umoja means "purpose and unity" in Swahili. I'm copresident. This year we are holding our first International Festival. It's a celebration of international diversity—there are a lot of students from many countries at my school. We are having a foreign film festival, dance classes, a talent show, a school assembly, and a special lunch, and we also put up lot of signs about busting stereotypes.

Our principal is kind of conservative. She didn't want a talent show, but we are sneaking it in and calling it a showcase. She didn't say why she didn't want it, but we figure she thinks it's gonna be a whole bunch of rap music and it's gonna get very rowdy. It's just Indian dance and French songs.

The film festival was my idea. I'm really into film. We are showing two Indian films, two Nigerian films, a South

they thought about the movie and how it made them feel. Talk about how the characters in the film experience racism and the way that you experience it in your own life. Ask your parents if the racism they see or experience today is different from when they were young. You don't have to come to any stunning conclusions during the discussion—you are providing food for thought that might inform later actions and reactions. What if your family is racist? It can be really hard if people in your family are racist or make racist remarks. You might be worried about bringing up the topic because it could start a fight or make others feel defensive and picked on. But if you approach your family members with respect, and talk to them, you might change their minds—even a little. Don't just yell at them and say that they are racist. Ask questions like, "Do you really mean what you just said?" or "I don't understand why you're saying that white people are out to get blacks when you have white friends and so do I." At the very least, you are demonstrating to the person that you are willing to act on your beliefs and challenge their bad behavior.

THE CAMPUS ACTIVIST

Invite a Speaker to Your School

Bringing someone in to your school to talk about racism at an assembly about racism can be really powerful, but it's a lot of work. If your school already has a lecture program or a history of inviting speakers, you've got it easy—just go through those channels. If it doesn't, you might have to jump through a few more hoops.

Your first step is finding a new speaker. One good way is to find someone who has a book out and might already be coming to your town to do an event at a bookstore. Visit local booksellers and ask them if they have a book signing schedule or if they have any authors they can recommend. The bookstore might even help you get in touch with the author. Another way to find an author is to search on an online site like Amazon.com or in the library. You can search by subject and then sort by release date to find the newest books on the topic you are interested in. Make sure you read the book and find out about the author before you decide on him or her! You don't want any surprises. The Web site Colors of Resistance (colours.mahost.org/) is a good resource as well.

Another way to find good speakers is to contact anti-racism institutions like the Southern Poverty Law Center and the National Association for the Advancement of Colored People (NAACP); their Web sites are listed

African musical, an Ethiopian film, and a European film—I think it's French. Entertainment is a good way to get people to actually listen. When people hear music or see a film they are interested, but when they hear facts, they're like, "We get that in school."

The festival was hard to organize. The hardest part is making sure everyone does all the work and makes the deadlines. As the copresident I end up having to nag people.

It's good to remember that when you are an activist, you aren't ever really acting alone. It's a cooperative effort between all of the human rights activists. Me doing what I'm doing in Nia Umoja is one thing. Challenging my parents is another. Poetry, reading your poetry, writing poetry—all of that is doing something. I think people have this huge misconception that they need to be a revolutionary leader, like Martin Luther King or Ghandi, and that's not true. Just standing up and saying, "I am a human rights activist" inspires people, and if you inspire people, you've made a difference.

at the end of this chapter. You can contact them and ask them to recommend speakers. Remember that speakers who are big names or who have to travel to get to your school might expect a speaker's fee and reimbursement for their expenses. If your school can't afford to do that, invite someone local or check out the fund-raising chapter for ideas.

Try to invite someone who can speak to the racial makeup of or issues at your school. If there is anti-Arab sentiment, someone from the American-Arab Anti-Discrimination Committee or a local mosque might be great. If your school is not racially mixed, try inviting someone who can talk about stereotypes that we are all exposed to and how we can resist them.

It's probably best to have a list of four or five speaker possibilities before you go to your school administration. See if you can get some teachers to sign on to your projects—that will bolster your case. You could also arm yourself with a petition signed by your fellow students to prove that this is something the student body wants to happen. Once you've gotten all of this together, set up a meeting with the appropriate school officia. Have a date in mind. It's good to tie the speaker to something in the calendar if you can: Martin Luther King Day (January 17), Asian American History Month (November), or the Muslim holiday of Ramadan (falls on the ninth month of the Muslim calendar—if you aren't Muslim, call a local mosque to ask) are all possibilities.

Explain to the person you are meeting with that you think it's important that the student body be exposed to all kinds of people, and that you think bringing this speaker to campus will foster tolerance and useful discussions about race. Have with you a neat, typed-up copy of your proposal, your list of speakers with their biographies, a copy of your petition, and some suggested dates, and leave them with the administrator after the meeting (leave *copies*—keep your originals).

If your school says no, check out alternative venues. Your local YMCA, library, or community center might have a room that you can use for your speaker. This can create its own hassles, but it does allow you to open the lecture up to the community and to invite a more controversial speaker, if that is what you are inclined to do. Make sure you publicize the event well, on campus and around town. Put up flyers and call the local media.

If your school says yes, you've cleared the first hurdle. Prepare to spend a lot of time on the phone now. Having a fax is helpful too. (You might be able to send faxes from your computer; if not, hit a Kinko's or use your school's fax.)

Get your list of speakers and rank them in order of who you

For more information on the groups Chika mentions, check out www.indymedia.org, www.iabolish.org, and www.amnestyusa.org.

EMMANUEL'S STORY

Emmanuel Tedder is eighteen and a senior at Governor's School for Science and Mathematics in Darlington, South Carolina.

I'm on the state board of a group called CAFE representing my youth chapter in Darlington, South Carolina. CAFE stands for Carolina Alliance for Fair Employment. It's a grassroots organization, designed to help working people, that grew out of the civil rights movement of the 1960s.

I first got involved with CAFE about seven years ago when I was really young. Carol Bishop, who is now the executive director, was a friend of my family, and she brought me to a meeting. I took part in the adult meetings, but I felt that there were important issues in the youth space as well, so I asked if I could start a youth component. They thought it

want the most to the least. Remember to be realistic—Russell Simmons might not have the time to come to your high school. To get the contact information for an author, you can call the publishing company and ask the publicity department how to contact the author. Another trick is to look on the acknowledgments page and see if the author thanks his or her agent, publicist, or editor, and then track them down. If you're targeting a celebrity, you can try looking on www.whoRepresents.com for management contacts. If your speaker-to-be is at a university, try the main number or look him or her up on the school's Web site. You will probably have to make a few (long-distance) calls to get to the right person, and you'll end up speaking with a lot of people's assistants.

Explain what you want to the assistant.

You could say something like "Hi, my name is Rachel. I'm a student at DeVille high school in Rochester, New York. I'm trying to encourage discussions of race and racism on our campus, and I'd like to invite Professor Stephens to speak. Our student body is very motivated to learn more about this topic, and I hope she can come."

The assistant will likely ask for more information. Don't worry if you don't have all the answers right that minute. Say something like "I'd be glad to e-mail or fax you that information." That way you will have time to get together what he or she needs and send it in a way that will make it easy for him or her to show the boss. Ask for the exact name and contact information of the person you are speaking with as well as the person you are sending the information to (if different). The assistant may also refer you to an agency that is responsible for booking all of the potential speaker's engagements. Call them up and give them the same spiel.

The information you are going to mail or fax will be an expanded version of your proposal to the school with a cover letter. You can use some of the stuff you said on the phone and to your school administrator, but remember that this is a total stranger—you have to make him or her care. Talk about your school and what it's like. Explain why you think this speaker is the perfect person for your school. If you can illustrate the story with some sort of incident or anything that makes it real, that can be really effective. Something like "We have a large group of Southeast Asian kids at our school who are all fairly new to our country. They keep to themselves, and they get teased a lot. With your background, you could really help us build bridges between the groups."

If you have a date in mind, include it in your letter. Be aware that the more flexible you are, the more likely you will be able to book

was a great idea, so we started the first youth chapter in Darlington County. Now we have fourteen youth chapters. The Darlington chapter has about 150 members.

The adult chapters handle adult issues like worker's rights, and the youth component deals more with youth issues such as student's rights, capacity building, and leadership development. We also do a lot of community service, like cleaning up the highways in the Adopt-A-Highway Program. Recently we've been really involved in Hispanic outreach. South Carolina, like the rest of the country, has a growing Hispanic population, and we feel that they are facing a lot of the same concerns and issues we are, so we want to bring them into our organization.

One of the Darlington youth chapter's biggest success stories was in addressing some racial disparities in our local school system. We have something called ALERT, which stands for achievement, leadership, exploration, research, and technology. It's a program for gifted and talented kids, and goes from third to sixth

the speaker you want. Once you've sent the letter, wait a week or two, then call back to see if a decision has been made. Don't pester, but be persistent. If it seems like it's not going to happen, move on to the next potential speaker.

If you get someone to say yes, congratulations! At this point, depending on how old you are, you might need an adult to help you with some logistics. If your speaker is going to have to make any travel arrangements or needs train or car directions, double check everything.

On the day of the visit, if your speaker is coming by public transportation, meet him or her at the station and escort him or her to the site of the lecture. If the speaker is driving, make sure you recommend a good place to park. Before he or she arrives, make sure the room you are using is clean and ready, and provide a bottle of water. If the speaker requested a lectern or AV equipment, ensure that it's working. Ask your friends to arrive early and sit up front. (You can even seed them with questions to ask during the Q and A if you want to.) You might also want to ask someone with a video camera to tape the event—you can give a copy to the school library.

Introduce your speaker. (Your principal or someone may want to say a few words of welcome as well.) After the talk is over, open up the room to Q and A A good question to ask is, "How would you suggest that our school, going forward, take greater steps toward tolerance?" Don't let the Q and A go on too long. When the Q and A is over, thank the speaker and everyone for coming. Announce that there is a sign-up sheet at the back of the room for anyone who wants to meet with you to plan future anti-racism events.

Make sure your speaker gets off campus and on the way home safely. Don't forget to send your speaker a thank-you note. Dealing with all that is involved in bringing someone to campus is a big task, and you should be really proud of yourself if you accomplish it.

THE COMMUNITY ACTIVIST

Mobilize Against Hate Groups by Writing a Letter to the Editor

A hate group is just what it sounds like: a group that wants to harm others because of their race, religion, sexual orientation, or gender. Almost every state in the U.S. has one or more active hate groups. Hate groups do everything from painting swastikas on buildings to beating up or even killing the people they hate. Tolerance.org, a project of the Southern Poverty Law Center, monitors hate groups throughout the U.S. Visit their Web site to see which ones are active in

grade. Every Friday the participants leave their regular classrooms and go to this program to learn things that are a little above what they would be learning in the other classrooms, such as mathematics, logic skills, geography, and technology. The school system selects students to take part in this program. The problem was that people of color and minorities were very underrepresented. Many people didn't even know about the program because the schools were not sending out any type of notice that told parents or students about the program. It was something the school system kept for the "elite."

The first thing we did was make sure that we had a case. We did a lot of research about the history of the program and what the school's responsibilities were. From our standpoint, the district denied access of information to everyone by not letting people know about the program. The school system was basically tracking out certain kids into a gifted track and just leaving everyone else behind. There were no set guidelines for how they

your state. Hate groups are also active on the Internet.

How can you fight them? One way is to expose them. These groups do not want publicity or attention—they prefer to work in secret. You can alert others in your community to hate groups operating nearby by writing letters to the editor of your local paper and lobbying your local and state government officials to issue statements decrying the presence of such groups.

Writing a letter to the editor is easy—writing a good one that gets published is a little harder. Here are some tips:

- Introduce yourself—your name, your age, where you go to school.
- Explain why you are writing. "I just learned that there are several hate groups operating in our state, including X, X, and X." (Name some that you got from the hatemap on Tolerance.org.)
- Explain why others should care. "This is an embarrassment to our community and to our country. I don't want to grow up where this is allowed."
- Cite statistics and say where you got them.
- If you have the time, research to see if any hate crimes have happened locally. You can go to the library and check out back issues of newspapers, which often print police blotters. Or you can ask the librarian to help you look through the crime statistics for ones relevant to your case. You can also call local or national civil rights groups like the ACLU for information.
- Give concrete suggestions to help fight the hate groups (this is sometimes referred to as a "call to action"). Some calls to action might be:
    - I call upon our civic leaders to issue a statement telling these groups they are not welcome in our state.
    - I recommend that our police forces undergo training so that they are able to recognize and deal with hate crimes when they occur.

- I ask our local school boards to create and implement a tolerance curriculum so that young people are not drawn into these groups, which actively recruit online.

Sign your letter, include your address and phone number, and send it off. The newspaper won't print your phone number—they will just need it to confirm that you are the one who sent the letter. You can ask them to withhold your name, too, if you are worried about reprisals.

It's a good idea to also send the letter to every state and local official you can. Look them up in your phone book or go to www.congress.org and enter your zip code. If you just get form letters back, you could even write a follow-up letter to the editor to say that you are shocked at the inaction of your elected officials. Be as vocal as you can—especially during an election year, the issue could take off as a topic.

You may be tempted to write to the hate groups or take them on yourself in some way. It's not a good idea. Unite your community, then act.

selected who was going to be in the program and who was not. It was a very ambiguous system. We wanted parents, educators, and students to know that there was this program out there, and to make the process of selecting students more fair.

We filed charges with the Office of Civil Rights in the Department of Education in Atlanta. Now the ALERT program is required to send out a yearly report to parents, teachers, and students telling them about the program and what qualifications are needed to be in the program. They are also moving toward recruiting more people of color into the program. It was a big success for our youth group. We took a very big stand. Speaking from personal experience, there were very few minorities in the program when I was in that age group, so I was very happy to see a change in the structure.

It is always a big challenge and a difficulty to be attending school at the same time that you are challenging the school system. It's something that keeps a lot of youth from

Other Ways to Fight Racism

• If you belong to a church (or mosque, or synagogue) that isn't racially mixed, ask your pastor or priest to work with you to set up an interfaith picnic or other event with a faith-based organization whose membership is composed of an ethnic group you don't ordinarily mix with. (There is more information about interfaith coalitions in the anti-war chapter.)

• Check out local community centers or organizations such as the Settlement Houses in New York City, which offers tutorial programs to kids in need. Become a mentor or a tutor. (Of course, you could end up tutoring a kid who is the same race you are! But it will be a good experience anyway.)

• Racism is a factor in many other issues of social justice, including poverty, education, and health care. You may choose to work on any of these, particularly in communities of color, and you'll be working to alleviate some of the terrible effects of racism.

THE 5-MINUTE ACTIVIST

End Homelessness Now

This site, sponsored by Amazon.com and other click-to-donate sites, links homelessness to social injustices such as discrimination and racism. Every sponsor donates half a cent to help change the lives of homeless people everywhere.
www.endhomelessnessnow.org

RACISM RESOURCES

Web Sites and Hotlines

All One Heart

This site is slightly sappy but has tons of good stuff. It's aimed at all forms of discrimination, not just racism. There's an interesting media section that highlights racist and intolerant things people have said in the press. It also has an electronic newsletter and a shopping area with anti-hate items.

www.alloneheart.com

American-Arab Anti-Discrimination Committee

Founded by a former U.S. senator, the ADC defends the rights of Arab Americans, promotes civic participation, and advocates what they call a "balanced Middle East Policy." (They are also quick to make the distinction between having some issues with Israel and being anti-Semitic. The ADC are the former, not the latter.) The site lists current issues of interest to Arab Americans, calls to action,

getting involved, because they are afraid of retaliation. There were times when we had difficulty getting a consensus among our members because they were afraid it could jeopardize their chances of graduation and their chances of getting a quality education, and that's understandable. Some of the parents were also expressing their concerns about the students pushing the school board and pushing the envelope. They didn't want to see their child being harassed by teachers or administrative people at school or on the school board level. In the end I think the youth realized that it could be a possible sacrifice, but they still made the choice to do it.

Another issue is that people think that they can't make a difference. What I like to do with these people is give them training and give them the skills and the tools to empower them, so that they lose this mentality of "I can't change anything" or "I don't think what I do matters." I think the biggest thing for people like that to know is that it's easier to make a change when you are a collective unit. When

legal services, and contact information to get in touch with your local chapter.
www.adc.org

Anti-Defamation League

The ADL has been fighting anti-Semitism and bigotry for almost one hundred years. Their mission is to stop the defamation of Jewish people and to secure justice and fair treatment for all. The site is comprehensive, covering recent ADL events, hate on the Internet, anti-Semitism in pop culture, the Holocaust, extremism in America, and terrorism.
www.adl.org

AntiRacism.net

A coalition of international anti-racism groups contribute to this site, which functions as a portal with links to fact sheets, social justice organizations, international events, and mailing lists. The main page is devoted to news stories—click on the directory button to get to the links. The site is run by the Anti-Racism and Diversity Committee of the Unitarian Church in New York.
www.antiracism.net

A.R.I.S. (The Anti-Racism Information Service)

A.R.I.S. was formed to support the anti-racism work of the United Nations. It's a free service that can send you documentation on any aspect of racism, from Holocaust denial to reparations for slavery. The documents include news stories, government reports, and books. A.R.IS. will e-mail,

fax, or send via regular post.
www.antiracism-info.org

The Art of the T-shirt

This is an artist's coalition that sells T-shirts with anti-racism slogans and designs made by inner city artists. They also have a yearly contest for new designs—you can submit yours or vote on the others.
www.art-teez.org

you have five fingers alone, it doesn't deliver a blow as strong as if those five fingers were together. So I think that people should realize that together they can make a difference. By themselves it's going to be hard, but together, as a unit, anything's possible.

To learn more about CAFE, check out www.cafesc.org.

Crosspoint

Crosspoint is an anti-discrimination megasite with links to organizations all over the world. You can search by location or by issue. Weirdly, racism isn't listed as one of the issues, but you can type it into the search box. Warning: The site is pretty slow.
www.magenta.nl/crosspoint

E.R.A.C.E. (Eliminating Racism and Creating Equality)

An anti-racism organization aimed at fifteen- to twenty-five-year-olds. While E.R.A.C.E. does a lot of community work (PSAs and campus outreach), the Web site focuses on transforming each individual and suggests adjustments you can make in your own life to fight racism.
www.erace.com

F.A.I.R.'s Anti-Racism Desk

F.A.I.R. (Fairness and Accuracy in Reporting) is a

watchdog group that tracks media bias and censorship. The anti-racism desk covers "misrepresentation, marginalization, and exclusion" of minorities in the news media. There are topical guides, links to recent racist remarks or behavior, and action alerts. www.fair.org/racism-desk

The Hate Crime Network

This site has resources and support for victims of hate crimes. You can sign up for a newsletter that will alert you every time a hate crime is reported. You can then read about the incident. In some cases, through the victim-support system, you can also respond directly to the victim with words of concern and encouragement (the victim remains anonymous). hate-crime.website-works.com

Hope in the Cities

This is an interracial, multifaith network dedicated to "honest conversations on race, acceptance of responsibility, and acts of reconciliation." Their work takes many forms, from a reenactment of the slave labor that built the United States Capitol Building to history tours for children, as well as more traditional community organizing. They explain how they bring about change in a lot of detail and provide resources like the "Connecting Communities" tool kit so that you can do similar projects. www.hopeinthecities.org

Jews for Racial and Economic Justice

Based in New York, this group is committed to connecting the Jewish community to anti-racism and
social justice issues they might not otherwise know
about. They protested the police shooting of
Haitian immigrant Amadou Diallo and have also
held alternative Jewish rituals, such as an "anti-
prison Passover." The site has fact sheets, inspiring
stories, and useful links.
www.jfrej.org

NAACP (National Association for the Advancement of Colored People)

Founded in 1909, the NAACP has been at the forefront of battles concerning segregation, discrimination, and racism ever since. The NAACP is responsible for pushing the passage of many civil rights
laws, including the Equal Employment
Opportunity Act and the Voting Rights Act. Today
it focuses its energy on protecting and enhancing
the rights of African Americans and other minorities. Visit this site to learn about the NAACP in
action, read past events in history, or educate yourself about the importance of voting in elections.
www.naacp.org

National Council of La Raza

NCLAR was established to reduce discrimination
and poverty and improve life opportunities for
Hispanic Americans. NCLAR is involved in everything from very local grassroots community work
to running a national policy think tank in

Washington, D.C. The site lays out issues of interest to Hispanic Americans, has links to local affiliates, and includes an action center where you can keep in touch with your Congressional representatives about policy issues relevant to the Hispanic community.
www.nclr.org

National Urban League

The Urban League's aim is to empower African Americans and let them fully participate in society, economically and culturally. The site doesn't have a lot of suggestions for things that you can do (other than donate), but it has tons of information about the work the League does in its three main areas of focus: education, economic self-sufficiency, and civil rights. It's useful for research and ideas—plus there are links to local groups you can join.
www.nul.org

Project Change

This site is supported by Levi's jeans—a form of corporate philanthropy. It describes their community work and has several downloadable publications such as an anti-racism resource guide and a community activist tool kit.
www.projectchange.org

Race, Racism, and the Law

This is a site put together by Vernellia R. Randall, a law professor at the University of Dayton. It's a bit dry, but it's a great resource if you want to make

some points about legal issues. It also has links, including one to a great survey called Race Relations in America.
academic.udayton.edu/race

Stop the Hate

This site has a great home page with quotes from many religions that express the need for tolerance, and resources for anti-racism and anti-religious discrimination work. It's also part of the Love Sees No Color Web ring, so it's a great starting point to surf around from if you want to. It also includes poems and stories from teens who have been affected by hate crimes.
www.stop-the-hate.org

The Southern Poverty Law Center

Another venerable institution that grew out of the civil rights movement of the 1960s, the Southern Poverty Law Center tracks hate groups and takes many discrimination and bias cases to court. They've been responsible for several landmark Supreme Court cases, including the Voting Rights Act of 1965. The site has information on civil rights history, current legal battles, ways to get involved, and links to their K–12 initiative, Tolerance.org (see below).
www.splcenter.org

Tolerance.org

A project of the Southern Poverty Law Center, this site is dedicated to students in grades K–12 (the

resources are separated into a teen section and one for younger kids). It has great discussions on hate language and racist lyrics, and a booklet called "101 Ways to Fight Hate." There are also profiles of teenagers who will inspire you, and substantive tips on how to discuss race and racism with your friends and your family. The "Mix it Up" project encourages teenagers to make friends with classmates of other ethnicities during lunch period.
www.tolerance.org

Youth Against Racism

Founded by three teenagers and geared toward their peers, this site has a message board so you can connect with other activists, a list of reasons you should get involved, and tips on how to get started. You can also sign various petitions to help stop racist events from occurring. Warning: It's not updated too often.
www.angelfire.com/rebellion/youthagainstracism

Youth Web

This site is aimed at uniting children, teens, and adults in the fight against racism, religious biases, and bigotry. It has a useful vocabulary-of-bias glossary that explains terms commonly used when talking about bias and racism. There's a hate-crime reporting form and a great reading list that includes books on LGBTQ issues, youth violence, and more. It also has tips on educating parents and teachers about prejudice.
www.youthwebonline.com

Books

Black Like Me
By John Howard Griffin
In this book, a Southern white man travels throughout the region disguised as a black man. Written in 1959, it offers a chilling look at segregation and discrimination in our recent history. (After the book was published, Griffin became a target of white supremacist groups, who branded him a "race traitor.")

The Hispanic Condition: Reflections on Culture and Identity in America
By Ilan Stavans
Discusses the history and future of Latino life in the United States by exploring history and literature. It gets into the interaction between minority or immigrant communities and the dominant culture. (Note: This is out of print, so it may be difficult to find.)

In the Name of Hate: Understanding Hate Crimes
By Barbara Perry
This book offers a comprehensive theory of hate crimes. Perry goes into the history of hate crimes and devotes chapters to minority violence and gender violence, giving possible explanations for this serious problem.

The Invisible Man
By Ralph Ellison
Ellison's novel tells the story of an unnamed black

man searching for the truth about race relations. The protagonist grasps at straws of truth and hope, only to have them exposed as shams. It's not an easy read, but it's a powerful one.

Racism Explained to My Daughter
By Tahar Ben Jelloun
It's aimed at preteens, but this book is still useful. The author tries to explain difficult topics—racism, bigotry, genocide, slavery, and anti-Semitism—to his curious ten-year-old daughter. It's in question-and-answer format.

Shared Dreams: Martin Luther King, Jr. and the Jewish Community
By Marc Schneier
A Long Island rabbi expounds on the relationship between Jewish people and African Americans. These interactions have often been hostile in recent years, but Schneier reminds us of the historic civil rights movement of the 1960s, which united the two cultures in a common struggle.

To Kill a Mockingbird
By Harper Lee
This Pulitzer Prize–winning novel about a black man charged with the rape of a white woman is told through the eyes of two insightful children. It is an honest and moving look at prejudice in the American South during the 1930s. (See also the movie listing under the At-Home Activist.)

Why Are All the Black Kids Sitting Together in the Cafeteria? and Other Conversations About Race

By Beverly Daniel Tatum

Tatum addresses race relations in today's schools and notes that there are "situations perceived as social segregation" at all grade levels. The book examines the evolution of racial identity and racial solidarity and also looks at issues in Latino, American Indian, and Asian-Pacific identity development.

Saving the Environment

THE ISSUES

The environment is a common concern for young people who want to become activists. The environment affects all of us through what we breathe, drink, and eat, whether we live surrounded by natural beauty or in an urban setting. Pollution, overpopulation, and destruction of natural habitats all contribute to a global crisis that never seems to get better. People who choose to work on environmental issues are motivated because they believe that every living being deserves a life free from pollutants and toxins, and that we should respect the natural world instead of destroying it.

Wanting to save the environment seems like something everyone could agree on, but unfortunately it isn't. No one is against the environment, but the issues of environmental justice can get very complicated. For example, economically disadvantaged neighborhoods are more likely to be located near waste processing plants, dumps, power plants, and other possible environmental hazards. Working to effect positive environmental change in these communities can mean challenging all kinds of power structures. Activists who work in this area need to be able to bring all sides together to form solutions.

A classic example of an environmental issue that

became political and divisive is the spotted owl controversy of the early 1990s. Under the Endangered Species Act, all logging on federal land in the Pacific Northwest was halted in order to preserve the owl's habitat. This made many local citizens unhappy because they depended on jobs in the logging industry. The issue was polarized and emotions ran high. The loggers accused the environmentalists of trying to take away their living, while the environmentalists portrayed the loggers as wanting to strip the forest for their own material gain. The conflict continued until 1994, when the Northwest Forest Plan was adopted. The plan, which was created by the U.S. Fish and Wildlife Service, had input from both environmentalists and the lumber industry. It allows for the preservation of some sections of old-growth forest and ecosystem management while allowing limited logging and instituting other types of economic development in the affected areas. By being open to a creative solution, both sides got some of what they wanted, and the controversy was resolved . . . for a while, at least.

Environmental issues often require global solutions. An oil spill in one part of the Atlantic Ocean could wash up on a shore thousands of miles away. Air pollutants can travel even farther. Who should pay for the cleanup? International environmental groups such as Greenpeace and UNEP, the United Nations Environment Programme, have adopted a global perspective. Part of their work is on this large scale, encouraging governments to sign or obey international environmental treaties. Other global perspectives on environmentalism focus on issues such as stopping the spread of nuclear power and nuclear weapons, protecting rain-forest land and other local habitats, and stopping the practice of "dumping," which is when rich countries send their waste to less wealthy countries for processing. The poorer country is in some sense forced to accept the waste in order to create some jobs, but it pays a heavy environmental price. You could choose to ally yourself with others working in any of these areas and know that you are helping the environment.

There are also tons of opportunities for you to take action in your local environment. That old saying "Think globally, act locally" is especially true here. Just changing your own behavior or that of your household, school, or community can have a major impact and inspire others to take action. Environmentalism also has a strong cultural component. Many great works of literature, art, film, and philosophy manifest a love of the natural world and a desire to celebrate and preserve it—you could get involved in this area. And because environmentalism is one of the oldest forms of activism, there are a lot of established and welcoming groups you can work with. Choosing to become an environmental activist will affect how you experience your world—every breath you take and every glass of water you drink are part of what you are working to save and restore.

THE AT-HOME ACTIVIST

Measure Your Environmental Footprint

Your environmental footprint is basically an aggregation of all the effects you are having on the environment: how much energy you are consuming and how much waste you are creating. There are lots of quizzes online to help you determine your environmental footprint. An easy one to find is www.myfootprint.org.

The quiz program will ask you a series of questions, like "How often do you use public transportation?" and then generate an estimate (sometimes expressed in acres) of how much of the earth's resources you are using. Along with your results, you will usually get tips, based on the answers you gave, on how to reduce your footprint.

Taking an environmental footprint quiz can be a great way to realize how much every single one of us is contributing to global environmental problems. It also will demonstrate really clearly what you can do to change things. Try implementing some of the measures the quiz suggests and then retake the quiz in six months. Is your footprint smaller?

ADAM'S STORY
Adam Donohoe is thirteen and in eighth grade at the West Branch Middle School in West Branch, Iowa.

Last year in my science class we did a lot of experiments with oil filters, figuring out the best way to recycle them. Now we are trying to get a law passed in our state about how to recycle them.

In Iowa about six million oil filters are disposed of every year. If they aren't disposed of properly, it's bad because the oil can drain out of them into the ground and then pollute our ground water and stuff. That's also why you should dispose of them right after you're done using them, so they won't leak everywhere.

When you dispose of used filters, you want to make sure that you get as much oil out of them as you can before you recycle them. That way the used filter is more easily recycled, and the used oil can be disposed of safely. The year before us, the eighth graders did a survey on what their parents do with used oil filters and found that fifty

Give Your House an Environmental Makeover

The house or apartment in which you live is your most intimate environment. Other than school, you probably spend more time there than anywhere else. But the average American household consumes far more energy than it needs to and produces waste at a rate unparalleled anywhere in the world. Luckily, it's not hard to improve your green quotient. With just a few changes, you can make the house or apartment you live in more energy efficient and less toxic to the environment—and you'll probably save some money, too. You don't have to do the whole environmental makeover at once; it's probably better to tackle it in sections.

Here are some questions to ask about your household, and suggested solutions.

What kind of light bulbs are we using?

You may be buying "energy efficient" incandescent bulbs at the store, but they don't actually save that much. It's much better to install compact fluorescent bulbs—they can last up to ten thousand hours and save seventy-five percent more energy than incandescent bulbs. Fluorescents cost more initially but they last so much longer that you will save about fifty percent over time. Some people object to the quality of fluorescent light, but recent reformulations have made them much softer. That said, the real energy savings for this type of bulb happens over time—like if it's left on for over an hour—so they won't do much if you install them somewhere like a bathroom or a garage where the light isn't

74

on for very long. They also won't work with timers or dimmers.

In situations where compact fluorescents won't work, try halogens. They are about twenty-five percent more efficient than incandescents are, and they are brighter so you can often use a lower wattage. Sometimes you have to go to a hardware store or a specialty lighting store to get them. Be careful where you use halogens—they can get very hot. Don't use them where they might come into contact with curtains or anything that could catch on fire.

Other lighting ideas: If you want lights on when you get home at night, install a timer. Choose light fixtures and lamps that use a lower wattage bulb. If your house has outdoor lighting, you can buy solar-powered outdoor lights that recharge themselves during the day. And don't forget, the best (and cheapest) light is sunlight. Maximize natural light in your house when you can and save artificial light for after dark.

percent of them were just throwing their used oil filters away.

Our experiment was to determine which recycling method recovers the most oil from the filters. We tried to figure out how much oil you can recover by draining them, by puncturing them, or by crushing them. Our teacher, Mr. Ibarra, bought some oil filters in different sizes, and we broke up into groups of three or four to do the experiments.

We had to wear goggles and rubber gloves. First we weighed the filters brand new, with no oil in them. Then we put the oil in and let them sit for two days. After that we drained them and weighed them again. They weighed a lot more than they did before because there's paper inside and the oil soaks into it. Then we tried to see how much oil we could get out by each of the three methods, and crushing them was the best. We had a crusher donated to us. It got the most oil out.

We sent our findings to the Iowa state senate and asked them to pass a bill about recycling oil filters. The bill will make it mandatory to recycle oil filters. People can take their filters to the landfill,

Do We Buy Bulk Food When Possible?

Sometimes your grocery bags contain more packaging than food. Something that comes in a paper bag inside a plastic bag inside a paper box, like microwave popcorn, is using up a lot of resources in the name of convenience. If you go to a health food store, you will find that there is more to bulk food than the candy and nut mixes you see at the supermarket. You can get flour, pasta, dry soup, popcorn, rice, and much more. As a bonus, it's probably organic.

Buying bulk food is cheaper and reduces the amount of wood pulp (i.e. mashed up forests) being used for packaging. And of course bringing your own bags to the store helps too. Some places will even let you bring your own container; you weigh the container when you come into the store, then weigh it again when it's full of what you are buying—no bag required.

Do We Have Houseplants That Help Clean the Air?

Yes, it's true! You can beautify your home and make it healthier at the same time. Plants not only release oxygen, they also clean the air of nasty things like formaldehyde, benzene, and other chemicals released by things like household cleansers and dry cleaning. The best plants for indoor air cleaning are Aglaonema (Chinese evergreen), Spathiphyllum (peace lily), Syngonium (arrowhead vine), Hedera (English ivy), Dracaena (cornplant), and Scindapsus (devil's ivy). Daisies and chrysanthemums are good too. You will need about fiften plants for every fifteen hundred square feet in your house. (Needless to say, check out some nontoxic and organic gardening resources so you don't have to use harsh chemicals on your plants and be back where you started.)

Could We Drive Less?

Ask your parents if they can take public transportation to work at least twice a week, or if they can carpool. Offer to do the same or better. Maintain your family car so it's as efficient as possible; keep it tuned up, change the air filter regularly, inflate the tires to the correct pressure, and look for "energy conserving" motor oil that contains friction-reducing additives. If your family owns or can afford to buy bikes, try running errands on them.

Do We Buy Organic Food Whenever Possible?

Organic farming is kinder to the earth and to our economy. Organic farmers don't use pesticides or artificial fertilizer, and they rotate their crops, which means that the soil won't be stripped of nutrients. Organic farms are also often small and family-owned, in comparison to government subsidized agribusinesses. In some parts of the country

but they won't go into the landfill. There will be a crusher there so you can crush your filters, and then they will recycle them for you. It's pretty cool.

Our whole class went to Des Moines, the state capital, to talk about our bill. It was a day trip—we left at the beginning of the school day and got back before school was over. We did a presentation of our experiment with PowerPoint for the state House Natural Resources Legislative Committee and explained why oil filters are so bad for the environment. The next day just a few of us went back to present the same thing to the whole state senate. That was in a bigger room. I wore a tie—my mom was kind of worried about what I was going to wear.

Right now our law is in a committee waiting to be passed. This summer we're going to Washington, D.C., to present this to more people. Our senator, Charles Grassley, came to our school, and we showed it to him, and he seemed interested. We hope they listen to us and maybe make laws to recycle used oil filters. Only five states now have the law that says you have to recycle oil filters.

you can actually join farm cooperatives where a local family farm will send you whatever is in season. Going all the way organic is a big step, but every little bit counts.

When We Buy New Appliances, Do We Look for the Most Energy-Efficient Models?

If your family is in the market for a new refrigerator, lawnmower, microwave, or car, check out the U.S. Department of Energy's Energy Efficiency and renewable Energy's Energy Savers section on their Web site (eere.energy.gov/consumerinfo/energy_savers) to see what the best options and models are.

Do We Unplug Appliances That Use Remote Controls When We Aren't Using Them?

Not many people know that televisions, DVD players, and other appliances that use remote controls are consuming energy even when they aren't turned on. It's true—part of the circuitry has to be always going in order to receive the signal when you want to power up. This creates what's called a "phantom load" that costs you about twenty dollars per year per appliance. Another thing to look for on your appliances is a little cube at the end of the cord that's always warm to the touch. These cubes are maintaining a constant (but weak) energy line so that the appliance will spring into action more quickly when you turn it on. Unplugging these types of appliances when not in use is the only way to really stop them from using power all the time.

Do We Look for Recycled Products and Packaging?

Recycled goods often take less energy to make and usually create less pollution in the manufacturing process. Buying recycled saves landfill space and is an efficient means of waste management. Be careful when you read labels: Just because the recycling symbol ♲ is on the package isn't a guarantee—it might just be a reminder to recycle the container. Look for products that have a high percentage of postconsumer content. That means it's something that's been used, and you are reusing it. Preconsumer content is also good, though less so—it's material that has been recycled because it is damaged, obsolete, or unsaleable.

If there is a product you like that doesn't use recycled materials in its formulation or packaging, write to the company. Tell them that you love it, but that you can't buy it anymore because you are committed to reducing waste and pollution. Ask them what steps they are taking to help the environment.

In West Branch we are trying to increase public awareness about oil filter recycling. We've put up posters in our school and around town about the oil filter problem. My dad is a farmer, and he drains his tractor and truck oil filters to recycle the oil, but he doesn't have anywhere to recycle his filters. They just pile up in the machine shed. I hope we can fix this.

I'm really happy with what we're doing. I've always liked science, and I like doing the hands-on experiments. I am going to stay involved with the environment.

To learn more about oil filtering recycling, checkout the Filter Manufacturers Council (filtercouncil.org), and the Web page describing Delaware's oil filter recycling program (www.dswa.com/programs/programs_oilfilter.htm).

Could We Lower Our Consumption of Power?

This is one your parents will really love because it saves money. You can estimate your household energy consumption by using the Home Energy Checkup at the Alliance to Save Energy (www2.ase.forumone.com /checkup/home/index.html). Some easy ways to reduce your energy use are: turning off lights and appliances when not in use, insulating (you can use old blankets in your attic if nothing else), using lids when you cook, and using a clothesline to dry your clothes when you can.

Investigate to see if "green energy" is available where you live by visiting www.greenmountain.com. Green energy is energy that comes from renewable sources like solar power or wind power. It's not just for hippies—even the White House has a solar electric system! You can also buy solar-powered radios, calculators, pool cleaners, and outdoor lights. Search for them on the Internet or try an outdoor supply store.

Do We Recycle Conscientiously?

Dig out your town's recycling rules and post them next to the trash bins in your house. If you don't have separate bins for the different types of waste, get them and mark them clearly. Make a special place for very toxic items like paint cans. Call your city to ask about what you can do with them. Before you throw anything away, consider if someone else could possibly use it—if they could, figure out where to donate it.

Could We Cut Down on How Often We Eat Beef?

Beef and beef products often use meat from cows raised on land that used to be rain forest. Furthermore, this beef has to be shipped or flown across the world to get to you, which adds to the waste. Eating fewer hamburgers and/or buying meat that is from sustainable farms will discourage the beef industry from ruining more of the ecosystem.

Could We Use Less Water?

Install an ultralow-flow showerhead in your shower, and request that family members cut down on the time they spend running water. If you have a lawn or a garden, don't water every day if you can help it, don't overwater, and always water in the early evening or early morning, when the soil is more receptive and the water is less likely to be burned off by the sun.

Do We Use Nontoxic Cleaning Products?

You can get your house just as clean as it has always been by using more environmentally friendly products. At this point, you don't even have to go out of your way to buy them—your local supermarket probably carries them. These products use natural solvents like citrus

DAVID'S STORY

David Cruz is seventeen and a senior at Menlo-Atherton High School. He lives in East Palo Alto, California.

I am a community organizer with Youth United for Community Action (YUCA). Our goal is to organize the youth around some of the problems we face in our community, like environmental racism and environmental justice. We really represent the unrepresented. Environmental justice means making sure that everyone's environmental rights are protected, not just those of rich people or white people. The environment we live in, where we live, work, and play, is something very precious to us. And when that is polluted or contaminated, as an oppressed class we have nowhere else to go. When we have a backyard full of arsenic, we want to clean it up. Justice is also getting regulations into state government and federal government that will protect our community. And justice probably means bringing some justice to the polluters. A lot of the polluters who

or almond oil to remove dirt. Your lungs will thank you, and so will your pets—small animals can really suffer from the toxic fumes some cleansers generate. You can even make your own cleansers, such as baking soda for scrubbing.

If your parents resist switching products, try looking up the ones you currently use on the National Institute of Health's Household Products Database. This will give you hard evidence that a change needs to happen. The URL for the database is householdproducts.nlm.nih.gov. When you do get your parents to switch, make sure you take the unused old products to a hazardous waste disposal site— don't put them in the regular trash.

Whenever you can, buy cleansers in concentrate form. It's usually cheaper, and since the bottle you are buying will last longer, you will reduce the need to manufacture more containers.

Do We Use Salt to Melt Ice and Snow After Storms?

Salt seeps into the earth and then is carried around by the groundwater: It makes soil unusable. Good old-fashioned shoveling is a better option, or you can look for products like "bare ground sprinkle" that use grain extracts and other nontoxic materials to achieve the same results.

These are just some checkpoints and suggestions. They may not all work for your family, or you might come up with even more. If you want to get hard-core and do an in-depth assessment of the environmental issues in your house, including possible lead paint exposure, air quality, and groundwater issues, check out the Federal Farm*A*Syst and Home*A*Syst programs at uwex.edu/homeasyst. They can help you assess any potential risks to your family's health and take action to improve your immediate environment.

THE CAMPUS ACTIVIST

Start an Environmental Mailing List

Is the environment something many of your classmates are concerned about? Students often cite the environment as their number one concern, but they don't have any ideas on what to do about it or how to educate themselves. You can do a great service by getting the word out that environmentalism is everyone's issue. Start an environmental mailing list that people can subscribe to.

The three main types of mailing lists are: announcement lists, like the kind bands have to announce shows and record releases; discussion lists, where anyone can reply to anyone else on the current topic; and informational lists that deliver

contaminate our environment aren't really held accountable, and that's something YUCA likes to take pride in helping with. We also go after the regulators who aren't doing their jobs.

I got involved with YUCA because I was a peer mediator at my high school. I went to a conference about it, and YUCA was there giving a workshop in environmental racism. I live in East Palo Alto (where YUCA is based), and I had no idea this was going on. A few days after the workshop, I was in their office working for them.

When I first came in, we were putting pressure on the regulators for one of the toxic waste plants that we have in our community. A lot of the waste comes from Silicon Valley—all of the microchips and the liquids that are used in making computers and things need to get recycled. It just so happens that it gets recycled in low-income communities across California.

We didn't feel that the regulators were doing all they could. One of them, the Air Quality Management District (AQMD), is the regulator that deals with airborne pollution. They were having community

tips or other useful things on a daily or weekly basis. Your mailing list should be a combination of the informational and announcement types. If you want to have a list where the subscribers can interact with one another, reply, and make comments, you can switch over to that kind later. It's probably best to begin with the simple type.

Start by gathering information for your mailing list. You'll want to have a bunch of info banked for the first few mailings, and identify good sources for more. Check out the Web sites at the end of this chapter for events and other things that you might want to announce (like Earth Day). Sign up for mailing lists from organizations like Campus Greens and Earth 911—then you can distill all the information you get and send it out to your friends. You'll be acting as an editor and just picking the things you think they will find interesting. Make sure you check the local paper for events around town such as park dedications, tree-planting ceremonies, or litter cleanups.

Other things to put in your newsletter are environmental tips. You can use some of the ones in the At-Home Activist section of this chapter or research new ones. Try doing product reviews of organic cleaners. Target your tips to your audience—if your subscribers are in high school and you know prom is coming up, do a newsletter on hair products that use organic ingredients and come in recycled containers.

Make your newsletter as reader-friendly as possible. You probably only want to send it out once a week, or even every two weeks so you won't clutter up everyone's inbox or make yourself crazy. Type it up carefully and resist the urge to use a lot of images or fancy formatting—you don't know what everyone's computer is like.

To manage your mailing list, you have several options. You could just do it yourself using your mail program's contact list function (sometimes called "address book") if it gives you the ability to create groups. You just create a group called "mylist" and enter your subscriber list into it. It's better to do this than to just send out the e-mail with everyone on the cc list, because it will keep the cc list private and prevent people from hitting "reply to all" and sending unwanted e-mail to everyone.

The advantage of doing it yourself is that it's the easiest way to start and you will control it all from your familiar program. The disadvantage is that you will have to do everything by hand—adding and deleting people from the list can get tedious if your newsletter takes off. Also, some ISPs won't let you do mass e-mailings because they are trying to stop spammers, so if your list gets too big you will have to switch to a mailing list program at that point.

meetings about their new plan to clean up the air. But you'd walk into a meeting and there would be maybe two people from the community there. The meetings were on weeknights, which are hard for working people to go to. My mom, for example, works from seven a.m. to seven p.m. every day.

So we hold our own forums. We hold them on the weekends, and we have them in both languages (English and Spanish).

We really try to reach out to the people. And then we take their input and use it to put pressure on the AQMD. We also presented a set of four demands about toxic waste in our community to the Department of Toxic Substance Control (DTSC). We went to their headquarters and had a meeting, and they agreed to all of them. The demands were things like making sure the company got an Environmental Impact Report, which they are required to do but hadn't done. And now we get a monthly update from the DTSC telling us what they've done on the matter.

At YUCA we work collectively. We try to represent what we'd want to

If you want to go with a mailing list program, there are some free options. Mailman is a freeware program available at www.list.org. There is also the old-school listserv option from L-soft Corporation. Go to their home page at www.lsoft.com, click on "listserv," then scroll down to the "listserv lite free edition." Both of these programs are only for use by nonprofit Interest-based e-mail lists.

Now it's time to start getting subscribers! Send an e-mail to all of your friends telling them about your list and inviting them to sign up. Have some sign-up sheets available at school as well. If your town has more than one high school or middle school, you could make some flyers and drop them off at coffee shops to spread the word. Look on the Web for appropriate bulletin boards where you can announce your list. Look for an announcements section or ask where you could post information about your list.

Remember that basic Net etiquette applies here. Don't send out spam or take people's addresses from Web sites or other lists without permission. Don't sign anyone up without asking. If someone requests to be taken off the list, do so immediately and graciously. It's good to put information on how to unsubscribe at the bottom of each mailing. Be safe: Never give out your name or any personal information to someone online you don't know.

Don't make your bulletins too long (or too short)— find a balance. Ask for feedback from people you trust. Once momentum builds, you could suggest some face-to-face meetings of the group. Have a pizza night, or do some environmentalism-related activity like picking up litter or going on a hike. If you keep your list going until you graduate, pass it on to a deserving younger classmate.

Find Out If Your School Spends More on Energy than on You

It's sad to think about, but this is true in many school districts. The cost of energy is so high that some communities now spend more on lighting and heating classrooms than on books and other learning materials. The problem can be exacerbated when school buildings are old and not energy-efficient. If you find that there is an imbalance where you live, you can use that information to see if some changes are possible.

Doing the research isn't that hard. The amount of money your school or school district spends on gas, water, and electricity is a matter of public record, as is the amount it spends on books and materials. Ask at your local library or at city hall to see a copy of the budget. You local PTA probably has a copy as well.

The terms "energy" and "classroom materials" might not appear

see in an ideal society, so we do everything democratically. Anyone can propose something, and then it goes through our decision-making process. There are some supervisors—they're the older people who just make sure that we're on track.

I know that there are people out there who think that they can't make a difference, and I don't blame them. The life we live, the things we watch, the media we read, it all conditions us to think we can't do anything. Everything tries to put a cap on what you're trying to do. And taking the power into your own hands in changing things that you want to change takes a lot of courage and passion. I think that every human being holds enough power to change things. The power to change is within ourselves. And there's no such thing as powerlessness.

For more information on YUCA and what they do, check out www.youthunited.net.

in the budget. You'll probably have to add together things like heating costs and gas bills to get the energy cost. For classroom materials, add up things like books, audiovisual materials, etc. The budget should also say how many students attend your school or are in your district.

Take each amount (energy and classroom materials) and divide by the number of students. For example, if the amount of oil and gas per year is $900,000 and there are 10,000 students, you divide 900,000 by 10,000. The school district is spending $90 per student on energy. Similarly, if the amount spent in that same district on books per year is $100,000, the amount per student is $10.

If you see a great disparity in the two numbers, with energy spending outweighing classroom materials spending, try publicizing them. Write to your school board and ask what can be done about this. Ask your parents to attend a PTA meeting and talk about the numbers. It's good to suggest positive action with your report: Maybe your school needs better insulation, or should install more energy-efficient windows. A small capital outlay now could save a lot of money in the long run—money that could be spent on books.

THE COMMUNITY ACTIVIST

Check Your Community Water Quality

Clean water is one of the most important factors affecting individual and community health. Water quality affects not only the stuff you drink and bathe in, but also the air you breathe and the soil where your food is grown.

As part of the Safe Drinking Water Act, the EPA requires that water providers send a water quality statement to residents in July of every year. This is called a Consumer Confidence Report. If you haven't gotten one, or if you want to review the report for your community, contact your water agency. You can find your agency at one of these sites. (It depends on whether your water comes from a state or municipal agency.): www.asdwa.org/state.html or www.amwa.net/about_amwa/members/index.html.

The report should list things like where your local water is coming from, a list of contaminants, the levels at which they were found, the likely source of the contaminants, and their potential health impacts. It should also have contact numbers for further information.

The EPA has a list of contaminants that it monitors to make sure they are at or below certain levels. The list includes chlorine, some microorganisms, and inorganic chemicals like arsenic. (The list is on the EPA Web site.) Each of these contaminants has a set level that it should be at or under when found in your drinking water. People disagree about whether these levels are set too high or not, but they are still a good guideline.

It can be useful to get the reports going back a few years to see if contaminants are on the rise. If you see contaminants that are steadily at or near the acceptable level, your community might be facing some health risks.

Another thing to do is check the health of your watershed. All of the water in your community comes from its watershed. The watershed is created by rain drainage, river tributaries or estuaries, and snowmelt. The watershed is affected by everyone in your community—if someone paints his or her house and doesn't dispose of the extra paint properly, it can get into the soil, and when it rains that paint and its chemicals will seep into the watershed. You can learn how to monitor the health of your watershed through the Earth Force Green Web site (www.green.org).

The environmental protection agency has a tool that will help you find your local watershed at www.epa.gov/surf. This site will also give you all the EPA reports regarding your watershed and links to local environmental groups.

If your research leads you to believe that your community's water is not healthy, you may want to do something about it like asking for better environmental regulation, or for better enforcement of existing regulations. But you don't have to act alone. Because water quality affects everyone, this is a great opportunity to do some coalition building. A coalition is basically a group of groups. Several organizations who may not otherwise always see eye-to-eye, and who may have different missions, all band together for one common goal they all agree on. For example, local merchants and tenant's rights activists could join together to stop a superstore from coming to their neighborhood.

Your coalition's goal is better water quality in your community. To find some good groups to hook up with, look in the community directory in your phone book, on your town's Web site if it has one, and on bulletin boards where people post flyers. They don't have to be environmentalists: Diversity is good.

Some possible groups are:

- Churches, synagogues, mosques, and other faith-based organizations
- PTAs
- Senior citizen groups
- Unions, such as the Steelworkers Union
- Youth groups like Big Sisters and Big Brothers, or Girl and Boy Scouts

What makes these groups ideal is that they have their own community that they can bring to your coalition, and they are already committed to service. They are fellow activists. Get in touch with their leaders and invite them to a meeting. Tell them you want to form a coalition to lobby for clean water in your community. At the meeting, show them your research and your results. Ask them to take the information back to their groups and discuss it with their members. Remind them that when communities come together, their voices are even more powerful. Get everyone's phone number and e-mail address, and also ask if they know of other groups that should be involved. Set a date for your next meeting.

At the next meeting, set up an action plan. Will you target local elected officials, or go straight to the EPA? Do you want to write letters, or picket and demonstrate near polluted sites? Decide what your strengths as a coalition are. If you have a lot of members, you might want to go with a petition because X-thousand signatures will say a lot. If you have a lot of passion but fewer individuals, a campaign that increases public awareness, like putting up posters around town, can publicize your cause and also draw more people into your coalition.

Put up a Web site that shows your water-monitoring

results. A good tool that will help you learn more about water monitoring and also store your data can be found at www.green.org. Through your group, adopt your local watershed and continue to let your community know about it. Here's the adoption site: www.epa.gov/adopt.

Identify Local Polluters

Pollution is sometimes invisible. You can see litter on the street, but you can't always look at a piece of land or a building and know whether it's toxic. Similarly, the people who create pollution are often invisible. Who exactly put the bad stuff into your local soil, water, and air? It's not that hard to find at least some of them.

Head to the EPA Web site (yet again). Click "Where You Live" on the left-hand menu, then on "Search Your Community." Enter your zip code and you'll get a street-by-street, block-by-block listing of every address near you that has ever been cited for violating environmental regulations. Go on a walking tour with some friends and check out some of the sites. Write down the names of the businesses located at the sites and write to them—tell them you found them on the EPA site and you want to know what they are going to do about the waste they are sitting on. Some of the listings on the EPA site may be out of date (i.e., the current resident might not have been the offender or even know about the citation), so be polite. Give them all the information you have and see if they act on it.

You could also do some educational activism about the sites listed by EPA. Make maps that identify all the addresses of concern and hand them out at local malls. Offer to take people on a "toxic tour" of your town. Publicize the businesses that are repeat offenders and ask people to stop patronizing them.

THE 5-MINUTE ACTIVIST

The Rainforest Site

Launched in 2000, this site focuses on preserving the world's rain forests. Every click protects 11.4 square feet of endangered rain forest. In 2003, visitors' clicks saved almost 73,000,000 square feet of land. You can only click once a day.
www.therainforestsite.com

EcologyFund

Save land, reduce pollution, plant trees, and protect coastal habitats on this site. Log on and you can click several buttons to donate to different causes such as saving sixty square feet of the Patagonian Coastal Reserve or removing two pounds of carbon dioxide from the air. You can only click once a day.
www.ecologyfund.com

I Want Clean Air

This site allows you to select an organization, such as the American Lung Association or the Clean Air Conservancy, who will benefit from your click. Each organization works to protect air from pollution. You can click once a day.
www.iwantcleanair.com

Tree4life

This site was started in 2000 to help save the rain forests in Brazil. Click on the button to help plant a tree in this critical area that is now less than five percent of its original size.

www.tree4life.com

Solar Site

The Solar Energy Light Fund helps villages in developing countries improve their lives through clean, renewable energy and modern forms of communication. Every click on this site is converted into one kilowatt of solar energy.

www.solarsite.net

RESOURCES

Web Sites

Earth911

This is a great site that provides tools and resources for individuals who want to live a more environmentally friendly life. There's info on how to recycle almost anything (including old cell phones), composting, and green shopping. You can also enter your zip code and get immediate information on local recycling resources and environmental events in your community. Toll free hotline: 1-800-CLEANUP

www.earth911.org

Earth Day Network

Every year on April 22, millions worldwide participate in Earth Day with actions, celebrations, education programs, and other events. This site will help
you set up your own event or locate ones near you
(it also lists events year round). There is a different
focus to every Earth Day that lasts throughout the
year, like clean energy or clean water. The site has
some tools, like an ecological footprint quiz, and a
great section of "fast facts" on environmental issues.
www.earthday.net

EnviroLink

This site is a great gateway to environmental
resources on the Web. There's a news section and a
database that you can browse by topic or by clicking on a map.
www.envirolink.org

Environmental Defense

This is a nonpartisan environmental advocacy group
that works to create solutions to environmental problems that have political, economic, and social support. They see themselves as protecting everyone's
environmental rights. Their broad areas of interest
are climate change, health, the oceans, and biodiver-
sity. The action center lets you send faxes and e-mails
to elected officials on environmental topics.
www.environmentaldefense.org

The Environmental Literacy Council

This group is dedicated to helping citizens, especially

young ones, learn how to participate in environmental issues in an informed way. The site also has detailed and easy-to-read explanations of environmental concepts and terms like ecosystems, acid rain biotechnology, and relative humidity. It's a great reference. www.enviroliteracy.org

Environmental Research Foundation

The ERF was founded to provide information to communities and individuals who are fighting for environmental justice. The Web site has a library of documents that you can search by topic or keyword; a search on "dioxin" brought up twenty-two documents, including a report from the American Public Health Association, a manual for doing online environmental research, and an explanation of how dioxin is produced when waste is incinerated. This is a great resource if you want background on things you've found in EPA reports or elsewhere regarding your community. (The site is also available in Spanish.) www.rachel.org

Greenpeace

Greenpeace is a nonprofit, global organization that focuses on worldwide threats to the environment. They have a subsite for almost every country and an international site. The U.S. site has an environmental newsroom, plus opinionated features on world events, information on their latest campaigns, multimedia, and even a games section where you can learn while playing "Nuclear Solitaire" or

"Crop Raider."
www.greenpeace.org

Natural Resources Defense Council

A prominent voice on a variety of topics, the NRDC
has more than a million members. They do a lot of
work with environmental legislation and have a great
magazine called *OnEarth*. The site has great information on nuclear energy, green living, wildlife, and
more. Almost every topic has an overview, an FAQ, a
how-to section, and the opportunity to act on the
issue from the NRDC action center. It has a fantastic
reference center, too.
www.nrdc.org

National Wildlife Federation

The NWF has been helping to preserve wildlife and
habitats, and promoting education about environmental issues since 1936. Their site reflects their many
issues and projects—everything from environmentally
friendly gardening products to eco-travel and a fascinating essay—not kidding—about whooping cranes.
You can learn how to attract wildlife to your backyard
and get it certified as a Backyard Habitat, or you can
check out various other action projects.
www.nwf.org

Rainforest Action Network

Founded in 1985, RAN works to save the world's rain
forests through education and direct action. One of
their more prominent successes was when they led a
boycott of Burger King, which resulted in Burger

King canceling its contracts in Central America and announcing that it would no longer use imported beef raised on former rain-forest land. The site has action alerts and a fantastic Activist Toolbox with tips on organizing demonstrations, passing resolutions, and more. You can also plug into their speakers bureau if you want to spread information about the rain forest in your school or community.
www.ran.org

Save Our Environment Action Center

The action center was created by a coalition of organizations dedicated to promoting environmental awareness and action. You can learn about a multitude of issues and do a variety of activities, like writing a letter to your local editor, with just a few clicks.
www.saveourenvironment.org

Student Conservation Association

The SCA is a clearinghouse of opportunities for environmental service. There are listings of volunteer and internship opportunities for high school, college, and graduate students to give their time and energy to environmental projects. You could end up building a trail or restoring a creek to health.
www.thesca.org

United Nations Environment Programme

UNEP's mission is "to provide leadership and encourage partnership in caring for the environment by inspiring, informing, and enabling nations and peoples to improve their quality of life without compromising that of future generations." They do things like administer the Convention on International Trade in Endangered Species of Wild Fauna and Flora, which has resulted in less killing of elephants and rhinoceroses. The youth section of the site, while aimed at younger kids, has a tree-planting campaign and some interesting stuff about sports and the environment. (Warning: Lots of the links in the youth section don't work as of June 2004.) www.unep.org

Books

Silent Spring

By Rachel Carson

Published in 1962, Carson's book is widely credited with launching the modern environmental movement. It's been reissued with a foreword by former vice president Al Gore, but any edition you can find is okay to read. Carson discusses (and documents) the effects of widespread pesticide use on our environment and the animals and humans who live in it. Still relevant and powerful.

My First Summer in the Sierra

By John Muir

John Muir was a Scotsman who explored the American West on foot in the late nineteenth century and was ecstatically transformed by the then-untouched beauty of the natural landscape he encountered. This book (one of many) is an account of his experience. He writes with great detail about every encounter—with trees, with mountains, with frogs. Muir became an early leader of the land conservation movement and helped preserve land that became part of our National Park System.

Walden

By Henry David Thoreau
You may have read or heard about Thoreau through his writings on self-reliance and his friendship with Ralph Waldo Emerson. While *Walden* does reflect his principles and beliefs, it is a very personal book—the story of a man living a completely austere life, yet who is intoxicated by the natural world around him.

Cartoon Guide to the Environment

By Larry Gonick
It's not *X-Men*, but this long-format comic book is pretty fun to read. It has drawings and text that explain almost every environmental term and concept, even "biome." Super easy to read, it will give you a good overview of environmental issues—and you could even pass it on to a younger sibling or a friend when you're done.

The Newman's Own Organics Guide to a Good Life: Simple Measures That Benefit You and the Place You Live

By Nell Newman and Joseph D'Agnese
You've probably eaten Newman's Own brand popcorn, pasta sauce, or chocolate. It's an environmentally friendly and socially responsible company started by the actor Paul Newman, whose daughter

is one of the book's coauthors. It's full of ideas on how to live a more "green" life, including using things like green power sources and organic pet food. It's also printed on one-hundred-percent post-consumer recycled paper.

Ending War

You might think that the American peace movement began in the 1960s, but it actually dates back much further than that, to at least the 1860s. At that time, many were against the looming Civil War and tried to prevent it by writing letters to politicians, distributing pamphlets, and holding public rallies. These protestors, sometimes called pacifists, were adamantly against slavery but did not want the conflict solved with violence. The peace movement continued through the 1930s, when student and campus activism became a strong component, and through both World Wars to the Vietnam-war era's protestors and finally to today's peace activists.

Peace activists don't only work to prevent and stop war—they also seek changes in foreign policy that will promote peace, advocate restructuring federal budgets that spend billions on the military, and try to help those who are suffering because of war. Peace activists work globally to support nonmilitary solutions to world problems, achieve nuclear disarmament, and help rid developing countries of landmines left behind from previous wars. Many pacifists act out of religious conviction; their faith spurs them to reject violence and war as options for human interaction.

When it became clear that the American government planned to go to war in Afghanistan and then Iraq, many teenagers became activists for the first time in their lives. Anti-war marches, petitions, and demonstrations took place all over this country and in many others. A revitalized peace movement was born. Old and new organizations and coalitions came together to urge our nation and others to lay down their arms and resolve conflicts through negotiation and other nonviolent measures.

Teenagers have particular reason to be against war. Not only are they on the front lines to be drafted and sent into battle, but teenagers are also large consumers of government services that are often cut in order to finance a war or a large military. Student loans for college, federal support for more teachers and smaller class sizes in high schools, even transportation subsidies and many other programs are reduced or put on hold while tax revenue is diverted to the war effort. Young people will inherit an environment scarred and polluted by wars.

Currently there is an increased military presence in American high schools—under the No Child Left Behind Act, military recruiters cannot be refused access to any high school campus. Student records are also available to the military unless the student's parent or guardian specifically requests they remain private. (For more information on the NCLB Act, see the chapter Promoting Civil Rights and Civil Liberty, page 227.)

Choosing to become a peace activist does not mean that you hate your country, or that you feel any animosity toward our armed forces. Working for peace is in line with deeply held American values that call for citizens to stand up for what they believe in. The men and women who serve in our country's armed forces deserve to be treated with respect—and they deserve to know that their lives are not expendable. (In fact, many peace activists are former military men and women who do not wish to see any more soldiers injured or killed.) Some peace activists feel that there is no such thing as a just war; others believe that force may be necessary at times. But all sides can agree that supporting and respecting the troops is the right thing to do.

Being a peace activist can sometimes be frustrating. Our country and many nations around the world are deeply invested in war as a tool of foreign policy. Our economy is tied to the war industry. Wars still happen. Peace activists try to take the long view, and to celebrate smaller victories while they work toward their ultimate goal. The huge demonstrations of the past few years, the student walkouts, and all the work that continues to happen further the cause of peace. Every action draws attention to the issue, sparks conversations, and encourages people to examine their own feelings about when war is justified, if ever. Now every politician running for office must justify his or her stance on the war in light of the fact that a large portion of the American people were vehemently against the stated rationale for the war and opposed sending our troops for this and many other reasons.

This chapter is being written after the war in Iraq is officially over but while the United States is still occupying the country and is engaged in daily combat. Other conflicts around the globe include Haiti, the Balkans, Iran, North Korea, Sudan, Colombia, the Congo, and Pakistan and the other parts of the Middle East. If you choose to become a peace activist whose main focus is ending and preventing war, you have many challenges ahead. But whether you concentrate on ending armed conflict, achieving nuclear disarmament, or any other pro-peace cause, you can know that your work is serving people all over the world. Every little bit of peace helps.

THE AT-HOME ACTIVIST

Put Up a Peace Poster

Hanging a sign in your window is a tiny peace demonstration that people will see every day. It doesn't mean you're a hippie, and it's really easy to do. Free downloadable posters are available at these sites:

Another Poster for Peace
www.anotherposterforpeace.org

Mike Flugennock's Mikey 'Zine

www.sinkers.org/posters/newwar/index.html
No More Victims
www.nomorevictims.org/posterdownloads.html

PeacePoster.org
www.peaceposter.org

ANA'S STORY

Ana Grady Flores is sixteen and lives in Ithaca, New York, where she is a senior at the Alternative Community School.

It began as a silent march. We were all dressed in black and we had signs pinned to our clothing that said "No War in Iraq." This was December 21, 2002—before the war had started. We wanted to say that if this war happens, many soldiers will die, many civilians will die, and we don't want that. We all had little pieces of cloth in our hands that had text printed on them reminding us of casualties from the war in Afghanistan, like "Five-year-old killed by U.S. bombs" or "Mother of four killed." That really personalized it. I remember mine was a little girl.

The march was my grandmother's idea. My family is very involved with the Ithaca Catholic Worker group. The Catholic Worker Movement is a nationwide group that provides places for homeless people to come and get clothing and

Protest Art Gallery (some in Spanish)
www.uglydesigns.info/projects/protest/others/stanton

Zama Online Design
www.zama.com/peace.html

If you don't want to use someone else's image, create your own on the computer. In most design programs there is an option to print the image out in tiles, which means you'll get a bunch of pages, each with a bit of the image on it, and you have to tape them all together to create your poster. Or you can always get some paint and poster paper and do your poster freehand.

Don't limit yourself to the traditional peace sign. You could make one with a dove, or the earth, the word "war" with a diagonal red line through it, or a slogan that you hope will make people stop and think. Some suggestions are:

- "An eye for an eye makes the whole world blind." (Gandhi)
- War is not the answer.
- I support the troops but not the war.

Put your peace poster in a window or on your front lawn—anywhere people can see it. If you've got the room, you could use an old sheet and make a big banner to hang from the roof or a balcony or large window. (Make sure your parents and your building or neighborhood association permit this.)

You could also get peace stickers for your bike or backpack, or peace buttons to put on your clothes.

This poster project can serve to remind you and everyone who sees your poster daily that there is another reality besides your own, where people are fighting for their lives. Maybe it will inspire you or others to do more work in this area. If people ask you about your poster, explain why you have it and see if a discussion about war and peace develops.

Don't underestimate the value of symbols. A peace sign is a visible representation of the fact that you are against war and for nonviolence.

Interview a Veteran of War

Talking to someone who has actually been in combat can be an emotional but valuable experience. If there are any veterans in your family, you can interview one of them, or try asking your parents if they know anyone who served in the military during wartime.

Another way to connect with a veteran is through a local vet organization or service provider like a Veterans of Foreign Wars chapter or a VA hospital. You can also try the Department of Veterans Affairs (www.va.gov) or the National

food for free, and a place to stay. My family is Catholic, but the Catholic Worker Movement isn't all Catholics—there are Jewish people, Muslims, and atheists. It's just people doing works of mercy. We were planning to go out of town to march, but my grandmother said that we needed to keep it local and inform our own community, and we agreed with her. So we decided to go to our local mall.

We spent the whole day before planning. We had kind of a retreat and we planned out how we were going to do the action, what we were going to do, who would be the spokesperson, and who would meet us at the police station if we got arrested. We picked December 21 because it was the last Saturday before Christmas, and we picked the mall because we knew a lot of people would be out shopping.

There were about three hundred people marching with us. It was really cold—sunny, but windy and freezing. People we didn't even know came and joined us in the march. After we'd been in the mall a little

Veterans Organization (www.nvo.org). There are some anti-war veteran groups listed at the end of this chapter. Tell the organization that you are a student learning about war and you'd like to interview someone who experienced it firsthand.

After you've set up the interview, prepare your questions. You might want to ask things like:

Why did you enter the military?
How old were you?
Which branch of the military were you in?
What was your rank?
Did you enlist or were you drafted?
If you enlisted, why did you do it?
If you were drafted, how did you feel about getting called up?
What kind of training did you have?
When did you get shipped overseas, if you did?
Were you scared?
What happened during your service?
Did you see combat?
What was it like?
How and why did you return home?
Did you stay in the military after returning to the states?
What was it like coming back?
Did you feel different?
How did your family and friends treat you?
How do you feel about war now?
What do you think about our current political situation?
How do you feel about anti-war activists and pacifists?

When you arrive at the interview, thank your subject for agreeing to meet with you, and shake hands. It's nice to bring some cookies or something as a sign of gratitude and to break the ice. After some introductory chatting, say that you'd like to begin the interview.

Let your subject answer your questions as fully as he or she wants to. Ask follow-up questions like "Why did that happen?" or "How did you feel when your sergeant said that?" Remember that you are there to listen. The person you are interviewing may have fond memories of the war and think that war is a good thing. There's nothing wrong with that—ask questions to find out why he or she feels that way.

It's a good idea to tape the conversation so you can transcribe it later or go back and listen to it. When you are done, thank your subject and leave.

There are several things you can do with your interview. You could play it for your family or friends and talk to them about it. You could transcribe it and give it to people to read. You could write an essay about your experience speaking with this person and send it to an essay contest or to your local news-

while, we were escorted out, and most of the group went out to the highway and held up banners and signs and pictures of kids. Thirteen of us went across the street to where the Army recruitment office is. My aunt Claire put red paint on our faces. It was time for the die-in.

We all went into the recruiter's office and lay down on the floor. My uncle went up to the officer who was working and said, "We come nonviolently and peacefully and we're here to recruit you into the peace movement." The officer was like, "What? What the hell? You're not allowed to be in here." He kept saying we couldn't be in there, but there were thirteen of us lying on the floor. I felt bad for the guy. Our spokespeople told him we weren't there to cause any trouble; we just wanted to send a message to the people who were thinking about joining the military. The recruiters target young [people], mainly minorities, who don't have much of an opportunity anywhere else, and you know, the military sounds nice because it will pay for your college and stuff. But it also means that you are not living a life of peace and

paper. You could invite the veteran you interviewed to come and speak to your club, school, or church.

Another thing you could do is interview a civilian war survivor—a refugee from a war-torn country, a Holocaust survivor, or a war orphan. Try contacting support groups that work with these people and reach out to them.

Actually speaking with someone who has experienced war is a great way to personalize an issue that can seem abstract to someone who is living in a war-free zone. You might end up befriending your interview subject and keeping in touch. Many war veterans feel forgotten or discounted, and reaching out to the person with whom you spoke could really make him or her feel that a new generation wants to learn about what happened in past wars.

THE CAMPUS ACTIVIST

Organize a Teach-In at Your School

A teach-in is an event that seeks to educate those in attendance about a particular issue. It's not a protest or a demonstration; it's more of a conversation between students and the speakers you invite. Organizing a teach-in can bring awareness about war to your campus and let students learn more about why some people oppose it and which war issues touch their lives in particular. A teach-in generally means that you invite some speakers to come and talk at your school, and you can also set up what's known as "tabling." This means you invite local activists, nonprofits, and political groups to set up tables in a designated area during the teach-in. At theirs table they can offer literature, sell T-shirts, have sign-up sheets, or whatever, and talk to anyone who stops by about their viewpoints on the war.

Note: Some schools will not allow outside organizations to come on campus and distribute literature, so tabling isn't always an option. If you can't arrange it at your school, you can still have a great teach-in.

Find out if your school has any provisions for having a teach-in, such as a speaker's program or other event series. If there is one, then you can probably squeeze your teach-in into the existing program. If there isn't one, you may need to lobby in order to have it. Get a few allies to go with you (people from student government or clubs like the history club or the politics club might be good) and make an appointment with the principal, vice principal, or whomever the appropriate person is.

Explain to the administrator that you want to have a teach-in about war, and that you think it will be beneficial to the student body. A

nonviolence.

We lay there for about an hour and a half. I was lying next to my cousin Marie and we were holding hands. That helped me a lot. I wasn't scared, but I was nervous about what was going to happen, like where they'd take us if we got arrested. My mom went out to where the other protestors were and invited them to come over to the recruiter's office and join us. They were all outside singing and praying. The office has big windows, so they could see us lying on the floor.

We read a sermon written by Martin Luther King Jr. months before he was murdered. In that sermon he talks about the Vietnam War and how it was illegal and wrong. The recruitment officers that were there stopped and listened, which was nice. They were quiet the whole time we read that. We also read a fact sheet on uranium, and the effects it has had in the past and today and in Iraq, and all the places we've used it and the weapons it's in and stuff. We all took turns reading.

The cops came, and the state troopers, and they said if we didn't get up and leave

teach-in might inspire students to take more notice of current events, and help them take some of their classes (like history and civics) more seriously. You can assure the administrator that the event will be peaceful, that it will just be speakers talking and other groups distributing literature. Tell him or her that you and your ad hoc committee will take care of the logistics and all school rules will be followed. You can offer to have the teach-in at lunch or after school so it won't interfere with classes.

You should have a rough plan with you of how you see your teach-in happening. Decide what you want, but be prepared to make changes in the planning process. One way to go is an all-day teach-in. This would mean that an auditorium or classroom would be devoted to the teach-in, and students could drop in during free periods or between classes. You would book a speaker for each class period, and teachers could even bring their classes to the teach-in to hear some of the views being expressed. The tables could be set up nearby for people to browse.

If an all-day teach-in isn't an option, after school or at lunch are the next best choices. You will probably want to book fewer speakers, since you'll only have an hour or so. (If your school has more than one lunch period, you can book more.) Maybe invite just one or two. That way a student could listen to a speaker, check out the tables, eat lunch, and get to class on time.

Your administrator might express concerns that the teach-in will be one sided. One thing you could say to him or her is that you will be very explicit to everyone involved that the viewpoints being presented are those of the speakers, and not those of your school or school district. Point out that a student who supports war could set up another teach-in on a different day. The administrator might ask you to book someone with an opposing point of view. That's not such a bad idea—having different voices never hurt anyone.

If your school admin says yes, that's great. If he or she says no, then you've got to be more persuasive. Try circulating a petition among the students asking for a teach-in. Get as many faculty members as you can to sign up too—and involve parents if you want. Make your teach-in coalition based. You can't have too many partners. Get as many campus groups as possible involved. Ask the debate team if they want to help. Any political clubs or student government entities are good choices too. If your school still says no, go off campus. Reserve a local community center, park, or church hall to have the teach-in.

Now it's time to book your speakers. If you have people who are already speaking out on this issue in your town, definitely consider asking some of them. They are members of your community and can address local issues and senti-

in ten minutes we would be facing a year in prison, and all this stuff which wasn't true—the most we could have faced was three months. They were really grumpy because it was a Saturday, and a lot of them were off duty already and they'd had to go back to work. They handcuffed the first three people and I was the third person. They used plastic cuffs and tightened them *really* tight, so my arms were basically, well, I couldn't do anything. My hands started turning purple. I had to keep asking the officers over and over again to take them off, until one of them finally did. They put us all in paddy wagons and cars and took us to the state troopers' barracks. There they took our mug shots and fingerprints and released us.

There was some coverage in the local papers, and when I got back to school (it happened over break) my principal came up to me and was like, "I heard what you did—good job!" I had a lot of people telling me that, but I also had to explain my story to a lot of other people who didn't know what happened. It created some good dialogues at my school. At least five

ments. Another source for speakers is the Iraq Speakers Bureau (www.iraqspeakers.org)—it can help you get in touch with policy experts, diplomats, former UN officials, human rights activists, and public health researchers. Local politicians who have expressed views on the war are also good. Remember that even among those who oppose the war, there are a variety of positions. For example, with regard to Iraq, some wanted the UN to lead the effort. Others felt that the entire war is based on a lie and should never have begun. (For more details on booking speakers, see the Campus Activist section in the Fighting Racism chapter.)

Invite organizations for the tabling. Reach out to as many groups as you can get—don't forget to consider veteran groups, religious organizations, and other groups who have viewpoints on pacifism, the current conflict, or war in general. Look them up online or in the phone book. Call and ask for the name of the public relations director or the youth outreach coordinator (if they have one). Write up an informational e-mail or letter and send it to that person's name at the organization's address. Your letter should say that you are setting up a teach-in at your high school about war, and that you are inviting representatives from local groups to come and meet with the student body. Explain how big your school is, why you feel it's important that this teach-in happen, and why you are inviting this group. Say that you will be setting up a table area where they can share information about their organization and their position on war. List what you can provide (a table and two chairs, or whatever), what the time frame is, and everything else they need to know.

A week or so after the initial contact, start calling your potential speakers again to confirm. Try to get a commitment as early on in the process as possible. You can say whom the other speakers are, or whom you are hoping to get, to give him or her a better idea of what you are planning. If the people you approached initially say no, thank them for their time and move on to your next group. If they say yes, thank them and send them all the information they will need to have for their experience at the teach-in to go smoothly, such as whether parking is available at your school.

Publicize the teach-in—leave flyers around campus, put it in the school paper, and ask for it to be announced on the daily PA announcement if your school does that. Put some eye-catching head-lines on your flyers, like "Billingsworth High School Says No to War" or "Peace Out! Come to the Anti-War Teach-In March 10th."

An important part of your pro-motional campaign is making sure that the students in your school know why this issue should be important to them. They might not

teachers talked about our action, and my cousins would come in and we'd talk to classes. We went to the main high school and talked to a big group of kids after school. We basically explained why we did the action, and continued to carry on our message of why we were there.

I've received e-mails from all over the nation, and from Europe, Africa, everywhere, saying "Good job." People in the military write me, or families with people in Iraq. This one girl wrote from the military, who was in the middle of becoming a conscientious objector, and she said we were an inspiration. So it's been really uplifting to get all the e-mails, because before I did it, I thought, "Well, this is just a little action," but now it's been huge.

The charges were basically dropped against the adults who were arrested, but the legal situation for the minors who participated—myself included—is ongoing. In a way, it's good that the whole court process has taken so long. Since the beginning we've said that this war won't bring any good or happiness to our nation, and it will only

realize why they should care. You need to appeal to your audience's own self-interest. Show your fellow students how the war is affecting them right now.

You could make a chart showing the amount of money being spent on the war vs. the amount of money that is going to student loans. If you make a bar graph, the war bar will be seven times higher than the education one. (For 2003, the U.S. Department of Defense budget was $396 billion. The Department of Education budget was $56.5 billion—roughly one-seventh of the military budget.)

Or you could publicize the effects of the recent legislation on your school. Under the No Child Left Behind Act your school is required to provide military recruiters with access to all facilities and to all student records and contact information. If your school does not comply, it risks losing federal aid. See the Protecting Civil Rights and Civil Liberty chapter for more on the NCLB Act.

In the week leading up to the teach-in, confirm with all of your speakers and organizations. Make sure they know what time to arrive and where to go. Ask the speakers how they want to be introduced. The day before, check on the facilities you are using (rooms, a podium, etc.) to see that they are in place. Put reminders in teachers' mailboxes and everywhere else you can think of.

On the day of the teach-in, everything should go smoothly, but don't freak out if it doesn't. Ask at least five of your friends to be on call for you throughout the event to do anything you might need. Greet your visitors when they arrive and show them to where the teach-in is happening. Make sure your speakers have some water, and that everyone knows where everything is (like bathrooms). You might not get to sit down and listen to any of the speakers for very long—you should be circulating to make sure that the next speaker is ready, that the tablers don't need anything, and that the students in attendance are finding everything.

When your speakers are done, thank everyone for coming, especially your speakers and any school staff who helped you out. Tell the audience that you hope they learned something at the teach-in, and that they will continue to have discussion on this topic among themselves and at home. Now is a good time to mention any upcoming peace activity, such as a rally or a petition you will be circulating.

After the teach-in, be responsible. Take care of your speakers, and make sure the campus is cleaned up. After a few days, you might want to call the organizations and the speakers to ask them how they think it went. Finally, write up your experience organizing and attending the teach-in and give it to your school librarian to keep. Maybe someone else will read it and organize another one, using your blueprint.

bring death and despair, and now we can see that that's what's happening, and that there's no point to the war. It's an illegal war, and now we are seeing the facts and statistics of the war. We're seeing that Bush planned this war before he was even in office. My cousins and I have taken every opportunity when we are on the stand or in court to speak our beliefs and express our support for peace.

I consider the action a success because it has created so much discussion and caused a lot of people to think about war and why we participate in it. It's given us a lot of opportunities to speak out about our beliefs. Next year I'm taking a year off before college so I can spend more time with the Catholic Worker group and do more of these kinds of things. Even when I go to college, I'm not ending my career in activism; this is something I will carry with me as long as I need to.

For more information about the Catholic Worker Movement, visit www.catholicworker.org

THE COMMUNITY ACTIVIST

Start a Faith-Based Peace Coalition

If you belong to a church, mosque, synagogue, or other religious group, you know that these are strong communities. Historically, such institutions have been at the forefront of the peace movement. One of America's oldest religious peace groups, the Fellowship of Reconciliation (www.forusa.org), was founded in 1915 and now includes members from nearly every faith. Forming a similar group in your town is a great—although challenging—way to act on your pro-peace beliefs.

Bringing together groups from different religions to work for peace can have the added benefit of promoting religious tolerance. Finding common ground is a classic start to conflict resolution. Any statement coming from a diverse coalition of faiths is very powerful because it itself is an example of acceptance of others who are different. So many conflicts are (or seem to be) religious in nature; therefore it is especially important for people of faith to speak out against hate and intolerance. Many great peace activists, such as Dr. Martin Luther King Jr. and Dorothy Day, came to their positions out of religious conviction.

Go to your pastor, rabbi, imam, or whoever leads your religious group and explain that you want your organization to make a statement for peace. Ask him or her to join you in doing this. (As with the teach-in idea, it might be good to bring some others with you to the meeting to show that you have support from the community.) Explain that you want to ally with other religious groups in your neighborhood to work for peace.

If he or she says no, ask why. You could possibly work through any objections and come to an agreement. If for some reason he or she is adamant, skip it. Ask a friend of yours who belongs to another group to try his or her leader. When you've got someone on board, work with him or her to send a letter to other groups in the area.

Here's a sample letter:

Dear Reverend Lee,

I'm Rabbi Ingall of the Shanker Street Synagogue here in West Elm. We're a congregation of about four hundred members, many of whom have been brought up in this synagogue.

Recently the young people of my group have become increasingly concerned about war—about our current involvement in Iraq, and about other conflicts worldwide. They've come to me to ask my help in creating a local religious coalition that will work for peace.

I'm very impressed that these young people want to act on the val-

HANNAH'S STORY

Hannah Verrill is sixteen and a senior at Packer Collegiate Institute in Brooklyn, New York.

My activism happened completely by chance. In October 2002, I was supposed to go to a concert with my brother Joe, and it was canceled. So instead I went to a panel about the impending Iraq war with my mom. This was my first introduction to the issues surrounding the war. Most of the panelists were Democratic members of the House of Representatives, and they were against it. The main thing they were saying is that it's not okay to start a preemptive war. We had no evidence that Iraq was going to attack us, and that made this war illegal. It really made sense to me. I thought, "This is so wrong." Then I thought, "What can I do about it?"

At the panel I got a flyer for the Stop the War Before It Starts March on Washington that was going to happen on October 26. You could buy a ticket and go on a bus from NYC, so I got a lot of my

ues of peace and tolerance that all of our religions espouse. So I'm writing to ask you to join us in this venture. The lead student's name is Andrew, and he will be calling your office soon to request a meeting to discuss this further. I urge you to speak with him, and to consider joining our coalition. There is nothing we can't do, if we do it together.

Respectfully,
Rabbi Ingall

Of course, if your rabbi already has a relationship with other local leaders, he or she can just pick up the phone and give them a call.

When you meet with the other leaders, tell them the same thing you told your own leader. Explain that you don't have a specific action in mind for your coalition, because you want it to come from within the group, but that your coalition could do things like hold a candlelight vigil together, have interfaith discussion groups to further tolerance, write letters to local leaders, or attend peace rallies and events together, just to name a few things.

Remember that there are some longstanding conflicts between certain faiths. People may be wary of your coalition because of this. If you think this might be a factor in any hesitation from a group, respect that position. Explain that you are asking them to put aside their differences in order to get to know other people of faith and work toward a common goal. In doing that, they may also form relationships that will allow for some misunderstandings and distrust to be resolved.

Call your first meeting as soon as you can. You might want to ask each group to send one adult and one teenager if possible. At the meeting welcome everyone— maybe have everyone introduce himself or herself and say something briefly about their hopes and expectations for the group.

A good first project for your coalition might be having a pizza night. A casual get-together can be a great way to start some relationships, let the various communities know about the coalition, and get more members who will be enthused to join in on bigger projects. Make sure that you schedule it on a night when people of every faith can make it—that there is no holiday or other religious obligation that night.

At the pizza night, encourage mingling. Introduce people to one another, and have everyone sign in. Remember it's a party, not a meeting, so don't have a big group discussion, but make a brief welcoming statement along with the other founders of the group. Tell them that you hope that this will be the first of many get-togethers and

friends and people at school to go. It was a completely beautiful day. First we gathered on the mall to hear the speakers. I was in this sea of people. I don't really know how to explain it. It was massive. I was just listening to the speakers, and looking at the people around me and reading their signs. It was eye opening. Then we marched through the city and that was pretty incredible as well.

I came back and flung myself into organizing. The panel I went to had been sponsored by ANSWER, Act Now to Stop War and End Terrorism, and that's how I'd gotten my bus ticket, so I started going to their meetings. I was completely new to activism, and ANSWER was the first thing presented to me so I took it. I went there and asked what they needed help with and they were like "KIDS!" They were so happy to have young people. They had a couple of college students but having young students come to organize against the war was really exciting for them.

In November I got involved in organizing a walkout at my school. It was a nationwide

IT'S YOUR WORLD—IF YOU DON'T LIKE IT, CHANGE IT

actions that will show that your town's religious community is against war.

Now that you have more of a base, you can plan a bigger action, like a peace vigil. Depending on the size of your town, you might want to do something like walk from one place of worship to another. One group starts at its meeting place and walks to the next one, carrying candles, then the two groups walk to the next one, and so on, until you arrive at the last one, with all of the faiths gathered together. If that isn't feasible, perhaps you can gather at the most centrally located address, or in the town square, or at a park. (Make sure you get permits for those if necessary.)

Your coalition can reach out to people who aren't regular churchgoers as well. Announce the vigil at services and post it on your church bulletin board, but also publicize the event around town so that anyone who wants to can join. Local politicians will probably jump at the chance. Everyone is for peace, right?

Depending on the sentiments of your group, you can do more pointed or polemic actions, or you may choose to just come together under the big tent of "peace." That's ok—it's still a powerful form of activism.

Go to a Big Protest

Check out some of the sites in the reference section of this chapter for an anti-war event near you. Get a group of people together and go. (And if there isn't one, think about organizing one.)

Feel free to make up your own chants. One of the most effective groups at an anti-war rally in NYC was a group called the Glamazons, fabulous drag queens who chanted "Le peace, c'est chic" and threw glitter on people. Some oldies but goodies are:

> One, two, three, four,
> we don't want another war.
> Five, six, seven, eight,
> stop the killing, stop the hate.
>
> Hey, hey, ho ho, you say war,
> we say no.
>
> What do we want?
> Peace!
> When do we want it?
> Now!.

Don't laugh, but you might feel left out if you don't know some of the songs or chants at the protests.

Bring water and a snack. Dress appropriately for the weather. If it's a planned march, stay in the area that the permit is for. Have phone numbers with you and an agreed-upon meeting point if you get separated from your friends. If the police are being cool, don't harass them. If they aren't being

student walkout to protest the war, scheduled for November 20. It was difficult because I go to a private school. There are schools in New York City where if you cut a class, it is no big deal; it is completely fine. My school is not like that. There's a possibility of suspension if you cut class.

So I knew no one would join the walkout if they had to cut. At my school it's just not acceptable—people wouldn't even consider it. I decided to hand out permission slips so people could have their parents approve them missing class. The permission slip basically said "I give my child permission to leave school for bla bla bla," and we explained the walkout. Some people thought that was strange because then it's not really a walkout, but I thought, "Well, what's more important? Do I want people to come?" Because no one would come if they had to cut.

I was handing these things out in the morning when parents were dropping their kids off and I had a huge misunderstanding with the administration. I had gone to the dean, and I should have gone to the head of the high

cool, get away from them. If you are near a group of people who you sense are going to engage in behavior with which you are uncomfortable—breaking down a barricade or interfering with a business along the route—get away from them and continue with the march.

A demonstration is a great place to publicize your anti-war group if you have one, and to connect with other groups. Bring flyers and cards to hand out to other protestors and to bystanders.

Going to a demonstration can be an uplifting and energizing experience. Seeing all these other people who believe as you do and who are willing to speak out is a good reminder that you aren't the only person struggling to make a difference.

THE 5-MINUTE ACTIVIST

Clear Landmines

Long after a war is over, landmines left behind continue to kill and injure thousands of innocent people every year. Every visit to this site helps to eradicate landmines around the world through the Canadian Landmine Foundation. Visitors are limited to one click per day. (You can read more about the global landmine problem at www.landmines.org; the UN also does a lot of work in this area.)
www.clearlandmines.com

RESOURCES

Web Sites

The M. K. Gandhi Institute for Nonviolence

Mahatma Gandhi was an Indian philosopher who espoused what he called "satyagraha," the principle of nonviolent resisitance. He personally worked with many groups in South Africa and elsewhere to overcome their oppression through peaceful means. In his later life Gandhi became a world figure, famous for his fasts and good works. The institute was founded by his grandson Arun Gandhi in order to keep promoting Mahatma Gandhi's ideas and writings on nonviolence. The site is a little bit disorganized, but the site has a good selection of articles by Gandhi and his followers, including a profound reponse to September 11 attacks written by Arun.

www.gandhiinstitute.org

The King Center

The King Center's mission is to

school, and he thought I was trying to undermine his authority. I got called into the office of the head of my school, and I was told that I was playing games, and that what I was doing was like passing out leaflets for a political party.

I was very confused by this. As a teenager and as a high school student I was being given the impression that I was just supposed to take my five classes a day and be okay with that. I try to educate myself in other ways. I'm not going to be tied down because of my age or my school. I think my school wants us to be unaffected instead of multifaceted, but for so many of us, that's not the way we are. It's not in us.

I did learn that if you are trying to organize, the first things to think about are where you're organizing from and the logistics. It was so new to me, it was my first month as an activist, and I just didn't know. In the end, I think twenty of us walked out. It's a really small school, so it wasn't a bad showing. We took the train to Union Square and then we marched to Washington Square where there was a little rally.

keep the work and ideals of Dr. Martin Luther King Jr. alive. They do this through producing educational materials, supporting research, and welcoming visitors to the center's Atlanta offices. The site has extensive information about the life of Dr. King, and a good explanation of his principles of nonviolence. You can take the pledge of nonviolence, read his famous "Letter from a Birmingham Jail," check out a great glossary of nonviolence, and more.
www.thekingcenter.com

National Youth and Student Peace Coalition

NYSPC was formed in the wake of the events of September 11. It's a national group with fifteen member organizations. NYSPC works to end war and to fight racism, cuts in education, and limits on civil rights. You can't join NYSPC as an individual, but you can join one of the affiliated groups, or just use the site—it's a great clearing house for youth anti-war activism and national actions like Books Not Bombs. If you have a project you'd like NYSPC to get involved with, there is a process for you to submit it.
www.nyspc.net

Nuclear Age Peace Foundation

This is a worldwide group that wants to abolish nuclear weapons and promote sustainable and ethical uses of technology. The site has a lot of great background on nuclear issues, which don't get much attention in the media anymore. The action center has letter-writing campaigns, info on press releases and other activism tips, and a really excellent detailed way to conduct your own civilian weapons inspection. There are also internship opportunities, a list of movies with nuclear themes, and a speaker's bureau.

www.wagingpeace.org

September Eleventh Families for Peaceful Tomorrows

Founded by family members of September 11 victims, Peaceful Tomorrows is an advocacy group dedicated to seeking nonviolent solutions to ending terrorism. It's members are also devoted to demanding a full investigation into the attacks that took the lives of those they love. The site has current news links, pictures from vigils and protests, and many heartfelt thoughts on nonviolence written by families who are working through their grief and trying to make a difference.

www.peacefultomorrows.org

The Student Peace Action Network

SPAN, formed in 1995, is one of

I kept doing a lot of activism right up until the war started. Throughout the whole process I'd thought that we really could stop it if people just understood, and when the war started I just couldn't believe it. It was surreal. It seemed impossible. I was dealing with a lot of disappointment, and I stopped going to ANSWER and going to rallies or doing big organizing things.

I don't feel like I've stopped being an activist, though. I guess I've started to realize that there are more ways to go about it. I wrote an article for a newsletter about street harassment. I consider that activism. I know activism is something I'll do for the rest of my life. Once you become conscious, there's no turning back.

I think that so many people think activism is going to a march and being cold and screaming. It's so much more—it's writing letters and writing articles, and even just having conversations. It's about having an open mind, and really believing in something and wanting more than anything to have it change. It's such a powerful thing to

the better-known student peace groups, and it's active on both high school and college campuses. Funded by the Peace Action Network, a large grassroots peace and justice organization, SPAN's aim is to fight to end social, economic, and physical violence, achieve nuclear disarmament, and promote alternatives to war. Currently its focus is ending the occupation of Iraq and getting the military out of schools. The site explains all of the issues with a special emphasis on why students should care about them. There's information on how to contact the SPAN chapter nearest you, or how to organize one on your campus.

www.studentpeaceaction.org

United for Peace and Justice

This is an anti-war coalition with more than 750 member organizations. It was launched during the buildup to the war in Iraq and continues to be very active, mobilizing for huge marches, posting calls to action from member organizations, and providing a great online space for peace activists to connect and share information, resources, and ideas. On the site there is a ton of information about how to organize, as well as background on the Iraq war, an activist tool kit, and information on potential speakers for your group.

www.unitedforpeace.org

Veterans Against the Iraq War

VAIW is a group of American veterans whose motto is "Support the troops, oppose the policy." Their

site lists every American soldier who was killed in the current conflict with Iraq, and also provides information about soldiers who were injured and then mistreated or neglected. The action page suggests things like participating in peace missions or lobbying Congress.
www.vaiw.org

Veterans for Peace

The members of Veterans for Peace want to end war as an instrument of foreign policy, educate the public about the costs of war, keep our government out of the internal affairs of other nations, and abolish nuclear arms. They are committed to achieving these goals through nonviolent and democratic means. The organization costs money to join, but the site, while troops-focused, is really worthwhile. It not only shows the perspective of veterans who want to stop war, but it also has powerful features, such as photos of "Arlington West," an art project that placed white crosses in a field, one for every

be involved in activism. It opens you up to being a more involved person, and how to make conscious decisions in what you do. Activism is feeling very passionate about something, and from that wanting to do something. It really comes down to just action.

To learn more about ANSWER, visit www.internationalanswer.org.

dead soldier, and the Iraq-o-meter, which looks like an arcade game but pings horribly every time a soldier or a civilian dies, while maintaining a big "0" over the weapons of mass destruction icon.
www.veteransforpeace.org

Women's International League for Peace and Freedom
Founded in 1915, WILPF works to end all forms of violence and promote equality for all, regardless of sex, race, or sexual preference. This site provides news and updates on issues concerning war and violence, and offers ways to get involved. WILPF's current campaigns, which will be the group's focus for the next three years, are dismantling the war economy, seeking racial justice, normalizing relations with Cuba, and reducing the power corporations have in America and the world.
www.wilpf.org

Books

A Force More Powerful: A Century of Nonviolent Conflict
By Peter Ackerman and Jack Duvall
Ackerman and Duvall trace nonviolent victories throughout history, highlighting the many times that significant social change was brought about by peaceful means. The stories are both gripping and inspiring—a reminder that nonviolence doesn't mean nonaction.

Gandhi on Non-Violence: A Selection from the Writings of Mahatma Gandhi

By Mahatma Gandhi and Mohandas Gandhi,
Edited by Thomas Merton
Merton provides a great introduction to Gandhi with this reader, taking selected passages from the famed pacifist's writings and interpreting them into easy-to-understand terms.

Nonviolence in America: A Documentary History

Edited by Staughton Lynd & Alice Lynd
This book is out of print, but your library might have it or be able to get it for you, and there are sometimes used copies for sale on Amazon.com. First published in 1966, *Nonviolence in America* compiles writings and texts from nonviolent activists, with selections from conscientious objectors, suffragettes, civil rights workers, and more. It's a great reminder that pacifism is an American tradition.

The Power of Nonviolence: Writings by Advocates of Peace

Edited by Howard Zinn
This is an anthology of essays on peace and nonviolence, with selections from Dr. Martin Luther King Jr., Arundhati Roy, and Ralph Waldo Emerson, among others. It's a great book to pick up whenever you want to read a little—the pieces are arranged in chronological order, but you can read them any way you like. Don't miss the contribution from Albert Camus.

A Testament of Hope: The Essential Writings and Speeches of Martin Luther King, Jr.
Edited by James M. Washington
King is probably our nation's greatest leader for the cause of nonviolent justice. His writings, speeches, and actions galvanized the civil rights movement of the 1960s and remain influential today. This book is expensive, but it's the best collection out there of his thoughts on nonviolence, civil disobedience, and equality. If you don't have access to this edition, there are many many other collections and reprints of his writing, and any of it you can get your hands on is worth reading.

Fighting the Spread of HIV/AIDS

THE ISSUES

HIV/AIDS affects everyone. It is not a gay disease—anyone can be infected, whether they are gay, straight, white, black, Hispanic, young, or old. Young people are one of the most at-risk populations: About half of all new infections, two million cases per year, are people who are between fifteen and twenty-four. Every minute, six people between the ages of five and twenty-five are infected with the virus that causes AIDS. Young women, particularly young women of color, are the fastest growing group of infected individuals.

HIV (Human Immunodeficiency Virus) is the virus that causes AIDS (Acquired Immune Deficiency Syndrome). HIV attacks the T cells, important cells in your body's immune system. Initially your body is able to replace those cells as they are lost, but eventually your immune system will shut down. At this stage, HIV infection becomes AIDS. Your body is very weak and vulnerable to catching other diseases like pneumonia, tuberculosis, and cancer.

When someone is tested and learns that he or she is infected with HIV (also called being "HIV positive"), it's essential that he or she access good health care and support services. Depending on how far the infection has progressed, that person might be put on an anti-HIV drug regimen (sometimes called a cocktail) aimed at slowing the growth and progression of the virus. There is no way to rid your body of the virus, but with good care HIV infection has become more like a chronic illness that you can live with for a long time before it develops into AIDS. When and if AIDS does develop, it, too, can be managed for a long time—much longer than in the past. However, AIDS is still almost always fatal. There is no cure or vaccine for HIV or for AIDS.

Preventing the spread of HIV is critical for everyone, and everyone should be aware of how you can be infected, and how to prevent infection. HIV is spread when an uninfected person comes into contact with the blood or the sexual fluids of someone who is infected. This usually happens through unprotected sex or through sharing needles used to inject intravenous drugs. Unprotected vaginal and anal sex are the most common ways that HIV is spread between partners; however, unprotected oral-genital sex has been shown to transmit HIV infection from one partner to another. Some children born to HIV-infected mothers will also become HIV positive, but this risk has markedly decreased in recent years due to the development of anti-HIV drug regimens. HIV-positive mothers are also encouraged to bottle feed instead of breast-feed to further reduce the risk. Before 1985, transfusions of blood products were also a significant risk, particularly for hemophiliacs, but improved procedures and test techniques have nearly eliminated this avenue of transmission.

The most common way that teenagers become infected is by having unprotected sex with someone who is HIV positive. This happens for a variety of reasons. Many teenagers don't know or realize how real the risk of infection is. Teenagers can often be in denial, thinking that they will live forever, and assume that for some reason "It won't happen to me." Many young people find it difficult to insist on condom use with their partners, especially if their partner is older. Some mistakenly think that oral sex is "okay" and that no precautions need to be taken. Many teenagers haven't taken the test for HIV, and as a result could be infected and not know it— and thus unknowingly pass the infection on to their partners. Other teens might believe their partner when he or she claims to be HIV negative, when it is more likely that he or she has never been tested. The common thread is ignorance. Too many young people don't know the facts about HIV/AIDS and how to protect themselves.

For this reason, most HIV/AIDS activism aimed at teenagers centers around education. Schools are not doing an adequate job. Federally mandated abstinence education, which forbids discussion of HIV/AIDS and safer sex practices, is the only sex education many students get. Activists get the word

LAURA'S STORY

Laura Cherkas is eighteen years old and a senior at San Marin High School in Novato, California.

The Marin AIDS Project has a thing called YouthReach that's their peer education group. I got involved with Reach because my school has an abstinence-only education policy. We weren't learning anything about preventing STDs or pregnancy or anything like that, so I wanted to educate myself and then teach others. Reach's main focus is to go into classrooms and talk to high school and sometimes middle school students about issues like HIV/AIDS, STDs, drug abuse, and sexual abuse. My goal was to try to get into my own school and work around the barriers that my school had put up.

We had about a month of training, but we packed a lot into the month. It was one weekday night every week for three hours, and then twice we had an entire weekend: two full days of training. It was kind of a bonding thing and education at the same time. We had "get to know

out through producing public service announcements (PSAs) to air on television, doing outreach to schools, and creating peer education programs so that youth can spread the word themselves.

Another arm of AIDS activism is encouraging everyone who is sexually active to get tested. Someone could be infected with HIV and not know it, which means he or she will not get the right health care as soon as possible, and that he or she may unknowingly transmit the virus. Other activists work with those who are living with HIV/AIDS by offering counseling, lobbying for better health care and funding for HIV/AIDS research, and speaking out about hate crimes and discrimination against those who are infected. There are fourteen million children who have been orphaned by AIDS, and many activists are working to help them. Some activists work at programs called needle exchanges; because intravenous drug users sharing needles often spread HIV, needle exchange programs allow users to trade in used needles for clean ones so the risk is reduced.

AIDS is a global epidemic. There are presently more than thirty-six million people worldwide living with HIV or AIDS. Seventy percent of the people who have HIV or AIDS live in sub-Saharan Africa. (Sub-Saharan Africa is basically the entire African continent and the surrounding islands, except for the countries that border the Mediterranean. It includes forty-eight countries. Among them are Sudan, Niger, Kenya, Ethiopia, Zambia, and Mozambique.) In these countries access to treatment is limited, drugs are often unaffordable, and the situation has become critical. One out of every ten people in sub-Saharan Africa is infected, and in some parts of South Africa one person in every five is HIV positive. The United Nations, the World Health Organization, and many other groups are very active in this area, but they are hampered by lack of funds and support from the international community.

Choosing to become an HIV/AIDS activist means committing yourself to fighting ignorance. It's ignorance of personal risk that leads to the spread of HIV through needle sharing and unsafe sex practices. It's ignorance of the global spread of the disease and the suffering it causes that prevents adequate funding for research, health care, and international aid. By speaking out on the subject—in your personal life, at school, and in your community—you can counter that ignorance with the truth about HIV/AIDS.

THE AT-HOME ACTIVIST

Get Tested

Getting tested for HIV is a great way to fight AIDS. If you are sexually active, you should be tested to

you" activities, and then we'd learn the different presentations that we do. We learned HIV basics, all about different STDs, and stuff like that. There were a lot of different kinds of kids in the program from all over Marin County. I got to meet kids that I never would have met otherwise—people who are from different social groups and different areas.

My first presentation was what we call HIV 101, at a high school in the next town over. The way it works is that schools contact Reach and ask for speakers, and then members of the group sign up to give that presentation. This time it was me and a girl named Danielle. I was very nervous. It was a class of freshmen, which is the worst—I've learned over the years that it's easier to talk to older kids about sensitive subjects because they are more mature. They're not like, "Ha, ha! She said 'ejaculate'!"

We had an outline of the presentation and guidelines for the activities and stuff like that, so Danielle and I studied them beforehand and decided who was going to talk about what. Once you get up there, you just freestyle it based on the guidelines. We explained

see if you've become infected. If you aren't sexually active, but you have friends who are, encourage them to take the test and offer to go with them and support them through the process.

There are specific risk factors that make it even more important to get tested:

If you've had unprotected sex. Ever.

If you've had sex with someone who has used drugs by injection or who has HIV

If you've ever had an STI or STD* such as herpes or gonorrhea

If you've ever had an unplanned pregnancy

If you've ever been sexually assaulted or been forced into sex against your will

If you've ever passed out or forgotten what happened to you, due to drinking or drugs

If you've ever shared needles or other things that pierce the skin (like piercing guns)

If your mother had HIV when you were born

If you've ever gotten a blood transfusion

*STI stands for "sexually transmitted infection," and STD stands for "sexually transmitted disease." Generally STI is used to refer to all infections that can be transferred by intimate contact. STD refers to an STI that has developed symptoms. The distinction was initially introduce to emphasize the fact that people are often infected without knowing it or without having any symptoms; however, many health organizations such as the Center for Disease Control and Planned Parenthood now use STI exclusively, while others stick to STD and some use the terms nearly interchangeably. In this book the two terms are distinct.

You can get tested on a visit to your regular doctor or at a public or private clinic. To find a testing site near you, visit the National HIV Testing Resources Web site (www.hivtest.org), the Web site for the Children's Hospital at Montefiore Medical Center (www.adolescentaids.org), or the Know HIV/AIDS site (www.knowhivaids.org). Many places offer the test free of charge, but ask about fees first to make sure.

It's natural to be concerned about privacy when you get tested. A teenager can get tested and treated for STIs in every state and the District of Columbia without parental consent; however, only twenty-nine states explicitly include HIV under their consent law. Physicians are not required to inform parents of test results, except in Iowa, where they must tell the parents if an HIV test is positive. In some states your right to consent to testing and treatment starts at twelve years of age, while in others you must be fourteen. (In South Carolina you must be sixteen.) In order to be clear on the laws in your state, check out the chart "Minors and the Right to Consent to Health Care and Make Other Important Decisions" on the Alan Guttmacher Institute Web site

the basics of HIV: T-Cell count, how the testing works, the difference between HIV and AIDS, methods of transmission, what to do if you think you may be infected, when you want to get tested, when you might not want to get tested, how the disease works, and some of the medications and therapies that are available for treatments afterward.

Basically, we try to get across the message that first of all HIV can happen to anyone; it's not a disease that can be stereotyped. You can't say "This is a gay man's disease" or "This is a black man's disease." And we try to get across the point that this is a very serious disease, but you can still have a life if you have HIV. Your quality of life may decrease, but it's not going to be the end of the world; there's still hope. We had a speaker, a man who was HIV positive, and he spoke for about a half hour about his experience.

My first presentation actually went really well, and since then I have done so many that I'm not nervous at all anymore.

I've been trying to do more things at my school, but it's hard because of the

(www.guttmacher.org/graphics/gr030405_f1.html) And ask what the policy is at the place where you plan to get tested; many states leave it up to the health care provider to determine if you are mature enough to make the decision about testing.

There are two types of testing practices: anonymous and confidential. An anonymous test means that your name will not be recorded and no one learns your results except you. A confidential test means that your name and results will be recorded in your medical chart, and they may also be reported to public health officials and/or become part of your medical record. In some states, if you test positive, your results may be reported to your current or previous sex partners without your permission. Because of these variations, if you choose to take a confidential test, ask what will happen with your results before you take it.

There are home HIV kits available by mail order and in many drugstores. Don't buy a kit that claims to show you your results right there before your eyes. What you want is called a home collection kit. These tests allow you to collect a sample at home, mail it in, and then call and get your results on the phone. Currently the only kit approved by the FDA is the Home Access Express HIV-1 Test System, manufactured by Home Access Health Corporation. It costs between forty and sixty dollars. Generally home testing is not recommended because it is best to get your results face-to-face, but not everyone has access to a testing site.

Before you commit to taking the test, there are some things you need to think about. It's a good idea to enlist a trusted friend or family member with whom you can discuss your test and the results—you might even invite him or her to go with you if you go get tested. You should consider what kind of support you will have from family and friends if you do test positive and what kind of access to health care you have. If you are in a very bad place in your life—if you are extremely depressed or under a lot of stress, for example—this may not be the right time to get tested. If you don't think that you can handle testing positive, you might want to wait. (If you do choose to wait, you should either abstain from sex or practice safe sex until you know your HIV status.) If you're worried about needles, don't be. Most tests now use oral swabs, kind of like Q-tips, and they just swipe the inside of your mouth.

If you go to a testing site for your test, a counselor will meet with you before you take the test. The counselor will explain the test to you and ask you some questions. Be honest with your counselor about your sexual behavior and the kinds of safe or unsafe sex that you've engaged in. He or she can alert you to things you might have thought were okay but

abstinence-only situation. There's no way there could be a Reach presentation there. I wanted to have a condom table for National Condom Week, and my vice principal said we couldn't do it. But then I talked to the school superintendent, and she gave me the go-ahead. She said it was okay because it wasn't in a classroom.

So we had a table in the lunch area. We had pamphlets that said "20 Ways to Say Just Use It," that encourage people to use condoms, but a school administrator wouldn't let us pass them out. People could only come to the table and look at them there. We were also telling people that there was Condom Pass going on off campus where they could get condoms. That really upset the administrator. She said it was illegal for me to tell people where they could get condoms, which I don't think is true. But it's things like that that make it difficult to work in my high school.

One thing that went off well was World AIDS Day in December. They couldn't really have an objection to World AIDS Day. We were able to have a table and pass out red ribbon pins, which

aren't and reassure you about other things. Your pretest counseling session is also your chance to talk to the counselor about any concerns you might have about your risk of getting HIV, what the results of the test might mean, and what will happen to your results. You should have all of your questions answered before you commit to taking the test.

Once you take the test, it usually takes at least a week to get your results. The test checks to see if you have certain antibodies in your blood—their presence means you have the virus, or are HIV positive. If there are no antibodies, then your test result will be negative.

Most test centers require you to come in and get your results in person from a counselor who will explain your results to you. If you test positive, your counselor will be able to help you with any feelings of fear or being overwhelmed that you might have. Testing positive does not mean you are going to die immediately, and it doesn't mean that you have AIDS. Many people live long healthy lives even though they are HIV positive. Testing positive does mean that you need to get health care to help you stay well. It also means you should enlist your loved ones in a support network to help you deal with your HIV status. You also need to take great care not to infect others.

If your test is negative, it's important that you realize that you still need to protect yourself from the virus. Because it can take three to six months to test positive after being exposed, you should get retested in six months.

Consider talking about getting tested with your friends. If you tell them that you have been tested and that it's something everyone should do, you might allay some nervousness they have about getting tested. Tell your friends that it was not a hassle, and that you will go with them if needed. Make sure that they make an informed decision to get tested, just like you did.

THE CAMPUS ACTIVIST

Fight for Comprehensive Sex Education

Does your school have a good HIV/AIDS awareness curriculum? Do you think that you and your classmates know all you need to about the virus and how to protect yourselves? Unfortunately the answer to this for many teenagers is no. Since 1996 Congress has funded only so-called "abstinence-only" sex education in schools.

Abstinence-only education is a sex-ed curriculum that, well, teaches only abstinence. Students are told that the only way that they can live a healthy life is to abstain from sex. These classes explicitly forbid discussion of HIV and AIDS, premarital sex, safer sex practices, contraception,

was pretty successful. A lot of kids took ribbons and it really warmed my heart; it was inspiring.

Everyone at my school knows that I do this—I'm pretty vocal about it. I've had people ask me for condoms, which I'm happy to give out. Sometimes people ask me for information. It feels good to be trusted about this kind of stuff. Plus I know that I'm giving them the right sort of information.

I don't think most high school students, especially young women, who are the fastest-growing population of people with HIV, know that they are such an at-risk group. Here in Marin, I think it's something like the second- or third-highest HIV rate per capita in the state, but no one knows it because it's so hushed up. A lot of things are like that here—pregnancy, for example. I think a lot of girls just don't know that they are the at-risk population. I've heard so many stories about people who were positive who thought, "I have a good life. It doesn't happen to people with good lives." And then it did. It's that disassociation—I think that's the most dangerous thing.

143

abortion, and homosexuality, among other things. Abstinence education is demonstrably harmful to teenagers. The sole focus of these programs is the benefits of abstaining from sex. Nearly all major health organizations agree that abstinence is an important part of sex education, and the only way to completely avoid pregnancy or STIs, but it should never be the entire curriculum. Teens who have only had abstinence education are less likely to use contraception when they do have sex and are more likely to get pregnant or be infected with an STI. These teenagers are also less likely to seek help when these situations occur.

Good comprehensive sex education (also called family life education) should include: information on abstinence and waiting to have sex; ways to reduce the risk of disease and unplanned pregnancy; and instruction on decision making, communication, and ways to say no if that is your choice. The program should have well-trained instructors and allow open discussion. Ideally, sex education is offered during freshman or sophomore years.

If your school uses an abstinence-only curriculum, or if it's curriculum doesn't meet the above criteria, there are thing you can do t make sure your peers are getting the information thet need. Don't go it alone on this project. Get a group together. You might want to involve student government or a gay/straight alliance club if there is one on your campus. Circulating flyers or calling for a meeting to discuss changing the curriculum can bring a lot of new friends out to work with you.

At the first meeting, have everyone sign in and give his or her e-mail and phone number. When everyone is together, go around the room for introductions. (Don't forget to introduce yourself.) Explain why you feel so strongly that your school needs a better sex-ed curriculum. It's a good idea to use a visual aid, like a chalkboard or a big piece of paper. On one side you can put the components of good sex education as outlined above; on the other you can check off whether your school is meeting this standard. This exercise will drive home the need for a change.

If your group agrees that you need to take action at your school, discuss your options. One is to institute a peer education program. That means that some students will get training and education on the issues, and then they will teach others. A good resource for setting up an HIV/AIDS peer education program is on the Advocates for Youth Web site (www.advocatesforyouth.org). Their program is called Teens for AIDS and STI Prevention and doesn't even need to be set up at school—it's adaptable to a faith-based institution, community center, or other setting. There might also be groups in your community such as local health centers or chapters of national

If I could change just one thing about where I'm growing up, I would want everyone to be educated. I want them to have the power to make an informed choice. We hope that most people who know how to protect themselves will do so, but it's very saddening to know that there are people out there who don't know how to protect themselves even if they wanted to. That's what I'm here for, just to get out any information I know about how to keep yourself healthy. I wish every high school student in Marin could have the opportunity to get all the education that I got from being in YouthReach.

If you want to learn more about YouthReach, visit the Marin AIDS Project Web site, www.marinaidsproject.org.

organizations like NARAL who already have peer education programs—call around and ask. If your school is a particularly hostile environment for HIV/AIDS education, this might be the way to go.

A more challenging but completely doable option is to change the sex-ed curriculum at your school or in your school district. Your best resource for this type of project is "The Roadmap: A Teen Guide to Changing Your School's Sex Ed," published by the Network for Family Life Education at Rutgers University. You can download the road map on the Sex, Etc. Web site (www.sxetc.org); click on "Take Action." It's got everything: a step-by-step program, sample flyers, press releases and school board resolutions, and tips on involving parents and the community. (You can read about one teenager's successful campaign to change her school district's sex ed in the "Defending Women's Rights" chapter—see "Erica's Story.")

When you've decided on your plan, divide up the duties so no one is overwhelmed and everyone is involved. Don't let anyone (including yourself) take on too much—they will just burn out.

Choose a name for your group. Something like "The Student Committee for Improving Education" is good. If anyone in the group is artistic, he or she could design a logo to put on all of your literature and materials. Set a date, time, and place for your next meeting and tell everyone that you are going to create a mailing list or phone list from the sign-in sheet.

This project will take time, so make sure that your group remains energized and inspired. Maintain a regular meeting schedule. You might want to ask people to bring snacks or tunes to meetings when appropriate, or invite guest speakers. If you've been split up into separate groups for a while, working on different things, have each group present their work to the others so everyone knows the status of the project.

Sex education, even education that is intended to prevent disease and unwanted pregnancies, can be a controversial topic. Just bringing up the subjects can make some people uncomfortable or even angry. Be ready for some opposition to your work. In many cases, resistance comes from ignorance, and once you explain your position, those who are challenging you might change their minds, but that won't always happen.

If you get discouraged, remember that your work is important for the public health and the public good. Educating your fellow students about their risks for HIV and AIDS and giving them the tools they need to protect themselves and others is a lifesaving cause.

HENRY'S STORY

Henry Schrader is seventeen years old and a senior at Francis W. Parker Charter Essential School in Fitchburg, Massachusetts.

I got involved with Ride FAR, the Ride for Aids Resources, through a family friend. Suzy Becker started Ride FAR in 1989 because she had friends who had HIV/AIDS, and she wanted to help them. It's a five-day, five-hundred-mile bike ride to raise money and awareness for people living with HIV/AIDS. So far it has raised over five hundred thousand dollars.

I grew up hearing about it, and when I got old enough I decided I wanted to be a part of it and be a crew member. The first time I went was in 2001, when I was fourteen, and then I went again last year when I was sixteen. The ride is every other year. Even though I had signed up, I was really hesitant my first year. I was thinking, "I don't know how this is gonna be."

Being a crew member means that you do everything to make sure the ride goes smoothly. We mark the routes and make sure that the rest stops are set up—we do

THE COMMUNITY ACTIVIST

Get Local Businesses to Sign an Anti-Discrimination Pledge

Those who are living with HIV and AIDS often suffer from discrimination and civil rights violations. Landlords might not want to rent to them and they sometimes have trouble getting custody of their children. They may not be considered for jobs they are applying for, or they may get passed over for promotions or get fired when their HIV status becomes known. Even hospitals and medical facilities have been known to treat them differently solely because they are infected.

Many states have passed laws making it illegal to discriminate against people based on their HIV status. Additionally, civil rights activists are fighting to make sure that those living with HIV or AIDS are covered under the federal Americans with Disabilities Act (ADA). However, none of these laws applies across the board—the ADA doesn't apply to businesses with fewer than fifteen employees, for example—and they are selectively enforced at best. Furthermore, many people don't even know the laws exist. Others are aware of the laws but break them anyway because they harbor prejudices based on misconceptions and ignorance about HIV and how it is spread.

Getting your local business community to sign an anti-discrimination pledge is a great way to raise awareness about this issue. While you're gathering signatures, you'll have the opportunity to talk one-on-one with business owners and other community members who can influence public opinion. And then when the petition is done and you are publicizing it, you can educate many others about HIV and HIV discrimination.

First you need to write the anti-discrimination statement. It doesn't have to be provocative—just a simple statement saying that each business that signs on will treat HIV-positive people just like they treat anyone else. Here's a sample statement:

Right now, there are more than 850,000 Americans infected by HIV, the virus that causes AIDS. Too often those who have the disease must suffer unnecessarily from intolerance, harassment, and discrimination.

HIV infection cannot be spread through casual contact and community members should have no fears about interacting with an HIV positive person. By signing this statement, I am affirming that my business welcomes those who are HIV positive as customers, as employees, as neighbors, and as valuable members of

everything so that the riders don't have to do anything other than ride. We also have a thing called "angels," where a crew member is responsible for a particular rider, and makes sure that rider has a few of the comforts of home during the ride. You call your rider up before the ride, introduce yourself, and ask them if there's anything that they really enjoy, and you try to get it for them. Some people like to read the paper every morning, so you would go to the store or whatever and get a paper for them.

Being a crew member is strenuous. On a typical day, we get up around 6 a.m. and make breakfast, then pack the cars with food, water, and medical kits. We help the riders with their bikes—tuning them up or finding parts. Then we have breakfast and get on the road. For the rest of the day we're on van duty until everyone's in at the next town, which is usually about five or six o'clock.

Van duty means that the ten-person crew is divided up into four vans: the lead van, the trail van, and two in the middle. We are driving along where the riders are riding.

the community—just as we would welcome anyone.

I promise to treat them with respect and courtesy, to maintain their privacy, and to ensure that everyone in my place of business does as well. I hope that everyone else in our local business community joins me in making this pledge. We are a town of tolerance, not prejudice.

Print up the pledge in petition form, with spaces for each business owner to sign and to put the name, address, and phone number of the business. Start with the businesses you think are most likely to sign your pledge. It will strengthen your case with those who are wavering if they see that a lot of others have already signed on. The rest is all footwork—you might want to enlist some friends, and just do a few square blocks every weekend, or hit all the malls before you go any-where else. In each place of business, introduce your-self and ask for the manager. If the place is really busy, come back another time.

When you meet the manager, shake hands and ask for a few minutes of their time. Say something like "I'm a student at Strong Valley High School here in town, and I'm going door-to-door asking local businesses to sign an anti-discrimination pledge. You may not know this, but some people discriminate against others just because they are infected with the HIV virus. Not only is that illegal, but it's also unnecessary, because the virus can't be spread through casual contact. There's no reason why someone who is HIV positive can't shop where they want to, live where they want to, eat where they want to, or anything like that. I know that our town is a tolerant town and I want to make it clear to everyone that our business community does not discriminate. I've written up this statement that basically says that your business won't violate the civil rights of someone who has HIV. Will you sign it?"

Hopefully he or she just says yes at this point. If they do, have them sign up, thank them, and you're on to the next place. It's a good idea to make up some cool posters or certificates to give to those who sign the pledge to display in their window or on their walls. These could say something like "This business does not discriminate on the basis of HIV-positive status." That will really help more and more people know about the issue.

The business owner may say that he or she needs to think about it or to talk to the boss. If this happens, leave a copy of the petition for review, along with an information sheet about your pledge drive. Ask for the boss's name and number so you can ask for him or her when you follow up. The information sheet should have basic information about who you are and how to contact you. You should make a state-

The first van goes ahead to make sure the route is not obscured in any way. The trail van makes sure that no one gets left behind, and then the other vans go from the back to the front making sure that people always have water and stuff. We drive alongside each rider and give them a thumbs-up, and if they give us a thumbs-up back then we know everything's okay. If they give us a thumbs-down, then we find somewhere safe and pull over.

Once we get to wherever we're staying that night, we unpack the vans, deliver the bags, and show the bikers where to put their bikes, or put them away ourselves. We have dinner, and then we have another crew meeting to talk about the next day's route. Most of the crew members have been on the route before, so they say things like, "Watch out for this section, it's slippery," or whatever. Then we go to bed. It's a long day.

Ride FAR has no overhead. Every penny we raise goes directly to services for children and adults with HIV/AIDS. Each rider and crew member commits to raising a certain amount of money, and the food and lodging, etc., gets

ment on the information sheet about why you are doing this—how you learned about this issue and why it is important to you. Then go on to say why you think it is important for your community and business leaders to support this project.

If a business owner flat-out refuses to sign the pledge, ask why. Listen to his or her reason respectfully. Point out that the pledge does nothing other than state that the business will treat everyone with dignity and respect, no matter who they are. If the person seems to lack knowledge about AIDS or HIV, offer him or her some information. Don't get confrontational. If the person just seems timid, let him or her know that you expect many other businesses to also sign this, and that you will be happy to come back in a month to see if he or she has reconsidered. Thank the business owner for for listening and leave.

This is a media-friendly project, so you might want to send a press release or letter to local reporters. They could send someone to go with you as you gather signatures, and possibly print a list of the businesses that sign.

Other activism ideas:

Volunteer at a free clinic or other service organization dedicated to those with AIDS. Organizations like God's Love We Deliver (www.godslovewedeliver.org) provide meals to homebound people, while others help them with errands or walk their dogs. Look through the charities and nonprofits listed in your local yellow pages for an opportunity to get involved—if it seems like there is nothing to help those with AIDS, suggest starting one to an appropriate group.

Get involved in a needle exchange programs. Needle exchange programs reduce the spread of HIV among injection drug users, their families, and their communities by providing clean, new needles in exchange for used needles. In some towns, they have reduced the HIV infection rate by as much as thirty percent. They are usually run by local health organizations and volunteers who go out into the community at set times and days. You can read more about needle exchange and find a list of programs on the Harm Reduction Web site (www.harmreduction.org).

THE 5-MINUTE ACTIVIST

FreeDonation.com

You can click more than once per day on this site, which also has areas for supporting the arts, fighting cancer, saving the rain forests, and housing the homeless. Not only that, but your nonprofit can apply to be a recipient of the money raised through the program. The site

donated. Some participants get really creative. One woman had an auction and sold a lot of her belongings, and another one donated one day's proceeds from her art gallery. Other people just write letters and raise money that way.

I wrote a letter and sent it to just about everybody I go to school with. I go to a small school so that's about a hundred students. I sent it to family and friends. It was a regular letter, not e-mail. The second time I went, my letter was really good because I could talk about my experience on the 2001 ride. I said that it had been a life-changing experience, and that I learned what it means to be part of something important. I got a ton of responses and raised a lot of money, over fifteen hundred dollars. I was overjoyed that people were willing to give that much to the cause.

The sum of all the money raised gets divided into three donation areas. One-third goes overseas to a pediatric AIDS organization. One third goes to Project Inform, which helps people with HIV/AIDS understand all of their treatment options, and the final third goes to community-based service organizations

also lists facts about HIV and AIDS, and pointers to AIDS activist organizations.
www.freedonation.com/aids

RESOURCES:

Web Sites

Adolescent AIDS Program at the Children's Hospital at Montefiore Medical Center
The Children's Hospital at Montefiore has been a leader in adolescent AIDS education and research, and its Web site is a great place to go for anyone who want the facts on HIV/AIDS and its impact on youth. It has a big list of youth-friendly testing sites, along with detailed information about what it's like to get tested. There's also a zine, lists of adolescent health links, and other resources.
www.adolescentaids.org

Advocates for Youth

This is an advocacy group dedicated to supporting programs and policies that help youth make informed decisions about their reproductive and sexual health. The site has great information on starting your own peer education program, actions you can take like signing a petition for better sex ed, and ways to connect with other youth activists. They also do international work and a lot of work connected to emergency contraception.
www.advocatesforyouth.org

AIDS Coalition to Unleash Power (ACT UP)

Best known for their slogan, "Silence=Death," ACT UP is a direct-action group fiercely dedicated to the cause of AIDS activism. ACT UP recently launched Youth Education Life Line (YELL), an advocacy and direct-action group aimed at improving HIV prevention education in New York City's Public Schools. Even if you don't live in NYC, you can gain inspiration by looking at this project and download materials like flyers and posters with condom use instructions. The non-YELL sections of the site are useful too, with information on what the critical current issues are, how to start your own ACT UP chapter, where to get civil disobedience training, and alerts on upcoming actions.
www.actupny.org

AIDS Education Global Information System

The AIDS Education Global Information System (AEGIS) is a massive database of information

that the riders choose.

My goal for the 2005 ride is to train and do the ride as a rider and not a crew member. I would totally recommend to other kids my age that they do something like this. It might be scary at first because you're doing all this stuff with people you don't really know, and you're a minority, being a young person. But it's really, really fun. After the first day or so I was really getting into it. We were having a good time encouraging the riders and doing funny stuff. It's just really fun, and it opens you up to new types of people and new experiences.

To learn more about Ride FAR, visit www.ridefar.org. There are many other bike rides to benefit HIV/AIDS throughout the country. Try searching on Google to see if there is one near you

relating to AIDS and HIV: publications, CDC info, conferences, treatment options, and legal and government news. It's huge, and amazing, and really easy to navigate. Bookmark it for the AEGIS daily briefing—global HIV-related news, updated hourly. www.aegis.com

The AIDS Memorial Quilt

The AIDS Quilt, sometimes also known as the NAMES Project, is one of the better-known and most moving activism projects connected to the AIDS pandemic. The project began in 1987 when a group of activists decided to create a memorial for their friends who had died of AIDS. They made a quilt composed of panels, each panel representing one person, with images and words telling a little bit about his or her life. The project grew and grew, and now the quilt has more than 45,000 panels, created by friends, lovers, and families in tribute to those they've lost. (The number of panels represents about seven percent of AIDS deaths in America.) Horribly, the quilt is now too large to be physically displayed in its entirety—but it lives on virtually on this Web site, which offers electronic access to nearly every panel, as well as information on how to contribute a panel in honor of someone you know. www.aidsquilt.org

AIDS Treatment Activist Coalition

ATAC is a national coalition of activists who are working to improve AIDS-related research and treatment and to mobilize more activists within affected communities. The coalition includes activists working to get better AIDS treatment to the incarcerated, groups protesting price hikes in HIV and AIDS medications, and others who lobby Congress for better government aid for people living with HIV. You can join a working group and immediately get involved in some of their campaigns, like sending letters to members of Congress inside of pill bottles to protest budget cuts on AIDS research.

www.atac-usa.org

American Foundation for AIDS Research (amfAR)

AmfAR has two goals: to stop the spread of HIV and to protect the rights of those who have been infected. They're extremely well funded and do things on a big scale, supporting research, clinical trials, public education campaigns, and training for health-care workers in Africa and Asia. The site is a nice way to look at how AIDS activism works at the top level. If you're ever in New York, visit their offices to view "Guests and Foreigners: Corporal Histories," an art piece about the spread of AIDS, by conceptual artist Joseph Kosuth. Call 212-806-1600 for more information or to schedule your tour.

www.amfar.org

Black AIDS Institute

AIDS has had a disproportionate impact on the African-American community. The infection rate is much higher among African Americans than it is among other groups. The Black AIDS Institute functions as both a clearinghouse for HIV/AIDS information specifically geared for this community and an advocacy group lobbying for their interests. The site has fact sheets about how HIV/AIDS is affecting African Americans, and insights into cultural issues that may be affecting the fight against the spread of the disease. They also put out a magazine called Kujisource, available on the site as a free download. www.blackaids.org

The Body

This site is a great resource with extremely detailed information on every aspect of HIV/AIDS, including prevention, treatment options, opportunistic infections, and an HIV/AIDS newsroom. There's also culturally specific information, like how AIDS is impacting the Latino community, although there isn't a section addressing the needs of youth. The site has a fantastic activism area with ways to get involved, a history of AIDS activism, and profiles of people who are making a difference. Try taking the quiz that allows you to assess your own risk for HIV.
www.thebody.com

Centers for Disease Control and Prevention Divisions of HIV/AIDS Prevention

The CDC is part of the Department of Health and Human Services, charged with protecting and promoting the health of the American people. Their HIV/AIDS Web pages are the place to go for statis-

tics and facts about the disease, who it's affecting, and trends in the infection rate. The site also has comprehensive information on prevention, transmission, symptoms, testing, funding, and more. (Ironically, the CDC gives out information that many schools are prevented from giving.) There's also a toll-free twenty-four-hour hotline: 1-800-342-2437.
www.cdc.gov/hiv/dhap.htm

Coalition for Positive Sexuality

CPS was founded by a group of Chicago teenagers in order to provide their peers with information about sexuality and their bodies and to create discussions about the availability of good sex ed. While their hands-on activism is local, the site has a lot to offer to any visitor. You can read "Just Say Yes," a comprehensive sex-ed booklet, hang out on the boards, and browse the resource guide. The whole site is written in a good conversational tone.
www.positive.org

Critical Path AIDS Project

Critical Path is an advocacy group focused on obtaining better treatment options for HIV/AIDS. The site has information on all of their work, along with state-by-state information on available treatment and benefits. It also features a link to the AIDS Library of Philadelphia, where you can access their extensive collection of research and literature.
www.critpath.org

The Henry J. Kaiser Family Foundation

Kaiser is probably the best known and most respected health research organization out there. Their HIV/AIDS Web area has a lot of research and information about the disease and how and why it's affecting different communities, genders, and age groups. There are also stats on AIDS treatment and research funding, a description of current testing protocols, and probably anything else you might be looking for if you want a broad view of the pandemic and the many ways people are trying to stop it.
www.kff.org

KNOW HIV/AIDS

This is a joint project between the Kaiser Foundation (see above) and Viacom, a media conglomerate that owns MTV, UPN, and CBS, among other properties. (Viacom also owns Simon & Schuster, the company that is publishing this book.) The site has clear and to-the-point information on HIV/AIDS, how to protect yourself, and what it's like to get tested. There's also a links area to connect you to activism opportunities. Best of all is the front-page feature that allows you to enter your zip code and get a testing site near you.
www.knowhivaids.org

The National Minority AIDS Council
The NMAC is dedicated to promoting leadership in minority communities who will join the fight against HIV/AIDS. They train activists and health-care workers, and also work in the public policy

area to promote national policies that are sensitive to the needs of communities of color. The site has lists of HIV/AIDS hotlines, links to treatment information organizations, and good commentary on public policy in this area. You can join NMAC in Action, a newsletter program that keeps you up to date on the issues and alerts you when action is needed.

www.nmac.org

Stop HIV

This is the Web site for the Pennsylvania Prevention Project at the University of Pittsburgh, but the site is useful for anyone, especially because it covers some stuff other sites don't. Check out the clear, detailed explanations of how to use a condom and dental dam and other safer sex practices.

www.stophiv.com

The Student Global AIDS Campaign

Just like the name says, this is a student-based organization fighting AIDS with a global perspective. They have chapters and individual members from both colleges and high schools. Their advocacy work is mostly about pressuring members of Congress through letter writing, meetings, and rallies. They've been part of several successful campaigns, such as winning treatment for Coke's HIV-positive employees in Africa. On the site you can join one of their working groups, which focus on various topics like Third World debt or women and AIDS, and you'll get updates and calls to action

delivered to your mailbox. You could also start a chapter at your school.
www.fightglobalaids.org

Sex, Etc.—a Web site by teens, for teens

Sex, Etc. is under the umbrella of the Network for Family Life Education, a group that fights for comprehensive sex education in schools. The site is written and edited by teens, and its goal is to provide balanced and accurate information to other teens so they can make informed decisions about their sexual health. There are great first-person stories about getting tested, being a player, learning to say no, giving a baby up for adoption—you name it. There's also an extremely frank glossary, an Ask the Experts section, and tons of info about all aspects of sexual health, including HIV/AIDS prevention and education. You can get involved too, by contributing a story or applying to be on the advisory board.
www.sxetc.org

Books

AIDS: Why Should I Care? Teens Across America Speak Out

Edited and with an introduction by Robert Starr
A collection of essays from teens whose lives have been affected by the pandemic. A great book to read or pass on to a friend who still thinks "It can't happen to me."

And the Band Played On: Politics, People, and the AIDS Pandemic

By Randy Shilts, with a introduction by William Greider And the Band Played On is a definitive account of the first five years of the AIDS pandemic in America—where the first reported cases turned up, why the scientific and medical communities were slow to react, and how, in Shilts's view, the Reagan administration chose to look the other way. It's a story about a disease, and also about activism, and Shilts chronicles how the climbing death toll ultimately politicized and enraged the gay community. The book is angry, meticulously researched, and completely tragic. Shilts himself was diagnosed with HIV after the book was written, and he died in 1994.

The First Year—HIV: An Essential Guide for the Newly Diagnosed

By Brett Grodeck This book is a reassuring and useful resource for anyone who's just been diagnosed HIV positive, or for anyone who is helping a friend deal with his or her diagnosis. It takes the first seven days one at a time, then goes week-by-week, and gradually month-by-month—the idea being that you need more support and information at first, then will gradually gain confidence as you learn to live with HIV and make good, informed decisions about your health.

Global AIDS: Myths and Facts—Tools for Fighting the AIDS Pandemic

By Alexander Irwin and Joyce Millen

This book is a great resource for any HIV/AIDS activist. Irwin and Millen pick apart various misunderstandings about the impact of AIDS on the international community, and discuss why those misunderstandings are hindering attempts to stop the disease. Most importantly, they demonstrate that change is possible, and illustrate this with examples of successful activist campaigns, including some student activism.

Human Rights and Public Health in the AIDS Pandemic

By Lawrence O. Gostin and Zita Lazzarini

The authors of this book link together two fields that haven't been historically connected, by arguing that human rights cannot be preserved without regard for human health, and that health needs cannot be addressed without considering the political and social welfare of the population or individual who is sick. They look at issues like partner notification with both of these concerns in mind. It can get a little theoretical, but raises important issues and questions for activists and public health officials to think about.

Out Here By Ourselves: The Stories of Young People Whose Mothers Have AIDS

By Diane Duggan

The author talks with three different kids about what their lives are like—all three have mothers with AIDS. Their stories are sometimes hard to read, and there is no happy resolution or vision of hope at the end, but the snapshot of these sometimes overlooked victims of the pandemic is unforgettable. It really shows how AIDS is intertwined with the social conditions of those who contract the virus, because the same factors that contributed to the mothers getting infected—drugs, lack of education, poor healthcare—are currently affecting the kids in the book.

Stopping School Violence and Bullying

THE ISSUES

Many students worry about the possibility of violence at their school. They fear being harassed by bullies or even being shot by their classmates. Often they are reluctant to speak out against bullies or other perpetrators of violence because they worry about not being taken seriously, or becoming a target themselves.

This is an issue that affects nearly everyone. One in twelve high school students is threatened with or injured by a weapon every year. Sixteen percent of boys and eleven percent of girls report being bullied at school every week. Bullying affects the entire school population; studies show that those who witness bullying experience feelings of helplessness, frustration, and rage similar to those of bullys' victims. When a campus environment becomes hostile, learning takes a backseat to just getting through the day hassle-free. Bullying is self-perpetuating: Those who have been bullied often become bullies themselves.

In the wake of horrific school shootings, bullying has taken on new meaning because it is often seen as a precursor to greater acts of violence. When conflicts aren't dealt with peacefully, and weapons are available, tragedies are more likely to happen. It's estimated that thousands of guns are brought into American schools every day. Some students bring them in order to feel safer—others intend to display them as a gesture of intimidation.

The most important thing to know about school violence is that it is often preventable. Students need to know that if they speak up and speak out, they can save lives and help others. Activists who work in this area have one overriding message: Listen to what your classmates tell you. If you have any reason to think that someone is planning to harm themselves or others, tell a responsible adult immediately. A responsible adult means a parent, teacher, or school counselor—someone who can help a troubled person see another way out of his or her situation.

School violence activists also work to create an environment where students feel comfortable asking for help or reporting fears that a violent event may happen. This often involves educating teachers and parents about what to do and how to react when a student

MISSY'S STORY

Missy Jenkins is twenty-two and a sophomore at Murray State University in Murray, Kentucky.

On December 1, 1997, when I was fifteen years old, I was sitting in my high school prayer circle when a classmate walked in. He pulled a .22-caliber gun out of his backpack and began shooting. He shot eight people that day, killing three and injuring five others. I was one of the most seriously injured. The bullet hit my shoulder and throat, and then it hit my lung and spinal cord and came out the right side of my back. It left me paralyzed from my chest down. I'm a paraplegic.

When I was in the hospital, the media wanted to talk to me a lot. I usually was just updating them on my condition, until the next shooting happened, the Jonesboro shooting in March, 1998. I got asked a lot about that, and that's when I realized that I could do a lot of good by talking to people about what gun violence can do to someone. I started out by going to little church

comes to them. Other activists create conflict management programs, hold anti-bullying workshops, and work to encourage responsible gun ownership that keeps guns out of the hands of minors.

Education is the key for activists working in this area. Many teenagers do not realize what they can do to prevent others from getting hurt.

However, while it's important to be aware of the risks, it's also important to avoid worrying too much. Make sure that your activist work isn't alarmist—give people the facts without scaring them.

Preventing others from being harmed or harming themselves is a socially responsible and caring cause. If you choose to be an activist in this area, your work can have a lasting effect on your classmates and your community. It's a great thing to spread the message that violence is never the answer and that we all have the power to prevent it.

THE AT-HOME ACTIVIST

Make an Anti-Violence Contract with Your Parents

Your parents are probably as worried about school violence as you are. A great way to relieve that anxiety is to discuss the issue, including what your family will do if anything happens. Writing up a little contract in which you and your parents promise to support each other and to be honest with each other is a great way to solidify trust. It helps ensure that if you ever need to confide in them about something, the situation will be handled in the best way possible.

Ask your parents if you can sit down and have a talk about school violence. Describe what your school is like. Bring up the potential situations that worry you the most, and explain why they concern you. Ask them what they worry about. It could be useful to have some statistics or information with you. Try looking on one of the Web sites in the resource section of this chapter. Tell your parents that you want to know you can come to them with your concerns about bullying and school violence, and that you want to be sure they are prepared to listen to you and will respond appropriately.

Draft your contract in the form of promises you and your parents are making to each other. Your part of the contract could say things like:

"I promise to be responsible and avoid situations that are potentially dangerous."

"I promise to let you know if I am worried

groups in the surrounding area and then went on to schools, and then bigger schools, and I'm still doing it now.

I just get up and I tell my story. I tell everything. I leave the details in because that's what I saw and I think that's what hits home. I don't want to baby it up and make it seem like it wasn't that big of a deal, because it was to me. I talk about the girls who died and the people who were injured, and then I talk about the boy who shot us. Like where he is now, but also why he thought he had to do what he did. He was bullied but he bullied people back, too. I think he just reached a point where he thought that the shooting was his only possible answer to his problems, and it wasn't.

I talk about the importance of telling [someone] if there's a gun or the potential for gun violence in your school. From what I've seen, in all the different school shootings, there've been so many times that the shooters have warned people that they were going to do something. It even happened at my school, but we didn't believe him because he was a jokester type and then we ended up

about my safety or the safety of others."

The part for your parents could say things like:

> "I promise that if you confide in me that you are worried someone
> else is planning a violent act, I will take you seriously and do all
> I can to prevent a tragedy and get help for those who need it."

> "I promise to trust you and that I will try not to let my own worries
> keep you from having a full school experience."

Add things that are specific to what you are worried
about. If you are apprehensive about walking home from
school when you are at school late, you could ask your
parents to promise to pick you up if you let them know
you'll be needing a ride. Your parents might want you to
tell them if any of your friends' families keep guns in the
house and whether they are properly secured.

Don't issue ultimatums or make demands—just bring
up things that concern you, and see if you can come to an
agreed-upon solution with your parents. Then when they
mention their concerns, listen to them and offer suggestions on how to deal with their anxieties.

When you've gotten all the promises down, type up
your contract and have all parties sign it. Drafting and
signing a contract like this might seem a little silly, but it
means that you and your parents are deciding to be a
team in the face of potential school violence. Your parents
know that you will do the right thing, and that they will
be kept in the loop about a serious issue. You know that
your parents will support you when you act to prevent
school violence.

THE CAMPUS ACTIVIST

Distribute a Flyer About the Warning Signs of Possible School Violence

Even students who know to go to a responsible adult or an anonymous tip line when they see signs of possible school violence might not entirely be clear on what those signs are. Giving students some examples of things to look for not only will increase awareness of warning signs, but also might relieve some of their anxieties about possible school violence because they will feel empowered to prevent it. Knowing when to speak up is as important as knowing that you should speak up.

Making a leaflet or a flyer with the warning signs of possible violent behavior will get the information into the hands of your friends and classmates. They can stick it in their lockers or keep it at home just in case they need it again. Even if they just read it once, some of it will stay with them and could help them spot potential trouble.

Begin by getting all the infor-

suffering the consequences.

I think that I'm effective as a speaker. For one thing, I'm in a wheelchair, and I am a powerful visual of what school violence can do. People think that school violence happens to other people, and they don't take the threat seriously. When they see me, I think it personalizes the issue. They can see what happened to me in a school shooting and hear the impact it's had on my life.

I really love talking to [kids in] schools because they listen attentively. I feel like I really grab their attention. I can relate to them and get to them and I feel like I'm hitting every one of them at different levels.

I always tell them not to take anything too lightly, that when they hear a scary rumor it's better to overreact than underreact. I have a friend who had heard that something big was going to happen at our school but he didn't say anything because he didn't believe it. Now he holds that heavy burden, that if only he had said something to somebody, maybe I would still be walking, or maybe the three girls that died would still be here. Maybe our entire

mation for your flyer together.

These are the warning signs that the American Psychological Association (APA) recommends being on the lookout for. Any of these signs means that violence is a serious possibility:

Loss of temper on a daily basis
Significant vandalism or property damage
Increase in risk-taking behavior
Enjoys hurting animals
Carrying a weapon
Increase in use of drugs or alcohol
Announces threats or plans for hurting others
Frequent physical fighting
Detailed plans to commit acts of violence

The APA also lists more subtle signs that you might notice over time. These signs indicate a potential for violent behavior, especially if the underlying issues aren't dealt with:

A history of violent or aggressive behavior
Serious drug or alcohol use
Gang membership or strong desire to be in a gang
Access to or fascination with weapons, especially guns
Threatening others regularly
Trouble controlling feelings like anger
Withdrawal from friends and usual activities
Feeling rejected or alone
Having been a victim of bullying
Poor school performance
History of discipline problems or frequent run-ins with authority

Feeling constantly disrespected

Failing to acknowledge the feelings or rights of others

Your flyer should also include information on what to do if someone observes any of these warning signs. If someone is concerned that violence is imminent, that person should not try to intervene with the person he or she is worried about, but get a responsible adult involved instead. In less immediate circumstances, he or she could try talking to the person, or seeing if there is some peer mediation or conflict resolution resource available. The National Crime Prevention Council (www.ncpc.org) has good information aimed at teenagers about how to manage conflicts peacefully.

Make a resource section on the flyer. List places to get help and report incidents, like counseling centers, anonymous tip lines, and school safety officers.

Remember not to scare people. You are making this leaflet about the warning signs for *possible* violent behavior, and you are distributing it so that any such behavior can be prevented before it happens.

community would not have had to go through this whole thing.

I tell them the importance of trusting adults and not thinking they're out to get you. You can trust a teacher and tell them when you think something's gonna happen. I also suggest that schools set up an anonymous tip line or a place where kids can go and feel safe about reporting things. I tell them about the PAX hotline, 1-866-SPEAK-UP.

I'm not anti-gun. My nephew, who is, like, a week younger than me, and I are really close, and he loves hunting. I don't talk down guns. But the shooter at my school had a .22, and that's not for hunting. The only thing you can use a .22-caliber for is to shoot people.

I actually am a pretty shy person. To get up and speak in public was a big challenge for me, but I've kind of gotten over it and I really enjoy speaking now. I feel like I was left on this earth for a reason. I could have easily died that day but for some reason I'm still here. It's given me a direction in life and a purpose.

Not many people find their purpose when they are fifteen years old, but every day

You might want to include some statistics about the probability and reality of school violence so no one blows the issue out of proportion. (Some of the sites listed in the resource section of this chapter have good fact sheets on this topic.) Bullying is common—homicide is not.

After you have all the information for your flyer gathered together, design it using a desktop publishing program. You don't have to go crazy, but make it look good (and don't forget to run the spell check). Break the information up in chunks, use little headlines, and make important stuff easy to find. Use clip art or drawings if you think it's appropriate and looks good. When you're done, print out a copy and then take it to a low-cost copy place, or run it off at school if they will let you.

The best way to distribute flyers varies from campus to campus. Some schools require that you run everything by the administration before you can hand it out, and others are cool with flyers and handouts if they are school-related. In some schools you can only post flyers in certain areas and you can't hand anything out or put anything in lockers. Find out what the policy is at your school.

If your school's administrators don't allow any distribution whatsoever, or if they take exception to your leaflet in particular, you can challenge them on free speech grounds (see the chapter on Protecting Civil Rights and Civil Libery), or just go around them. Distribute the leaflet off campus—right outside the school, or at the library or coffee shop (ask first). Put them on cars where you know students park. Take them to a PTA meeting and ask the members there if they'd like to help you distribute them.

If you can distribute on campus, great. Bring your flyers to school and start putting them up and handing them out. Be respectful of other people's time—don't disrupt the school day by passing out leaflets in the middle of class or in a doorway when people are trying to get by. It might be tempting to put your flyers in piles and hope that interested people will take one, but that's not the most effective way to get your message across. Handing them out one by one to people means that every flyer provides you with an opportunity to have a conversation about school violence.

Try walking up to people and saying, "Hi, I'm Trini, and I'm distributing this flyer about how to stop violence in schools. Would you like one? It's got lots of information about warning signs and what you should do if you see them." Make eye contact, smile, and have a few flyers in your hand.

Chances are, most people will take one. If they do, thank them

when I go and speak I feel like I'm really fulfilling what my life is meant to be. I think it makes the fact that I'm in a wheelchair much easier for me, because I feel like it was all for a purpose.

To learn more about how you can prevent gun violence at your school, check out the PAX Web site (www.pax.com).

BRITT'S STORY
Britt Hinchcliff is seventeen and a senior at Poway High School in Poway, California.

When I moved to Poway in eighth grade I was shocked at how disrespectful the kids were to the teachers and to themselves. I just sat in my Basic Ed classroom and watched kids argue with the teacher about an assignment. She had assigned it two weeks before, and they were saying that they wanted the deadline pushed back, even though we'd had plenty of time. What can the teacher do? Punish the whole class? Send all the kids to the office?

There was a lot of bullying, too. If you were different in any way, kids wouldn't talk to you and they'd pick on you.

and move on to the next person. If they say no, try pushing back a little. Maybe they just think it's "uncool" to take a handout or to act like they care about something. You could say, "Well, why not just take it? Maybe you will feel like reading it later." Don't push it too far—you don't want to be obnoxious, and you don't want to waste your time on people who won't listen.

You might get discouraged if you see some people looking at their flyers and then tossing them—or, even worse, tossing them without looking at them. Try not to focus on this. Even if they don't read the sheet, you've still heightened awareness of the issue. And if they do read it, then they know more than they did before you distributed the flyer. You've made a difference.

When you're done, remember not to leave any undistributed leaflets where someone else will have to clean them up. Put them in the recycling bin.

Create a Bully Box

Especially in the higher grades, victims of bullying are often reluctant to come forward. They may not want to be perceived as weak, or draw attention to themselves. Suggest that your school create a bully box (you can call it an "anti-harassment box" if you want to sound less playground-y).

A bully box is just a box with a hole in the top, where students can anonymously report instances of bullying. It's probably a good idea to have more than one, and to have them scattered around the school so that people can use the boxes without being observed.

First make sure that your school administration will honor the anonymous aspect of the bully box. If you can get an agreement in writing from the principal or guidance counselor, that's the best scenario. Tell the administrators that students won't use the box if they are worried that they will be exposed, and that then the boxes will be worthless. The important thing is to have information about potential violence, not to know who said what about whom. If you don't think your school will maintain privacy for those who use the box, you probably want to consider another option, like spreading the word about an anonymous tip line.

If your school does agree to set up the boxes and keep the reports anonymous, you are set. Get some shoeboxes, or whatever you want to use, and put signs on them explaining what they are for, that they are anonymous, and when to use them. You could also put paper and writing materials nearby. Let the student body know about the boxes in any way you can—put an ad in the school paper, talk on the morning announcement, whatever.

The school system here is really racially mixed, about eighty percent white, ten percent Latino, five percent African American, and five percent Asian American. The financial backgrounds are varied—some kids live in trailer parks, and others live in two-million-dollar homes. So there are a lot of cliques and stuff.

Sophomore year, my friend Courtney decided to start a Students Against Violence Everywhere (SAVE) club at our school. She'd heard about it from someone at another school. I thought it was a great idea, and I joined right in. We got our principal to approve and got started. The national office of SAVE sent us a lot of material and information.

Our mission is to bring the school back to where it's more of an educational facility, rather than a place where kids are going to school in fear. They shouldn't be thinking, Am I going to get beat up today? or, Is this one kid going to pick on me? School isn't for that—it's for kids to learn and go on in life.

SAVE works through peer-to-peer communication, and I really believe in that. It's much easier for peers to

Your school counselor, or whomever the principal designates, should go through the boxes at least once a week and keep on top of the reports, acting when necessary. You might want to check in with him or her to see if the boxes are working out—if people are reporting things and all is going as planned.

A bully box is a low-tech way to ensure that those who want to report incidents without exposing themselves are free to do so. It encourages more people to come forward because they can do so without fear of reprisal or being stigmatized as a narc. It's also a visible reminder that your school is not going to tolerate bullying behavior.

THE COMMUNITY ACTIVIST

Connect with an At-Risk Youth

Young people who have suffered from abuse, live in high-crime or high-drug-use areas, or are economically disadvantaged are at a higher risk of becoming violent. None of these factors mean that a person is definitely going to act violently—never assume that. But it is true that kids from these backgrounds may need more help in learning ways to express themselves and communicate with others. Providing that help by mentoring or connecting with someone younger than you not only will be beneficial to the both of you, but also will serve your community by reducing the chance of any potential violent behavior in the future.

One way to connect with at-risk youth is by becoming a Big Brother or a Big Sister. Big Brothers Big Sisters of America was founded in 1904. The organization believes that pairing at-risk kids with responsible older people can help those kids avoid self-destructive behaviors, improve their self-esteem, and even help them do better in school. The main program pairs children with adults, but they also have a program that hooks up high school "Bigs" with elementary school "Littles."

As a Big Brother or Big Sister, you'll meet with your partner once a week during the school year. Basically you just hang out. You can play sports, read, or talk about school, friends, and family—whatever feels right. Make sure that your little sister or brother knows that you are there to listen and to give advice and share your own experiences. You could try talking about what things were like for you at that age in order to get him or her to open up.

To find out more, visit the BBBS Web site (www.bbbs.org). Read about the program, and if you choose to participate, click the Volunteer link and enter your zip code. You'll be asked to supply your name, phone, and e-mail, and then

change their campus, rather than adults, because peers are going to listen to their peers. If an adult tells me not to do something, I won't take that into consideration as much as I will a student telling me not to do something.

One of the first things we did was put on a battle of the bands at the community center. We had a local DJ from a radio station host it and the bands were local bands. It was great; it let people know what SAVE is about. It also gave people a way to get together and be friendly, and have something to do rather than go vandalize something or get high or something like that. We promoted it by putting up flyers and posters, and by telling people—word of mouth.

Throughout the year we do educational workshops. We work mainly with middle-school students, although we do work with high-school students sometimes. I think it's important to talk to the younger students because middle school is really where the big-time bullying and things like that start happening, so we just want to get to the kids and educate them. We tell them that there

submit your applicaton electronically. Later a BBBS representative will call you and talk to you about what you want to do, so they can pair you with the right kid. If you are under eighteen, you will have to get a parent's permission.

You don't have to go through BBBS to become a mentor and helper to a younger student, although it is the most well-established option. Maybe your school or a local community center has a program. Whatever way you choose to reach out, connecting with an at-risk youth is a great way to help someone fulfill his or her potential and get on the road to living a peaceful life. You'll make a friend and also know that you are contributing to your community in a meaningful way.

THE 5-MINUTE ACTIVIST

The Brady Campaign

Jim Brady, the former press secretary to President Ronald Reagan, was seriously wounded by a gunshot to the head during an assassination attempt on the president. Since his recovery, he and his wife have worked tirelessly to end gun voilence. In the Brady Campaign Action Center you can quickly get up to speed on current gun violence issues, like victim's rights and background checks at gun shows. Then you can go to a "click to e-mail" page where you can write to your congessional representatives with your views. www.bradycampaign.org

RESOURCES

Web Sites

Common Sense about Kids and Guns

This project was put together by gun owners and non–gun owners who want to protect youth from gun deaths and injuries. They work to encourage safe gun storage, and to educate the public about the risks of gun violence due to a lack of adult supervision. The site has good resources, especially an interactive map where you can click on your state and you will get news about recent gun-related crimes, a synopsis of your state's crime laws, and links to organizations working to end youth gun violence in your area.

www.kidsandguns.org

Keep Schools Safe

KSS is a new site aimed at students, parents, and schools. The student section is small, but it has good information, especially about fighting—how to avoid are alternatives to bullying, what you can do if you are being bullied, and what you can do with your anger rather than punch someone. It really stems from education and prevention.

Another thing that we focus on in middle school is that it's okay to tell. If some kid brings a knife to school, it's better to save lives than to feel guilty for narking. It's okay to tell people like a teacher, a trusted adult, or an administrator.

For high-school students, it's a bit different. We talk about ways to resolve conflicts peacefully, and we also encourage them to step outside their comfort zones a little bit and get to know other people. It's a lot of getting kids to realize that different is okay. Once you get kids to realize that, a lot of the problems disappear.

I know that one of the Muslim students at our school was very affected by 9/11 because people started looking at him differently and things like that. If you knew this kid, he's one of the nicest people that I've ever met. So we've just been trying to let people know that stereotyping isn't the way to go. You have to look at each individual

fights and how to be a "positive bystander" and try to calm the situation.
www.keepschoolssafe.org

National Youth Violence Prevention Campaign

This site was created to promote National Youth Violence Prevention Week, an initiative that asks schools to dedicate a week in late March or early April to raising awareness about youth violence. The organization provides material and ideas for every day of the week, planning guides, and discussion boards where you can connect with others planning similar weeks in their schools. Whether you decide to launch such a project at your school or not, the site has extremely useful content. The front page has a cool thing: a wheel with segments that have labels such as "senior citizens," "parents," and "media." You click on each and read how that part of the community can help with school violence.
www.violencepreventionweek.org

National Youth Violence Prevention Resource Center

This site is huge but well organized. It has a daily news brief, tons of info for educators (conferences and stuff), and sections for parents and teens. The teen section has fact sheets, information about what you can do, and some great reports on things like dating violence and bullying.
www.safeyouth.org

PAX: Real Solutions to Gun Violence

PAX is a group working to end gun violence through

major educational campaigns. There is one aimed at parents, called ASK, and one for students, called SPEAK UP. SPEAK UP has an anonymous national hotline (1-866-SPEAK-UP) and stories of incidents that were prevented because someone was responsible enough to warn others.

www.pax.com

Report-it.com

This is a low-cost service that will set your school up with an anonymous reporting system to report violent incidents and warn about potential violence. The fee is about $325 to set it up, and there is a $40 per month maintenance fee. When it's implemented, anyone at your school—student, teacher, staff—can anonymously and safely let others know what's going on. About 350 schools nationwide are already using it.

www.report-it.com

Report Someone

Report Someone provides a nationwide, anonymous, and free Web interface where people

person. People from other countries might think that all Americans are fat and they eat McDonald's all the time, and that's not true either. You have to look at the individual person.

I'm really glad I got involved with this. I'm on the national board of SAVE now.

I just found my passion and I went with it. I think that's the key. You need to find something that really interests you and then take it to the next level. If you do that, you're going to enjoy what you're doing, and you'll be amazed at what you can accomplish.

It's amazing what teenagers can do nowadays because there are opportunities to change your community and get involved in your community, whether it's through community service, or getting involved with a club on campus, or whatever you choose to do. Anyone can make a difference.

To learn more about Students Against Violence Everywhere, visit www.nationalsave.org.

can report threats and incidents of violence. It was launched by a mother who heard about a gun at her son's school and then realized her son knew more about it than the police. If you file a report, it will go to the school principal, the school resource officer (if there is one), and possibly the police. One interesting feature of the site is that you can look to see what sorts of incidents have been reported in your state.
www.reportsomeone.com

School Violence Resource Center

SVRC is a federally funded project aimed at reducing school violence through research, education, and the creation of a school violence education curriculum. The site has information on community preparedness, fact sheets on risk factors and crime statistics, and a really big resource section organized by topic.
www.svrc.net

Students Against Violence Everywhere

SAVE, though an initiative of MAVIA (Mothers Against Violence in America), doesn't have a parental vibe at all. Its members work to empower students so they can solve their own problems and help one another prevent violence on campus and off. The main way SAVE operates is through clubs— you start a SAVE club or chapter at your school, and you get support from the national center to run campaigns, implement peer education, and work with your school administration to raise awareness. For

more on SAVE, see "Britt's Story" in this chapter.
www.nationalsave.org

Student Pledge Against Gun Violence

Every year on the National Day of Concern about
Young People and Gun Violence, in October, millions
of students sign the pledge, promising to refrain
from gun violence and to prevent others from using
guns to solve disputes. The site has information on
how to run a pledge drive at your school, with ideas
for events and outreach (there's even a special section
for people who start their campaigns at the last
minute), and lots of support material.
www.pledge.org

Teens, Crime, and the Community

TCC, a Department of Justice–funded operation,
works primarily through this Web site. It has crime
stats, a quiz to test your knowledge, and a big list
of suggested action projects that you can do in your
school or community. There's also Community
Works, a guide to getting the community involved
in whatever you do—really useful.
www.nationaltcc.org

Warning Signs

This is a project put together by MTV and the
American Psychological Association. It delivers info
in short shots—why violence is a problem for
youth, how to spot warning signs, and what to do
about it. There's also a good quiz you can take to see
if you yourself are at risk for violent behavior, and

some anger management tips. The information is also available as a downloadable brochure, or you can order a hard copy.

www.helping.apa.org/warningsigns

Books

The Bully, the Bullied, and the Bystander: From Preschool to High School—How Parents and Teachers Can Help Break the Cycle of Violence

By Barbara Coloroso

Coloroso, who spent decades working with troubled youth, takes a scholarly look at bullying. The book's written for parents and teachers, but it's worth reading because she is one of the few writers who addresses the problem in a holistic way, dealing with bystanders as well as victims and bullies.

Days of Respect: Organizing a School-Wide Violence Prevention Program

By Ralph Cantor with Paul Kivel and Alan Creighton and the Oakland Men's Project

This book has everything you need to set up a violence awareness event at your school—flyers, handouts, training exercises, and more. It's pretty ambitious—definitely not something you'd want to take on alone—but a fantastic resource for anyone who wants to do some anti-violence work at his or her school. You also might want to check out their other book (aimed at teachers and without Ralph Cantor, but still good), *Making the Peace: A 15-Session Violence Prevention Curriculum for Young People.*

Kids Working It Out: Stories and Strategies for Making Peace in Our Schools

Edited by Tricia S. Jones and Randy Compton

The authors take the position that teaching peaceful conflict resolution is something that schools have to do for the benefit of students and society. They explain how others have made changes within themselves and at their schools, and provide great suggestions and ideas for how to make your school a safer place.

No Easy Answers: The Truth Behind the Death at Columbine

By Brooks Brown and Rob Merritt

Brooks Brown was friends with Dylan Klebold and Eric Harris, the gunmen who killed twelve students and one teacher and wounded many others at Columbine High School in April 1999. Brown argues that the culture of constant harassment and injustice in the halls at Columbine not only was a deterrent to learning, but also was so poisonous that an event of this magnitude was bound to happen at some point. He wants America to know that and to focus on fixing these problems, rather than worry about video games and music lyrics. Brown is writing from an emotional ground zero—the book was published just eighteen months after the tragedy, when his anger and grief were still raw.

Things Get Hectic: Teens Write About the Violence That Surrounds Them

By Youth Communication, and edited by Philip Kay,
Andrea Estepa, and Al Desetta
This is a powerful first-person book put out by
Youth Communications, a New York–based group
that also published a youth newspaper. The authors
are brutally honest about the violence they've
seen—what they've suffered and what they've seen
others suffer. It's a dose of reality that will stay with
you long after you are done reading.

Defending
Women's Rights

ISSUES

Although the American women's rights movement has had many significant victories, including the right to vote, we are still very far from reaching equality in this country. A full-time working woman earns only seventy-three cents for every dollar earned by a man. Thirty percent of American women report being abused by their partner, and three women are murdered every day by a husband or a boyfriend. *Roe v. Wade*, the landmark decision legalizing abortion, is under attack. Women are more likely than men to be harassed at work, to receive poor health care, and to live in poverty. Young women are also struggling—they have a higher risk of getting infected with HIV than young men, their reproductive rights are curtailed, and eighty-three percent of high school age females report having been sexually harassed at school.

Women's rights—and their lives—are at stake around the world as well. Of the world's 1.3 billion people living in poverty, it is estimated that nearly seventy percent are women. Women are twice as likely to be illiterate as men are. On average, women earn about three-fourths of the pay of men for the same work in both developed and developing countries. Worldwide, twenty to fifty percent of women experience some degree of domestic violence during marriage. And the primary victims of today's wars are civilian women and their children, not soldiers.

The women's rights movement, sometimes also called the feminist movement, works to bring an end to these political, social, and economic inequalities. Some people have misconceptions about what it means to be a feminist, but it's really very simple. A feminist is someone who believes that everyone should be treated equally. If you believe that, then you are a feminist. Among feminists there are many types of women (and men!) with many different opinions and ideas, but they all share that same fundamental belief.

Although there have been amazing women throughout history—women who refused the gender roles society tried to force them into and who instead became pirates, warriors, poets, and politicians—the organized women's rights movement is only about a hundred years old. In the west, particularly in America, feminism is often discussed in terms of waves. Each "wave" is a period that was particularly active or notable, although feminism didn't stop between waves.

The first wave of feminists were the suffragettes, who were active in the late 1800s and early 1900s. The suffragettes, activists such as Elizabeth Cady Stanton, Susan B. Anthony, and Lucretia Mott, fought to get women—white women—the vote. Many of these women were seasoned activists; they had been active in the abolition and temperance movements, and they knew the pressure that a populist campaign can bring to bear on a government. They often employed civil disobedience tactics. They would attempt to vote, go limp and allow themselves to be dragged away when they were arrested, then go on hunger strikes while in jail—all of which gained them a lot of attention. Women finally did get the vote with the passage of the Nineteenth Amendment in 1920.

The second wave of feminist activism occurred in the 1960s and 1970s. Like the first wave, the majority of second wave feminist leaders were middle-class, educated white women. Second wave feminists had a broad agenda including pay equity, access to education, health care and reproductive rights, domestic violence issues, protecting women against rape, workplace issues, civil rights, and even the right to wear pants instead of skirts. These activists, who include Betty Friedan, Gloria Steinem, Germaine Greer, Margaret Sloane, Robin Morgan, Shulamith Firestone, Susan Brownmiller, Marilyn Webb, Kathie Sarachild, and Rita Mae Brown, often described themselves as fighting to liberate women from oppression, and were sometimes called "women's libbers."

This was a turbulent time in American culture, and the second wave was right at the forefront. Some women were allied with radi-

SARA'S STORY

Sara Ahmed is seventeen and a senior at Woodward Academy in College Park, Georgia. She lives in Stone Mountain, Georgia.

I've been working with Raksha for about a year and a half now. *Raksha* means "protection" in several South Asian languages. We are a nonprofit for the advancement of women and families in the South Asian community in and around Atlanta. There is a big South Asian Community in the Atlanta area—recently arrived immigrants as well as settled families. I am first generation; my parents moved here thirty years ago.

Raksha tries to bring up issues that aren't easily talked about in our community, like domestic violence and sexual abuse. Women in the South Asian community are raised believing that their role in the household includes sometimes taking abuse. It's something that's not talked about and not brought to the surface. Raksha is trying to create an atmosphere within families as well as in the community at large where sexual violence and domestic

cal groups like the Black Panthers and the Students for a Democratic Society, while others fought for liberation in more traditional ways. They filed legal briefs, formed collectives, issued manifestos, marched, demonstrated, published, spoke out, and did everything they could to expose and end the sexism they identified in every aspect of society. Some aspects of the second wave are criticized today, but there is no question that most women in America, and many women around the world, live fuller and better lives today due to the work of these feminist activists.

Today's women's movement is the so-called third wave of feminism. Third wave feminism is much less personality-driven than its predecessors, although some of its notable voices include Amy Richards, Ophira and Tali Edut, Kathleen Hanna, Jennifer Baumgardner, Marcelle Karp, Rebecca Walker, Farai Chideya, Debbie Stoller, and Sonia Shah. This moment in the women's movement is often described as having a sort of mother-daughter relationship with second wave feminism, in that third wavers are descended from and benefit from the work of the second wave, but at the same time they often challenge its institutions and values, which they see as old-fashioned. An important aspect of third wave politics is its striving toward diversity—finally American feminism is starting to represent and give voice to women of all classes, races, and sexual orientations.

Feminists now have a global network that fights for the human rights and civil rights of all women, including the struggle to end horrific traditions like female genital mutilation. The women's movement is active within the legal system and in the malls, in the government and in the schools, in magazines and zines, in coffee houses and rock clubs, in homes and on the street. Women's rights activists run free clinics, support women's sports, help women-owned small businesses, critique misogynist media, advocate for maternity and family leave, support pro-choice candidates, and more. Individually and collectively, these activists are making a difference.

If you choose to become a women's rights activist, you have many options. You could work with one of the many well-established feminist organizations or a more radical new one. If you see that the needs of women on your campus or in your community are not being served, you might want to form your own women's group to assess those needs and respond to them. Joining the feminist movement is an action that will benefit you and the young women around you, as well as generations to come. Be proud to be a feminist.

violence are not a silent crime. We want women to feel comfortable talking about their situation and helping each other through situations like that.

I work with a group within Raksha called Art and Activism. We try to create awareness through art. I wrote a couple of articles on domestic violence and surviving sexual assault in intimate relationships because I wanted to debunk the myth that when women are raped or sexually assaulted, it's by a stranger. The stories I wrote are trying to bring up that it's actually more common in the home. Then I started going out and reading these pieces in public. I read them at coffee shops and sometimes at more-organized events. I read at the International Day for Women event in Atlanta.

I think it's really powerful for women to hear stories about other women who have survived sexual assault, because when you are in that situation you can start to feel really desperate and make some very dangerous decisions. I feel like people need to hear that you can get out of it; there is a way to overcome your situation—

THE AT-HOME ACTIVIST

Learn About Feminist History

Although the modern feminist movement is an important part of American history, you probably won't learn about it in school. Most history classes mention when women got the vote, and that's it. But the history of feminism is much richer and deeper than that, and it has influenced every area of our culture as well as helped strengthen or launch other women's movements around the globe. Reading about the feminist movement's growth and its many internal struggles and debates on topics ranging from race and class to literary criticism, the role of marriage, and the politics of pornography is a great history lesson in women's rights, and in activism.

Below is a short reading list to get you started with your feminist history education. You could suggest that your history class (or another appropriate class) study some aspects of feminist history, or you could ask if you can do a paper on the subject. Another idea is to form a book club with your friends and read a book every month, then meet and discuss it, or you might prefer to just do some reading on your own.

There's no need to go in any special order, or to read all the books on the list—just pick ones that appeal to you. You may not agree with everything that every feminist says or does, but you will likely appreciate their passion and dedication. One thing to look for as you read is how the goals of feminism and the strategies for achieving those goals have changed. Another thing to note is the changing makeup of the movement—what began as a group of white, straight, middle-class women has grown and struggled to become more inclusive of all women. It's also interesting to think about how feminist institutions such as the National Organization for Women and the National Abortion Rights Action League were formed, and how (or if) they continue to serve their constituencies.

Reading Suggestions

Abortion Wars: A Half Century of Struggle, 1950–2000

Edited by Rickie Solinger

The right of women to control their own bodies and to choose to terminate an unwanted pregnancy has probably been the most controversial issue in modern feminism. This is a collection of eighteen essays, all written by abortion rights supporters. The pieces discuss various aspects of the abortion rights movement, from underground abortion providers who helped women before the procedure was legalized, to the issues of

you're not stuck where you are. There's always a way out and there are people willing to help you and to listen to you. You need a community to fall back on and Raksha is trying to provide that.

Raksha also does other types of outreach—a lot of public service things. We had one program where we flew in a group of young Indian singers from Pennsylvania. They came in to do a show, and during the intermission, I read and performed along with other people.

We have posters up with the number for our hotline. We try to get the message out wherever we can—there's a lot of Indian hangouts around Atlanta, different Indian shopping plazas, so we put stuff up around there. There's an Indian TV channel, so we put public service announcements on it. Also there are Indian magazines, the equivalent to, like, *People* magazine, and we have ads in there.

Raksha is doing good work, but I feel like it's going to take a lot longer than we anticipated to really change women's lives. It's years and years of culture and tradition that we're trying to break,. and the response hasn't been

abortion rights for poor and minority women and the rising militancy of the anti-choice movement.

Dear Sisters: Dispatches from the Women's Liberation Movement

Edited by Rosalyn Baxandall and Linda Gordon
This is a collection of documents from the second wave of feminism—specifically the years 1968 to 1977. It has cartoons, essays, newspaper editorials, and many other types of documents. Dear Sisters will give you an insight into the joy and hopefulness of the women who were engaged in the fight for equality.

Feminism: The Essential Historical Writings

Edited by Miriam Schneir
Schneir collected an amazing range of documents dating back to the 1700s that reveal the origins of American feminism and follow it through the 1940s. (She later edited another volume covering World War II to the present.) The anthology includes excerpts from letters, books, and speeches—they are great to read because you are actually hearing the voices of women from those times, something you don't get from history books. The earlier documents give a bit of insight into how a nation founded on the principle of equality nonetheless excluded women and blacks from citizenship and other rights.

The Ladies of Seneca Falls: The Birth of the Woman's Rights Movement

By Miriam Gurko
In July 1848, Susan B. Anthony, Elizabeth Cady

Stanton, Lucretia Mott, and more than two hundred other women's suffrage activists gathered in Seneca Falls, New York, to draft and pass a statement declaring women's rights as citizens and calling for the reform of laws that perpetuated the inferior status of women. (You can read the historic declaration here: www.ukans.edu/carrie/docs/texts/seneca.htm. You'll note that it's explicitly modeled on the Declaration of Independence.) Gurko traces the women's rights movement from the Seneca Falls Convention through the passage of the Nineteenth Amendment, giving women the right to vote. The book is a great encapsulation of an activist campaign that articulated then achieved its goals despite great resistance from the government and society at large.

Outrageous Acts and Everyday Rebellions

By Gloria Steinem
Gloria Steinem is a feminist icon—active from the 1960s to the present day, she has been a leader in many feminist organizations and, as a writer, has

as overwhelming as we wished it would be. There is a slight change. You see a change in men's attitudes when they watch a girl who tells a story about domestic violence and it hits home. There are a lot of calls in to Raksha, and there are a lot of women who need Raksha.

I feel that if you have the ability to do something that could help, you should. What I write best about are situations that women are put in and even though I haven't been put in a lot of those situations, I've seen a lot. I've worked at a lot of different places, volunteered at a lot of different places, and I've seen a lot of different people and different situations. I feel like I have the ability to make a difference by writing other people's stories down. I'm putting something out into the world that other people can read and understand and relate to.

It's rare to find someone who's really passionate about change and making a difference, and if you are that type of person you should definitely go out there and do it. Even you help just one person—by listening or by creating something, by coming to an event or by

been instrumental in articulating American women's frustration with their lack of equality. This is a collection of her brilliant—sometimes funny, sometimes angry—essays and writings from 1963 to 1983. From describing what it was like to go undercover as a Playboy Bunny to the founding of Ms. magazine, Steinem brings an adventurous spirit and a questioning mind to her work that makes it really accessible.

The Power of Feminist Art: The American Movement of the 1970s, History and Impact
Edited by Norma Broude and Mary D. Garrard

Feminism and visual culture have confronted, challenged, and enriched each other in various ways. Feminist art historians have criticized a male-dominated canon and pointed out misogynistic practices of representation. Feminist artists have made similar points with their work, while also struggling to articulate aspects of women's lives that had rarely been seen in museums and galleries. This anthology not only reproduces over two hundred and seventy works, but also discusses their impact and their contribution to the feminist cause. It's a great way to look at the ways art and activism can work together.

Sisterhood Is Powerful: An Anthology of Writings from the Women's Liberation Movement
Compiled, edited, and with an introduction by Robin Morgan

Published in 1970, this anthology is especially useful because it shows which writings were considered influential at that time by Morgan— a poet, radical activist, and, eventually, editor-in-chief of Ms. Magazine. Sisterhood includes work from Kate Millett, who wrote the ground-breaking book Sexual Politics, Alix Kates Shulman, whose Memoirs of an Ex-Prom Queen outlines a suburban girl's path to a feminist self-realization, and even Valerie Solanis, who is perhaps most famous for attempting to kill Andy Warhol in 1968.

Unequal Sisters: A Multicultural Reader in U.S. Women's History

Edited by Vicki L. Ruiz and Ellen Carol DuBois

Unequal Sisters is an anthology of more than thirty essays that reconsider American history and women's history with a sensibility that includes factors such as race, class, privilege, gender, sexuality, and ethnicity. The women's movement has long been criticized for being too middle class, too straight,

passing out flyers—then you've made a difference. And everyone that you touch will touch someone else. I love being an activist. I can't imagine doing anything else. It's who I am.

To learn more about Raksha, visit www.raksha.org.

ERICA'S STORY

Erica O'Brien is sixteen and a junior at Woodside High School. She lives in Emerald Hills, California.

We had a problem with the sex ed in my school district, the Sequoia Union High School District in California. Basically it wasn't really required and any teacher could say, "I'd rather not have that in my class." Or the teacher could just give his or her version of it. Then those students wouldn't be getting the same education as other students and some wouldn't get it at all. Sometimes they wouldn't get it until their junior or senior year.

Not having good sex ed is bad for the students. The rates of teen pregnancy and STDs are much higher if they're not given proper education about what kind of

and too white; this book collects the best of those critiques and gathers them in one place, where they provide not only a great way to look at the history of American feminism, but also some ideas on how to make the movement of the future a more inclusive and tolerant one.

Discuss Feminism with Someone from Another Generation

You might be surprised at what a difference feminism has made in the lives of women you spend time with every day. Did you know that as recently as 1974, women living in some parts of the country couldn't get their names in the phone book? They could only be listed under their husbands' names. Speaking with your mom, grandmother, a teacher, or a family friend about how feminism has affected her life is a great way to see how a mass movement has touched individual lives. It will likely also inspire you to continue to advocate for women's rights.

Ask your interview subject what her life was like growing up. Did she expect to get married, or to have a career, or both? What were the career and education options available to her, compared with men her own age? Did she feel equal to men in school and in the workplace? What kind of health education did she get—did she know about birth control, STDs and STIs, and abortion? How much interaction did she have with women from other classes and races? Ask her if she was aware of feminism when she was younger. Does she feel it has affected her life in any specific ways? In what ways has feminism failed her? This conversation might guide you in your choices for further activism.

THE CAMPUS ACTIVIST

Speak Out About Dating Violence

Dating violence is a growing problem among teenagers. Chances are, you know or will know someone in an abusive relationship. Although dating violence affects both young men and young women, young women are more likely to be the victims of abuse, and they generally experience more violent forms of abuse than young men do. One in five female high school students reports having experienced physical or sexual violence in a dating relationship, and nearly half say they know of someone who has been in an abusive relationship. The types of violent acts young women report include being punched, shoved, cut, and forced to engage in sexual activity against their will. Young men are more likely to report being pinched or slapped by their partners, and often report that their own jealousy or inappropriate sexual

contraception to use and how to protect themselves. It's especially important for girls—they are the ones who get pregnant, and they are at such a high risk of getting HIV.

My freshman science teacher, Ms. Handler, knew I was interested in this stuff. I'm a feminist and I'm pro-choice. She asked me if I was interested in joining a group that would be doing a project for this cause, and so I sent in an application. I got in and we started meeting in January 2002.

The project was put together by the Teen Pregnancy Coalition of San Mateo County. Our group was called ASsET, Advocating Sex Education Together. There were about twenty of us, some from every high school in the district. We met every other Wednesday at the TPC center. Toward the end of the project we met every week. We worked with a health educator from the center, Kris Popplewell. Our main resource, besides the center, was "The Roadmap: A Teen Guide to Changing Your School's Sex Ed," put out by the Network for Family Life Education. It has ideas and flyers and everything in it—all

advances may have caused the incident. Both sexes report many types of emotional abuse, such as being constantly criticized, intimidated by frequent rages, and feeling controlled by their partners. (Dating violence can also occur in same-sex relationships.)

Unfortunately very few teenagers talk to health care professionals, responsible adults, or even one another about this topic, which means that they aren't aware of how widespread it is, or that there are ways for them to get out of an abusive situation and into a healthy one. Breaking the silence about dating violence at your school can be a first step toward transforming the lives of those who are in abusive relationships. Young people who have been victims of dating violence are more likely to abuse drugs, attempt suicide, and grow up to be adults who are abused, unless they get the help they need when they need it.

Speaking out about the problem will also help educate your campus community about the issue, so that your classmates can be sensitive to signs of dating violence and be better equipped to help themselves and their friends out of a bad situation. It's estimated that close to half of dating violence incidents take place on campus, so it's a great place for this kind of "word-of-mouth activism."

Deciding to speak out about dating violence means that you will no longer treat the subject as taboo. You'll arm yourself with the facts, and you will share them when appropriate. You'll say something if you see the warning signs of abuse, and you will say something if you see someone being abused. If the subject of dating violence comes up because a character on a TV show or a movie is the victim of dating violence, you might point out that it is a very real problem, and possibly create a discussion about it among your friends. There might even be an appropriate time to discuss dating violence in class—if your health or sex education classes discuss relationships, for example.

Here are some warning signs of dating violence to be on the lookout for. Someone might be in a potentially abusive relationship if he or she:

- has sudden loss of self-confidence and a growing difficulty with making decisions
- is engaging in risky behavior (such as binge drinking or unsafe sex) as part of a new relationship
- begins doing poorly in school and dropping out of activities
- becomes increasingly isolated from his or her friends
- makes excuses for the bad behavior of his or her partner

Someone might become abusive if he or she is:

- extremely jealous or possessive
- exerting pressure to make the relationship very serious, very fast
- using forms of emotional abuse such as

you need.

We spent most of the spring educating ourselves about comprehensive sex education. Comprehensive sex education teaches you a variety of ways to protect yourself, unlike "abstinence only" education, where they preach just abstinence. Comprehensive sex education covers protecting yourself as well as abstinence. The curriculum also covers homosexuality, family and lifestyle, sexuality, rape . . . all those kinds of things. Toward the end of that year we also did some public speaking and we formulated our plan to lobby the district for comprehensive sexuality education beginning in the ninth grade.

In the 2002–2003 school year we focused on the community. In the fall we did a survey of teachers, students, and parents to ask their thoughts about sex education in the schools. There were different surveys for the students and the teachers and the parents. They had about eight questions each. The questions were like, "Do you feel that sex education should be required in your student's school?"

yelling, swearing, or throwing tantrums
- trying to make all the decisions in the relationship
- separating his or her significant other from other relationships, even longstanding friendships

If you are seeing one or more of these signs in a friend, or in his or her partner, then you might want to raise the issue of dating violence. Sometimes it's tempting to dismiss verbal harassment or other types of humiliating behavior—but trust your instincts. Calling someone a bitch or yelling at her if she spends time with her friends can, bit by bit, break down her self-esteem and create a controlling relationship. The verbal abuse can then escalate into physical violence.

When you decide to raise the issue of dating violence with someone, do so thoughtfully and with respect. You will probably want to talk to the individual privately. You can say, "I'm concerned about you, and here's why." Citing specific incidents can be helpful. Explain that a lot of people don't realize they are being abused or won't admit it, and that you want to help. The important thing is to raise the issue and to let your friend know that you are there, and that there are things he or she can do to take control of the situation. It can be good to have a hotline number to give out or some literature (see the resources at the end of this section). Avoid issuing ultimatums—pushing your friend into a choice between you or his or her significant other is just going to alienate your friend.

If the person isn't someone you know very well, then the situation is slightly more delicate, but you can still do something. Don't act like a stalker, but you can strike up a conversation at some point about school or whatever, and then say something like, "You know, I noticed that your boyfriend/girlfriend was really yelling at you the other day. Does he/she do that a lot?" This person might have been wondering to whom he or she can talk about what's going on. It's common for abusers to isolate their victims—becoming friends with this stranger means you can be his or her lifeline.

Don't be surprised people are sometimes resistant to what you are saying. Victims of many types of crimes feel ashamed and guilty, as if the situation is their fault. With dating violence, because the relationship was originally a romantic one, it can feel like a betrayal to admit that a partner has become abusive. Add this to the controlling dynamic mentioned above, and you've got a lot of reasons for denial.

If your friend doesn't want to deal, be patient. Keep in touch and keep suggesting activities that you two can do together. Remind your friend that this situation is not his or her fault and that you are there.

We administered them on Back to School Night, and we handed some out at football games. We had to get permission from the principal of each of the schools, but they were pretty comfortable with it. I handed some out at a football game. A lot of students were eager to take them, as well as parents.

We tallied all of the surveys, which took three long meetings. It was kind of a pain and there were papers everywhere. Then we calculated everything and put it all together into one big set of statistics.

Next we held a forum for the community to ask questions. We handed out flyers, posted some flyers in the schools and gave them to the teachers, and got a pretty good turnout with a lot of students and quite a few parents as well as a few teachers. Everyone in our group had a job at the forum. Four people were on the panel and answered questions, and others talked a little bit about what our purpose was. Some others took notes on what questions were being asked and who was asking them. That's what I did.

The most common

However, if you see signs that the abuse has become physical—if you witness an incident, or if your friend begins having frequent injuries and mysterious bruises—call a violence hotline yourself. They can help you find resources in your area and a responsible adult who can step in.

After you've been speaking out about dating violence for a while, you might find that you become a kind of resource yourself. Friends and acquaintances could start coming to you with questions and concerns. At that point you could take your activism to another level and make flyers to hand out at school, or some educational posters to hang up, or even invite a speaker to discuss the issue with the entire student body. (See the "Fighting Racism" chapter for tips on how to bring a speaker to your campus.)

Dating Violence Resources

In Love & In Danger: A Teen's Guide to Breaking Free of Abusive Relationships

By Barrie Levy

This is a great book to read, whether you are in an abusive relationship or helping someone else who is in one. It starts with three personal stories, but then it turns into more of a workbook, with checklists to determine if a relationship is abusive, explanations of behaviors and terms, coping strategy suggestions, and ways to get out of a bad situation. Want to know the diff between healthy love and addictive love? It's in here.

The National Domestic Violence Hotline

In most public health discussions, dating violence comes under the heading of domestic violence, which also includes child abuse, spousal abuse, and other types of violence within a family or household. This hotline can talk you through a crisis, help you find local resources such as counseling or shelters, and give you guidance if you're unclear on whether to act or not in a particular situation.

1-800-799-SAFE

Love Is Not Abuse

The main focus of this site (funded by the Liz Claiborne clothing company) is older women in domestic abuse situations, but there is good information on dating violence as well—click on the "Just for Teens" button. You'll find information on how to discuss dating violence, listings for teen-friendly resources all over the country, and stories from real girls who have been abused or who have helped others. There

question was from people wanting to know exactly what their children would be taught and how it would make a difference and what kind of effect it would have on them. We told them what our goal was, and once they knew what this comprehensive sex education would contain, they saw that it would benefit their children. So we just kind of rallied a lot of support from them.

After the forum we had a wrap-up meeting to discuss what had happened. We talked about all the issues that parents had brought up and what they wanted to know most—basically, what their general opinion was. The forum had reinforced our beliefs that this project was needed.

Our next step was a letter campaign. We thought that it would help to get the idea out there and have people speaking about it and realizing the importance of this. We sent out letters to newspapers and companies and stuff. The letter said exactly why this issue was so important, what we were proposing would actually do, and how teens would benefit from it. We said we would like them to support us. Most

is a downloadable brochure about dating violence and one for parents as well.
www.loveisnotabuse.com

See It and Stop It

This is a fantastic site created by teenagers and wholly devoted to the issue of dating violence. It has tips on how to fight dating violence as an individual, among your friends, or in a group. There's also an organizing tool kit with a lot of ideas and materials to do more. You can also join the Teen Action Campaign to hook up with other activists who are working on this issue.
www.seeitandstopit.org

Find Out If Your School Is Title IX Compliant

If you are female and you play sports in school, you have Title IX to thank for it. In fact, many of the world's top female athletes, including Sheryl Swoopes and Mia Hamm, wouldn't be where they are today if it weren't for Title IX. Title IX is a federal law that was passed in 1972 banning gender discrimination in any extracurricular program or activity. It applies to all public schools and any private schools that receive federal money.

At the time it became law, Title IX was completely radical because at most schools, sports programs for young women either didn't exist or were tiny and had few resources. With Title IX's passage, every school had to be Title IX compliant, meaning that women's sports had to be treated in a manner equal to men's sports at the same institution. If there is a men's junior varsity basketball team, there should be a women's junior varsity basketball team. If there is a bus that takes the men's track team to their meets, there should be a bus for the women's track team as well. (A common misconception about Title IX is that equal amounts of money must be spent on men's and women's sports—it is not true. Scholarship money must be equal. Other than that, the language requires that women's programs receive equal "treatment" and "benefits.")

Title IX has created a sports culture for women and provided role models for female athletes. It is directly responsible for college women's sports programs, high school programs, and even the WNBA. (Where do you think all the athletes learned to play?) Millions of young women have opportunities now that they never would have had without the law's passage. In 1970 only about three percent of female students played varsity sports, compared with forty percent today. Studies show that playing sports not only improves physical fitness, but also improves the lives

of the responses were very good. They were in full support of what we were doing and offered all kinds of help. We asked people to write to the school district and say they wanted the requirement too.

In the fall of 2003 we worked on our proposal for the school board. The proposal was that the current policy be amended so that comprehensive sex education would be required in at least one year, preferably in the ninth grade. We didn't want our proposal to be too demanding, so we left it open that they could choose the course that it would be taught in. We had a couple of pages of background and some specifics about what the community thought about it. We also had a petition signed by students that we had distributed in the fall.

By December we were ready. We called the schools' superintendent and had him look over our proposal. He had to okay it and put it on the agenda so we could present it for a vote. At the meeting I was nervous. But I thought that if they voted in favor of our proposal, it would help a lot. I didn't see any disadvantages to it.

of those who participate at the high school level. Female high school athletes are less likely to get pregnant, are more likely to graduate, and have higher self-esteem than their peers who do not participate in sports.

Unfortunately many high schools and most colleges are still not in compliance with Title IX. Young women currently have still 1.1 million fewer opportunities to play sports than young men do. Finding out if your school is in compliance is a great way to support the right of young women to participate in sports on an equal level to young men.

To determine if your school is complying with its Title IX obligations, start by looking around you. Are the women's sports at your school treated equally in terms of resources and opportunities? One good thing to do is count the number of young men participating in sports (fifteen on JV basketball and fifteen on varsity, plus thirty on JV football and thirty on varsity, etc.) and then count the number of young women. Are the two numbers equal, or close to it? Now look at the sports programs in terms of resources. Do the teams of both sexes have the same number of coaches? The same kinds of equipment and uniforms? If you note a lot of inequities, your school might not be doing all it could to support women's sports in accordance with the law.

At this point you might want to go online and download a formal checklist to organize your research. There is a good one on the Women's Sports Foundation Web site (www.womenssportsfoundation.org—click on "Issues and Action," then on "Geena Takes Aim" and then on "Grade Your School") and another one on the site for the National Women's Law Center (www.nwlc.org—click on "Athletics" and then scroll down to "Is Your School Complying with Title IX?"). Print out the checklist of your choice and get going filling it out. You might want to enlist some friends or athletes so you don't have to do the whole thing by yourself.

If you complete your checklist and feel that your school is not in compliance with Title IX, it's time to set up a meeting with your school's Title IX coordinator. Every school is required to have a coordinator—you can look on your school's Web site or call the office to ask who it is. If your school doesn't have a Title IX officer, you can report it to the Department of Education's civil rights department. Here's the contact information:

U.S. Department of Education
Office for Civil Rights
Customer Service Team
Mary E. Switzer Building
330 C Street, SW
Washington, D.C. 20202
1-800-421-3481
Fax: 202-205-9862
TDD: 877-521-2172
OCR@ed.gov

The board seemed a little confused at first because they thought their policy was sufficient. But we pointed out that the policy was outdated and also that it didn't exactly say what it needed to say. It was open to interpretation so teachers could take it the wrong way and not teach what they needed to teach. It didn't say much about contraceptives, and it used terms like "venereal disease," which is a term that's not even used today.

We had a PowerPoint presentation. Kris spoke and then some of us took points from the presentation and talked about them and kind of elaborated on those points. During this the panel had our proposal in their hands and were looking through it and looking at the evidence that we had to support that. Surprisingly there was not really much opposition. There was one panel member who kind of thought it was unnecessary at first but then later voted in favor.

They voted at the next meeting. We weren't there but we got an e-mail right after that said we had won. They voted to start implementing the change right away, in the fall. Then that following

If your school does have a Title IX coordinator, request a meeting. Bring your research, and some notes if you need them. Taking a few friends and/or star athletes with you to your meeting is a great idea—it will show the person with whom you are meeting that this is something bigger than one individual.

Ask the Title IX coordinator if he or she thinks your school is in compliance. If the answer is yes, then ask how he or she knows this. Is there a yearly report, or some other kind of information you can look at? In the unlikely event there is such a report, check it out and compare it to your research. You could ask to take it with you, and request a follow-up meeting, or just look at it side-by-side with the coordinator. It's possible that the report is incomplete, inaccurate, or misunderstands the requirements of Title IX.

If there is no report, then tell the coordinator that you've done some research and hand over your checklist. Don't just hand it over and wait for a response—keep the conversation going. You could say something like, "Well, we looked into it, and we saw that two hundred and forty-five guys are playing sports here, but only one hundred girls, so it seems like noncompliance to us," or "The guys' teams all get preferential time slots for practice, so every girls' team practices in the late afternoon or at night—that doesn't seem fair to us." Don't be mean or accusing—just state the facts.

Your Title IX coordinator might be feeling a little defensive at this point, so try defusing the situation with some positive suggestions. You can say something like, "We'd love to work with you to get our school in compliance with the law." It's good to have a list of proposals also. Your proposals could be things like:

- introduce JV teams for all women's sports (because all the boys' sports have them)
- upgrade the women's locker room, which is leaky and unusable when it rains
- set up a scheduling lottery for practice fields, so every team has an equal chance to get desirable slots

If the coordinator is open to your proposals, he or she will probably want to look into it and get back to you. Agree to a meeting in a week or so, and ask who else should attend—maybe some coaches, or the principal. After the meeting send copies of your findings and your proposals to the principal and the athletic director if you have one (and if it isn't who you met with). Say that you just had a great meeting with the compliance officer and you look forward to discussing the topic further at the next meeting. From here on out, you just keep pushing until your proposals have come to pass.

If the coordinator dismisses your research and your proposals, or makes promises and doesn't keep

Wednesday we had a meeting to discuss what they did and how they voted. We were very happy and we had a little celebration. We got a certificate signed by a local politician congratulating us and extolling our work.

My parents thought it was great that I did this. They were in full support of what I was doing and proud that I was involved with changing the policy. They knew that I was helping create a better environment for future students. I think it was a good experience that helped me to get more involved with my community. I definitely want to keep doing things like this.

For more information on comprehensive sexuality education, see the HIV/AIDS chapter. You can visit the Teen Pregnancy Coalition of San Mateo County at www.teenpregnancycoalition.org

them, then you might want to try going to the PTA or to another influential group at your school. Set up a meeting with an officer of the group and explain the situation. Ask if you can bring up the topic at the group's next formal meeting. At that meeting, again present your findings and your proposals. Tell the group that you know they want every student to be treated equally and do not want the school to be breaking a federal law. Suggest that they use their influence to bring the school into compliance.

If even that doesn't work, you can take legal action. Try contacting the ACLU (www.aclu.org) or the Women's Sports Foundation. One of these organizations can help you get the resources you need to file a complaint with the Department of Education. You might be in for a big fight—but think about what Title IX means, and why it is so important. Helping your school to comply with Title IX not only will benefit you and every female athlete at your school, but also will honor those who first fought for the passage of this law, and for the idea that every athlete deserves a chance to compete.

THE COMMUNITY ACTIVIST

Have a Letter-Writing Party to Fight for Women's Reproductive Rights

The reproductive rights of women are in danger, especially those of teenagers and women living in poverty. Several different pieces of recent legislation combine to make access to information and services difficult, if not impossible. In a country that cherishes freedom, restricting basic health care and education is wrong. Here are two examples of the situation.

Only ten percent of American students get a comprehensive sex education. (For more on comprehensive sex ed and how to get it in your school, see the Educating Others About HIV/AIDS chapter). In order to qualify for federal funds, many schools are forced to use what's called "abstinence-only" education, which forbids any mention of contraception, disease prevention, or homosexuality. Seven out of ten Americans oppose abstinence-only programs, which have not been shown to be effective in reducing the number of teenagers who are sexually active, and may be linked to teen pregnancies and STDs. The sex education that has been shown to work discusses both abstinence and birth control.

Thirty states have some form of a parental consent law, which affects the ability of a minor to get an abortion. A parental consent law requires that a minor (sometimes defined as under eighteen, sometimes as under sixteen) get the permission of one or both parents before seeking an abortion. (Some states require parental notification, and others require consent.)

Additionally, some state attorneys general contend that parental notification and consent should also apply if a minor seeks birth control. Nearly half of all minors in one study said that they would discontinue using contraceptives if their parents were notified. They did not, however, say that they would stop having sex.

Consent and notification laws severely limit the access teenagers have to reproductive health care. They not only put young women at risk of being thrown out or punished by their parents when the situation becomes known, but also they can force young women into carrying unplanned pregnancies to term or into seeking out illegal abortions. A teenager who has an unwanted child is at a high risk for dropping out of high school or developing substance abuse problems, and is more likely to become the recipient of government funds.

You can find out what the laws are in your state by checking the NARAL (National Abortion Rights Action League) Web site at www.naral.org. Every year they publish "Who Decides? A State-by-State Report on the Status of Women's Reproductive Rights," which explains what the restrictions are in every state. There's also good information on the Center for Reproductive Rights Web site (www.reproductiverights.org /pub_fac_restrictions.html).

A great way to get your voice and the voices of others heard on this subject is to have a letter-writing party. It's got some of the elements of a regular party (food, drinks, music, friends), but while you are there, you also write letters to educators, government representatives, and others to let them know that you want your rights restored and protected.

The first step is logistics. Pick a place (at someone's house or a local coffee shop or pizza place—make sure it's somewhere with lots of writing surfaces or you'll need to provide clipboards) and set a date and time. Invite all of your friends, and encourage them to invite more people, depending on the capacity of the room. Tell the invitees that the party will combine good times with good work—that they will be speaking out for what they believe in while hanging out with their pals. You could encourage friends with laptops to bring them so they won't have to handwrite their letters. (Having a printer available at the location is above and beyond, but if you can pull it off, go for it.)

Before the party make a list of the people to whom you want to send letters, and their addresses. Some good ones are your local school board, all of your local high school principals (get these addresses from the phone book), your state government representatives, and your members of the House and Senate. You can get most of those addresses on www.congress.org.

Get all of your supplies together. You'll need pens, stamps, and a lot of nice paper and envelopes. Stamp the envelopes, and print out several copies of your address list. Make a fact sheet to hand out so everyone knows what the issues are.

Write a sample letter for people to use as a template. It could be something like this fictitious example:

Dear Senator Bender:

I am a student at Davis Park High School in Davis Park, Nebraska. I believe in women's rights—they are part of this country's values of freedom and equality. Therefore I am adamantly opposed to the parental notification law and the abstinence-only education policy currently in place in our state. These laws directly affect my life and the lives of others, and they can contribute to teen pregnancies, STDs, etc.

One quarter of the American public is now under eighteen. We can't vote. But you should know that we watch to see who protects our rights and fights for us, and who does-n't. We influence the way our parents vote, and when we can vote ourselves we will not be voting for anyone who supports this type of legislation, or who fails to fight against it.

I'm writing this letter to alert you to this problem, and to the growing dissatisfaction among young people toward civic life in general. Why should we participate in a system that doesn't respect our rights? You have the power to inspire us by standing up for reproductive freedom. We want to believe that our government and our country belong to us—we need you to prove to us that this is true.

Thank you for your time. I would love to hear back from you on this matter.

Sincerely,
Mike Guillermo-Vega

Print several copies of the sample letter as well.

On the day of the party, get to the location early to set up. You might want to make a packet for each attendee, so each person gets some paper and envelopes, a fact sheet, a sample letter, and a list of addresses. Don't forget to bring the snacks and drinks too, unless you are meeting at a place where people can buy food. If there is a way to have music, go for it—that will make the party more festive.

Give people packets as they arrive and explain what to do. They should read your fact sheet and your sample letter, then write their own letters. Urge everyone to per-sonalize the letters if they can, with things like, "At my school, we aren't taught about birth control. As a result, many kids are having unsafe sex. I'm worried they will get pregnant or sick. If we had good sex ed this wouldn't be happening." Or, "My sister wanted to get an abortion but she had to get permission from my dad. He got mad about it and kicked her out. Now she's living on welfare in a group home and about to have a baby that she doesn't want, because of this law." Stories like this will bring the issue to life for the letter recipients; they will also remind your friends why this action is so necessary.

While everyone is working on their letters, be a good host. Circulate the snacks, and offer to help anyone who is stuck. It's important to write the letters, but it's also a party, so have fun! Play music and tell jokes, whatever you usually do at parties with your friends.

Some people might question if writing letters actually makes a difference. It does. Letter-writing is an important and effective form of advocacy. It is the job of every elected official to represent the people who voted for them. Letters can educate officials about issues, and also let them know how their constituents feel about a particular issue. E-mails may be easier to send, but studies show that actual letters sent through the mail are given greater weight by members of Congress and other government officials.

When the letters are finished and put into signed, addressed envelopes, collect them all for mailing. Congratulate everyone on a job well done, and keep the party going. When it does start to break up, thank everyone for coming and for standing up for women's reproductive rights. If the event goes really well, you might want to consider making these parties a regular event, and choose a different topic to write about each time. Writing letters is an important part of participatory democracy, and doing it regularly is a great way to make sure that your government listens to you.

THE 5-MINUTE ACTIVIST

Feminist Campus

Feminist Campus is a pro-choice student network. In its "1-Click" action center (under "Act" on the home page), it presents topical women's rights issues with links for you to fax or e-mail key politicians and urge them to act in order with the ideal of equality. Topics range from nominating and confirming pro-choice judges to emergency contraception and the protection of Afghan and Iraqi women. Okay, it takes more than one click, and you have to enter your zip code, but it's still a great tool to make your voice heard in just a few minutes. www.feministcampus.org/act/oneclick

The Breast Cancer Site

Mammography is one of the best methods for early detection of breast cancer, but many women don't have the resources to get a mammogram as part of their health care program. Click every day and you help pay for a free mammogram for an underprivileged woman, provided by the National Breast Cancer Foundation.
www.thebreastcancersite.com

RESOURCES

Web Sites

Advocates for Youth

This is an advocacy group dedicated to supporting programs and policies that help youth make informed decisions about their reproductive and sexual health. The site has great information on starting your own peer education program, actions you can take such as signing a petition for better sex ed, and ways to connect with other youth activists. The group also does international work and a lot of work connected with emergency contraception. www.advocatesforyouth.org

The Alan Guttmacher Institute

AGI is a nonprofit devoted to sexual and reproductive health research and rights. It does research and issues public policy reports. The site is a good place to get facts and stats on nearly anything related to sexuality or sexual health, and there is a special youth section. The state center will let you see what the laws and issues are in your state. You can even use the tablemaker to draw information from the AGI databases to create your own reports. www.agi-usa.org

Association for Women's Rights in Development

AWID is an international group focused on sustainable development and on fostering gender equality in the development process—making sure that

women's rights are not neglected. The members, who are on the ground in developing countries, promote women's access to technology, help to form feminist groups, and work with feminist organizations that are unfamiliar with international issues. Use the site to see what it's like to be a feminist activist in the developing world—if you're interested, AWID's Young Women and Leadership Program can get you started.
www.awid.org

Feminist Majority Foundation

Over fifty-six percent of American women, and nearly seventy percent of young women, identify themselves as feminists—a true feminist majority. The FMF is dedicated to representing those feminists and to advancing the rights of women everywhere. This site—probably the biggest feminist site on the Internet—is an invaluable resource for anyone interested in women's issues and gender equality. In addition to all of the information and news, the site also provides lots of ways to connect to other activists and activist groups, through the Internet portal and the listings of professional women's organizations, domestic violence shelters, and campus activist groups.
www.feminist.org

The National Campaign to Prevent Teen Pregnancy

Despite the recent decline in teen pregnancy rates, the United States still leads the industrialized world in the number of teen pregnancies per capita. A

teenager who gets pregnant is less likely to graduate from high school or to hold down a job, and the children of teen parents often do poorly in school themselves. The National Campaign to Prevent Teen Pregnancy wants to reduce the number of teen pregnancies through education and outreach, working with many types of groups (including religious organizations). The teen section of the site is great, with tips on how to avoid pregnancy (including how to say no), a quiz to test your knowledge, polls, stories from real teens, and support for teenagers who are active in this area.
www.teenpregnancy.org

National Center for Policy Research for Women & Families

This site is a great clearinghouse for information on studies done on children, women, teenagers, and families. You can see what the latest research says about young women and obesity, depression, or various other health issues. There isn't a straight-up activism component, but reading up on this stuff will probably give you a lot of ideas for issues you want to work on.
www.center4policy.org

National Committee on Pay Equity

Even when you account for education and experience, women still lag significantly behind men in how much they earn, and the gap is much greater for women of color. The NCPE is a coalition of labor unions, workplace groups, and individuals dedicated to closing the wage gap. The site has info and stats about pay equity, and ways for both individuals and businesses to get involved in the solution. www.pay-equity.org

National Partnership for Women & Families

National Partnership is an advocacy group with three main areas of interest: health care, workplace fairness, and work and family (which includes things like allowing parents to take medical leave when a child is sick). The site's legislative center will inform you and help you take action on issues such as at-home infant care, affirmative action, genetic testing, sexual harassment laws, and other issues connected to the group's mission. www.nationalpartnership.org

Planned Parenthood Federation of America

Planned Parenthood's mission is built on the idea that every individual has the right to manage his or her own fertility. It acts on this mission by providing comprehensive health care, including prenatal and birthing classes, abortion and contraception services, research and educational programs, and a vigorous public policy advocacy arm. The Web site has information on the many, many things Planned Parenthood does, an interface to reach your local clinic (or call the hotline at 1-800-772-9100), and information on how to get involved with reproductive rights and health care activism. www.plannedparenthood.org

National Abortion Federation

Did you know that forty-three percent of American women have an abortion in their lifetime? It's critical to women's lives that the right to choice be defended. The mission of the NAF is to keep abortion safe, affordable, and legal. The site has a really valuable section on how to be pro-choice in your daily life, as well as an edited list of online pro-choice resources. There are also comprehensive facts and statistics about abortion, information about violence against abortion providers and clinics, and good explanations of the legal issues surrounding abortion. The site is in Spanish and in English, and it has a hotline: 1-800-772-9100. www.prochoice.org

Religious Coalition for Reproductive Choice

You don't need to choose between your faith and your belief in a woman's right to choose, according to the Religious Coalition for Reproductive Choice, which has more than twenty million members, mostly from Christian and Jewish backgrounds. On this site you can read about how different people have come to their pro-choice and pro-faith positions, connect with member congregations and groups, and join the youth group, Spiritual Youth for Reproductive Freedom. www.rcrc.org

UNIFEM: A Portal on Women, Peace, and Security

When violence erupts around the world, women are killed, raped, mutilated, displaced, abducted, and tortured. UNIFEM is the United Nations

Development Fund for Women, intended to protect women who are caught in armed conflicts and to promote equal rights in post-conflict nation building. The site is rather shocking—it opens with a map covered with dots, each one representing an armed conflict or somewhere where UN Peacekeepers are deployed. From there you can choose from a long list of locations or issues and read about how women are being affected daily by armed conflict. The UN doesn't have suggestions for what individuals can do to help—if you want to work in this area, try the Sisterhood Is Global Institute (www.sigi.org) or Amnesty International (www.amnesty.org).
www.womenwarpeace.org

Books

The Abortion Conflict: A Pro/Con Issue

By Deanne Durrett

Although abortion is legal and the majority of Americans are pro-choice, abortion remains an extremely divisive issue in this country. This book goes through the history of the procedure and presents the arguments on both sides in a neutral way. It hasn't been updated to include the recent morning-after pill controversy, but it's still worth reading.

Colonize This!: Young Women of Color on Today's Feminism

Edited by Daisy Hernández and Bushra Rehman

This anthology of essays is a great way to see the sometimes uneasy relationship that the feminist establishment has with women of color, as several authors take the movement to task for not being more inclusive. But you will also read about the flipside—the difficulty of bringing a feminist ethos into some communities of color, as when one Indian woman decides to refuse an arranged marriage.

Deal With It!: A Whole New Approach to Your Body, Brain, and Life as a gURL

By Esther Drill, Heather McDonald, and Rebecca Odes The founders of gURL.com changed a lot of lives when they released *Deal With It!*, a combination handbook and manifesto for young women. The book offers frank information and advice about all aspects of physical and mental health, from drug use and spirituality to boobs and birth control. If you think you're too old for it—you're wrong. Demand that your school library get a copy as well. (Note: The author of this book contributed to *Deal With It!*)

Feminism Is for Everybody: Passionate Politics

By Bell Hooks bell hooks has been an outspoken feminist since her first book, *Ain't I a Woman: Black Women and Feminism*, appeared in 1981. Since then, through her writing and her poetry she has often functioned as a sort of feminist conscience, complaining when the movement lets her down and urging activists to do the right thing. (She's also well known for refusing to capitalize her name.) *Feminism Is for Everybody*, written in 2002, not only is an inspiring introduction to feminism if you don't know a lot about it, but also will revitalize any old-schoolers whose spirit is flagging. hooks argues passionately that feminism is still relevant, as well as vital to both individual and global well-being.

The Feminine Mystique
By Betty Friedan

First published in 1963, Friedan's book is widely credited for galvanizing the second wave of feminism. It's worth reading to see where that generation was coming from and what sorts of things made them sit up and take action to fight for equality. Friedan describes the dissatisfaction she and her contemporaries have with their lives and connects that dissatisfaction to the systematic discrimination against women in American culture.

Manifesta: Young Women, Feminism, and the Future
By Jennifer Baumgardner and Amy Richards

In their powerful opening chapter, "A Day without Feminism," Baumgardner and Richards illustrate the ways that the victories of second wave women's rights activists benefit every woman today. But after establishing what today's feminists owe their elders, the authors go on to discuss the resentments that some young women feel toward older feminists, and the many ways that some in the feminist establishment have belittled young women, focusing on issues like clothing styles rather than core feminist values. Manifesta provides a clear-eyed look at contemporary feminism, then goes on to provide a cogent vision of feminism's future—one in which a new generation assumes responsibility for fulfilling the promise of equality. The book also has a lot of great info in the appendices on feminist books and how-tos for grassroots organizing.

When Chickenheads Come Home to Roost: A Hip-Hop Feminist Breaks It Down

By Joan Morgan

Morgan writes about what it's like for her to be black and a feminist today, dealing with the misogynistic aspects of hip-hop culture as well as feminism's racial missteps. As she straddles both cultures, Morgan insists that she and other black women can forge a new political identity that incorporates both race and gender issues. It's all written in a chatty voice, full of pop culture references that make it fun to read now, though it may seem really dated in a few years.

Protecting Civil Rights and Civil Liberty

THE ISSUES

America prides itself on the freedom of its citizens. Our country was founded with freedom in mind, and those freedoms are enshrined in our Constitution. But freedoms often need to be fought for, and then vigilantly defended. Many citizens are denied their most basic freedoms, which are also known as civil rights and civil liberty.

Your civil rights are what allow you to be yourself—to express yourself and to act on your beliefs. In America, civil rights are generally considered to be the ones guaranteed by the Bill of Rights, the first ten amendments to the Constitution of the United States. The list of civil rights includes but is not limited to:

Freedom of speech
Freedom of assembly
Freedom of the press
The right to petition
Freedom of religion
The right to vote
The right to a fair trial

Civil liberty is the right to live your life without

government interference. Civil liberties are guaranteed by the Thirteenth and Fourteenth Amendments, which abolished slavery and enumerated the rights of citizens, respectively. A good way to think about it is that your civil liberty is the ability to enjoy your civil rights without any government agency getting in your way. For example, you should be able to express your political views without fearing repercussions from the police. Groups such as the American Civil Liberties Union use the term "civil liberties" to refer to both civil rights and civil liberty.

The American civil rights movement of the 1950s and 1960s was focused mostly on racial equality. Under the 1892 Supreme Court case *Plessy v. Ferguson*, it was legal to distinguish between races, as long as the results were "separate but equal." However, things were not equal. African Americans were being denied their civil rights. They had difficulties voting, attended substandard schools, and were segregated from whites even at drinking fountains. Activists such as Rosa Parks and Dr. Martin Luther King

ASHLEY'S STORY

Ashley Shaw is fifteen and a sophomore at Longmeadow High School in Longmeadow, Connecticut.

I write for my school paper, the *Jet Jotter*, which comes out every other month. We do a thing called "Centerfold," which is three different stories all on the same topic. When we did the January 2004 issue, the topic was drugs, and I wrote a story for it. I wrote about a girl I know, a girl who goes to my school, who told me that she and her mom do drugs together. The story was called "High Class Parenting." The mother has been on drugs since she was in high school and she didn't really want her daughter to start, but the daughter found her drugs and started. The story was about how they are more like friends, not a mother-daughter relationship. I didn't say the names of the people in the story—they were anonymous.

I am friends with the girl in the story. She is not my best friend, but she is one of my closer friends. She knew our topic for the issue was drugs, and that I wanted to write

Jr. led the struggle for voting rights, education, and desegregation. There were legal challenges to racist laws, sit-ins and demonstrations to protest racist institutions, and unprecedented community mobilization— often spearheaded by religious leaders. Activists from all over the country traveled to the Southern states to register African-American voters.

This period of civil rights activism was heavily influenced by thinkers like Henry David Thoreau and Mahatma Gandhi. In 1849 Thoreau outlined the principle of civil disobedience as an activist tactic. Civil disobedience means symbolically and publicly breaking an unjust law in order to bring the matter into the court system and to create public discussion. When Rosa Parks refused to go to the back of the bus, that was civil disobedience. Gandhi's activist work elaborated on the idea of civil disobedience and introduced concepts like passive resistance and noncooperation. Actions such as sit-ins, strikes, and boycotts are examples of passive resistance and noncooperation.

While the civil rights leaders of the 1950s and '60s explicitly espoused nonviolent resistance, civil rights activists were often in great physical danger. Violent clashes with the police were commonplace, and some activists were even killed while working for the cause they believed in. Dr. Martin Luther King Jr. was assassinated in Memphis, Tennessee, in 1968. Despite this, there were many successes, including school integration, and the activism of this period continues to inspire civil rights activists today.

Teenagers do not have the same civil rights as adults. You don't have the right to vote until you are eighteen. Your parents have the right to search your room and read your e-mail. Your school can search your backpack and your locker. In some cases, your school can dictate what you can wear and what you can publish in your school paper. Your school can also prevent you from accessing certain Web sites when using school computers. You can't drive without your parents' permission until you're eighteen. You can't drink. Some towns have curfews that only apply to teenagers.

These restrictions on youth civil rights are often challenged. There is no definitive case law regarding a high school student's right to free expression or a minor's right to privacy. Even when significant cases have been decided, the courts have been divided in how they apply the standards. For example, the Supreme Court, in *Bethel School District No. 403 v. Fraser*, 1986, ruled that while students have a right to express their political views, public schools also have the right to prohibit vulgar and offensive speech. Some courts feel that the *Fraser* decision means that

about someone doing drugs with an older person. She came to me and said I should write about her and her mom. She wanted the story told. She and her mom both wanted to do it, but only anonymously.

I went to the advisor for the paper. He teaches the journalism class also. I said the people in my story wanted to be anonymous and he said okay. He told me the guidelines and rules I should be following, and then we talked to the editor of the paper. He also thought it was a good idea.

I interviewed my friend and her mom together. I had all my questions written out beforehand. I was kind of uneasy at first, but then it wasn't hard to do. I didn't tape the interview—I took notes. I asked them why they got started on drugs and how they got started. They weren't worried at all about the story coming out. My friend is a quiet girl and no one would ever think this was about her, but it seemed a little weird to me that the mom wasn't worried.

When the story came out, I got positive and negative reactions. People were saying, "Good job, you're

schools may prohibit *all* types of offensive speech, while others have ruled that schools have jurisdiction only over school-sponsored speech. Therefore, if you were to wear a T-shirt that says "Libertarians suck" and your school thought your shirt was offensive, the outcome of your case would depend on which way the court interpreted *Fraser*. If the court felt *Fraser* covered all speech, you'd lose. If the court interpreted *Fraser* more narrowly, you'd probably win.

Since September 11, 2001, there have been significant challenges to the civil rights and civil liberty of all Americans. Both the Patriot Act and the No Child Left Behind Act allow the government to engage in activities not previously allowed, and both have specific impact on the lives of young people. The Patriot Act allows extensive government monitoring of Internet and phone communication, surveillance of political and religious groups, and access to university student records without the students' knowledge. International students are forced to register with the FBI, are entered into a database, and are often intensely monitored. The NCLB Act allows military recruitment on high school campuses and military access to middle school student records. In combination, these acts have increased the military presence on American campuses and reduced the rights of students, as well as all citizens, to control their own personal information. (The full text of each act is available on the ACLU Web site, www.aclu.org.)

There are other restrictions being made on civil rights, and on free speech in particular. The proposed Broadcast Decency Enforcement Act will allow the Federal Communications Commission to levy large fines on broadcasters that broadcast "indecent" material—even if the viewer specifically sought out, subscribed to, or purchased the material. Low-power or noncorporate radio stations are being forced off the air while radio conglomerates prevent their DJs from discussing certain topics. Police officers and FBI agents are covertly attending political and religious gatherings to monitor what is being said. Recently in New York City, the mayor threatened to withdraw funding from a museum because he was offended by a piece of art on display.

The Internet is the site of many free speech and privacy battles. The FBI is currently attempting to extend phone surveillance laws to allow them to wiretap networks. Libraries and schools are under pressure to install filters that may prevent users from getting the information they are seeking. These filters block some offensive sites, but they also block sites that supply health care and other types of useful, nonoffensive content.

Civil rights activists take on all of these battles and more. In fact, many of the issues in this book—the rights

waking up the community and letting people know there are problems out there." And then the negative people were just downing it and bashing it. I don't even know why they didn't like it. Everyone was trying to figure out who the people in the story were.

About two or three days after the story came out, the principal called me to his office. He told me that I was shaking things up, and that I didn't have to tell him who the people were but that he was going to try to find out. I was like, go ahead and try. The local newspaper and the TV did stories about it. The DA's office said they were going to get involved but they never contacted me. People in the community kept calling my house. Everyone just kept saying, "Who is it? Who is it?" and trying to figure it out.

I had mixed feelings about not telling. I felt that I was doing the right thing by not telling, because they didn't want me to tell. But then I felt that I was doing the wrong thing because they actually needed help. We talked about the First Amendment and freedom of the press in class, and I knew that what I was doing was part of that. My advisor told me to hold my

of women and minorities, the right for same-sex couples to marry, the rights of those infected with HIV—can be discussed in terms of civil rights. Anti-discrimination activism is always founded on protecting the underlying civil rights of those being discriminated against. Being a civil rights activist could mean filing a lawsuit to force your school to comply with the Americans with Disabilities Act and install wheelchair ramps, attending a march to protest recent infringements on a woman's right to choose, or organizing in low-income neighborhoods to demand better bus service.

Choosing to become a civil rights activist requires passion and an incredible amount of patience. Legal challenges often mean a great deal of bureaucracy to wade through, and results can hinge on the wording or interpretation of laws written hundreds of years ago. Getting those laws changed (or even enforced) can be a long, grinding process. Participating in civil liberty projects directly contributes to the strength of our democracy and ensures that others will also have the right to voice their opinions.

Civil Rights, Civil Liberties, Human Rights—What's the Difference?

Both civil rights and civil liberty are determined nationally, and not every nation grants its citizens these freedoms in its constitution and national laws. The civil rights and the civil liberty that an American citizen enjoys are not the same as those of a citizen of Great Britain, South Africa, or the Dominican Republic.

Human rights are meant to apply to all people, regardless of nationality. Some human rights and civil rights overlap, such as the right to free speech. A good list of human rights is enumerated in the Universal Declaration of Human Rights, a document adopted by the United Nations General Assembly in 1948. Some of the human rights it lists are:

The right to be free from torture
The right to a trial
The right to seek asylum
The right to own property
The right to freedom of opinion and expression
The right to move freely within a country and to travel to other countries

The struggle for human rights is being fought in many places around the world, including right here in the United States. If you want to know more about human rights and human rights activism, visit Amnesty International (www.amnestyusa.org) or the Human Rights Watch (www.hrw.org).

head up high and to hang on to my integrity and my pride. My parents also supported me.

When my friend and her mom saw all the publicity the story was getting, they decided to enroll themselves in a drug treatment program. They have been receiving help, and now they have been off drugs for three and a half weeks. I think when the mom realized how many people were worried about her in the community, it woke her up so she could get help.

I'm glad I wrote this story. I would write it again. I did something to help the community out, to make people aware and realize that there are problems, that there are drugs everywhere. I will never tell the names of the people in it.

If you'd like to read more about a reporter's right to protect his or her sources, (sometimes called a shield law), visit the Web site for the Reporters Committee for Freedom of the Press (www.rcfp.org). You can download a publication called "The Reporter's Privilege," which is both detailed and easy to understand. There is also information on this topic

IT'S YOUR WORLD—IF YOU DON'T LIKE IT, CHANGE IT

THE AT-HOME ACTIVIST

Find Out What Data the Government Has on File About You

Under the 1966 Freedom of Information Act (FOIA) and the 1974 Privacy Act, you have the right to obtain copies of the records any government agency has been keeping on you. Looking at your files can be an eye-opening experience. If you've been active in politics or in certain religious groups, you may find that noted in your file. There could be copies of your grades and information on any foreign travel that you've done. If you've ever written a letter to the president or any elected official, that could be there too. When you see how much information has been collected in just your short life, imagine how much could be compiled by the time you hit forty or fifty.

To get copies of your records, you need to write a letter to every government agency you think might have such a record. If you are in high school, the most likely places to have collected info on you are the Army, the Department of Defense, the Department of Homeland Security, the Federal Bureau of Investigation, the Selective Service System, and the Department of Health and Human Services. Each of these agencies is required to have an FOIA office where you should direct your query. Contact information for these agencies is below—look for information on other agencies in the federal register at the library or online.

You need to write one letter for an FOIA request, and another one for a Privacy Act request, although you send both letters to the same address. The FOIA request will return all publicly available records. The Privacy Act request will return all records that pertain to you, public or private.

Before you write your letter, you might want to call the FOIA office of the agency or agencies you are interested in to ask about fees. When you are requesting your own records for personal use under the FOIA, agencies are allowed to charge you only for the cost of searching out and copying the documents. However, different types of searches have different costs, and even photocopying costs can vary from agency to agency. Since your request is for noncommercial use, fees for the first two hours of searching and the first one hundred pages of photocopying are waived. When you file under the Privacy Act, you are responsible only for copying costs. It's unlikely that a teenager will have a file more than one hundred pages long, so you probably won't have any fees, but ask anyway.

Whether you are making your request under FOIA or the Privacy

on the First Amendment Center Web site (firstamendmentcenter.org).

ALAN'S STORY

Alan Newsom is fourteen and in the eighth grade at Jack Jouett Middle School in Earlysville, Virginia.

In April 2002 I went to a weekend sports shooting camp put on by the National Rifle Association. I wanted to learn how to shoot. We learned all about how not to get hurt with a gun and how to be safe and make sure that nobody else gets hurt. We learned how to aim and to be careful and to hit the bull's-eye.

When I went back to school I wore my camp T-shirt. It's a purple shirt that says "NRA Sports Shooting Camp," and it has outlines of three men aiming firearms. One has a rifle, one has a shotgun, and one has a pistol. I wanted people to know I went to the camp. It was fun. Nobody really noticed the T-shirt, except some of my friends asked about the camp.

Then at lunch the vice principal asked me to remove my shirt. She said it was against the rules. I asked

Act, address your letter to the FOIA department or officer. Give as much information about yourself as you can: your name, your nickname if you have one, your age, your Social Security Number, your phone number, your current address, and any former addresses to help them with their search. You don't have to tell them why you want the info, but you should state that your purpose is noncommercial, because that will reduce some of the possible fees. State which act you are filing your request under, the Privacy Act or the FOIA. Keep a copy of your letter. On the outside of the envelope write "Attention: FOIA Request" or "Privacy Act Request."

Here is contact information for the Army, the Department of Defense, the Department of Homeland Security, the Federal Bureau of Investigation, the Selective Service System, and the Department of Health and Human Services. Each record includes the address and phone number (when available) of the FOIA department, the agency's Web site, and a direct link to the FOIA section of their Web site.

Army
Department of Army
Freedom of Information and Privacy Act Division
7798 Cissna Road, Suite 205
Springfield, VA 22153-3166
foia@rmda.belvoir.army.mil
army.mil
www2.arims.army.mil/rmdaxml/rmda/FPHomepage.asp

Department of Defense
(All branches of the military except the Army)

Office of the Secretary of Defense
Director, Freedom of Information
Room 2C757, Pentagon
Arlington, VA 20301-1400
202-697-1180
www.dod.gov
www.defenselink.mil/pubs/foi

Department of Homeland Security
Departmental Disclosure Officer
Department of Homeland Security
Washington, D.C. 20528
202-772-9848
www.dhs.gov
www.dhs.gov/dhspublic/display?theme=48
FBI
David M. Hardy, Chief
Record/Information Dissemination Section
Records Management Division
Federal Bureau of Investigation
Department of Justice
935 Pennsylvania Avenue, NW
Washington, D.C. 20535-0001
202-324-5520
www.fbi.gov
foia.fbi.gov

Selective Service System
National Headquarters
FOIA Officer
Arlington, VA 22209-2425
703-605-4048

what would happen if I didn't do it, and she said I would be suspended. So I turned my T-shirt inside out and wore it that way the rest of the day. I'd never been in trouble in school before, except for sometimes talking too much when I was little.

I went home and told my parents, and we looked in the school rule book and the dress code but we couldn't find anything about T-shirts like mine. My mom said I should get a petition to show that lots of people didn't think the T-shirt was wrong, so I made one. I asked my friends and teachers to sign it, but then I didn't turn it in. Some of my friends asked me not to because they thought they would get in trouble, and I did not want to get my friends in trouble.

My dad e-mailed the NRA and eventually they e-mailed us back. We are NRA members. The NRA attorney wrote to the school on our behalf and asked them to change their minds. Then the school changed the dress code so the T-shirt was against the rules. The attorney wrote again and said we were going to sue.

We filed a U.S. district court case against my school

www.sss.gov
www.sss.gov/freedomhome.htm

Department of Health and Human Services
HHS Freedom of Information Officer
Room 645-F, Hubert H. Humphrey Building
Department of Health and Human Services
200 Independence Avenue, SW
Washington, D.C. 20201
202-690-7453
www.hhs.gov
www.hhs.gov/about/infoguid.html

Once your letter has been received, the agency has twenty days, excluding Saturdays, Sundays, and holidays, to decide whether it will comply with your request and to let you know its decision. You have the right to appeal if the agency refuses to comply. If it does comply, it then has twenty more days to fulfill your request, unless it can prove that unusual circumstances apply, such as a backlog of requests. The agency may assign you a wait number.

The agency may claim it is unable to fulfill your request on the following grounds: if your request was inadequately detailed, if the material does not exist, or if the material you've requested is exempt from disclosure. If your request was inadequately detailed, you can rewrite it and refile. If the agency claims the information does not exist or is exempt from disclosure, you have the right to challenge that claim by filing an administrative appeal with a higher agency official. As a last resort, you can file a lawsuit in federal court. If you are under eighteen, have never been in foster care, opted out of the NCLB Act, and have never engaged in any political activity, it's probably be true that you don't have a file. If the agency is claiming that your file is exempt from disclosure, you might want to consider filing an appeal to see what your file contains.

When your files begin arriving, read them. Look through and note what's there. If there is anything that isn't true, you have the right to challenge it.

If you're surprised at all the data that's been collected, you could decide to do something about it, like write an editorial in your school paper, or send a letter to your local congressional representative urging him or her to curb government intrusions on your privacy. You could also show your parents the information you've gotten and ask them if they'd like to file Privacy Act and FOIA requests themselves.

For a more detailed description of how to file an FOIA request, check out the ACLU's "Using the Freedom of Information Act: A

asking for damages for violating my civil rights. Lots of NRA members gave money so my family wouldn't have to pay for it. They told me it was the most money ever given by members for a case. The attorney general of Virginia and the ACLU were also on our side, and some Constitution experts. The attorney general said that the new policy meant I couldn't even wear a T-shirt with the Virginia state seal on it, because the state seal has weapons on it (a sword and a speak).

I went to court every day for the case. It was very formal. I talked to a lot of reporters and TV cameras. I was pretty nervous, and I was surprised how many people wanted to know about the case. We were saying that my T-shirt was speech and I have a right to free speech, but the school was saying that I was being disruptive by wearing the shirt. The judge ruled against us. I felt pretty bad.

We appealed the decision and we won on appeal. That made me feel like I was right. We lost the first battle but we won the war. Now the school dress code says that NRA T-shirts and shirts with

Step-by-Step Guide," available at archive.aclu.org/library/foia.html.

THE CAMPUS ACTIVIST

Start an Alternative School Paper

If you're tired of reading a school paper that does nothing but report football scores and review movies, do something about it. An alternative school paper is a great way to let the student body express what it really thinks.

If everyone is talking about the disgusting bathrooms, but the school never does anything about them, putting a picture of one of the bathrooms on the front page of your paper can bring the issue to the fore. It's even better if you back up your attention-grabbing picture and headline with a story that reveals that bathroom cleanups have been reduced to once per month due to budget problems, or that the janitor seems to spend a lot of time out back smoking instead of cleaning up. Back up what you say—if you say the janitor is out back smoking, take pictures of him or her throughout the day to prove your point. Get copies of the school budget for the past few years to see if the budget has changed, and read the minutes of the school board meetings. Don't print anything that isn't true—free speech is protected, but lies are not.

Let people know you are starting a new paper and have a meeting to get started. At this meeting you can choose a name and discuss the kinds of things you want to put in your paper. It's up to you how you want to structure the group—you could let things happen kind of free-form, or have each person take on a defined role, like photo editor or managing editor. By the end of this meeting, try to have a date set for publication, a story list, and a date for everyone to turn in their stories. You will probably want to agree to keep meeting every week.

At your next meeting, get an update from everyone on their stories, and then turn to publishing matters. Where will you get the paper, printing, and copying facilities for your newspaper? Depending on how the club system works at your school, you could make your paper a club and get access to school supplies and computers that way— but it may curtail your ability to publish what you want to. If you want to be truly indie, you'll have to encourage everyone to use their home computers, and then ask for donations or have some fund-raisers to pay for printing.

When all the stories are in, you might want to have everyone read one another's and give feedback in a constructive way. If that's too messy, try pairing people off to do

weapons are okay. I'm going to the NRA convention this year to thank everybody who helped.

The T-shirt is actually too small now for me to wear. I keep it in my drawer. I have one like it that I've worn to school and some other NRA T-shirts. I think people should be able to wear any T-shirt they want to as long as it is not racist or vulgar or violent.

I kept going with this for so long because I knew I was right. I'm not a hero or anything, just a regular guy who fought and won. We learned about the First Amendment and our rights in school. I always thought rights were something you just got, but sometimes you have to fight for your rights.

You can read more about Alan's legal battle, and see a picture of the T-shirt, on the NRA Web site at nrahq.org/youth/enews/hqnews.asp. (Scroll down to the bottom of the page.)

it one-on-one. Have a group meeting to decide which stories are going on which page and how many pages you can afford to print. Solicit someone with some design skills to do the layout—or quickly develop some skills of your own. When you put the paper together, use images and graphics where you can so it looks exciting.

Once you've got it all laid out in electronic format, call printers for quotes. Be ready to tell them the page size, how many pages it has, what kind of paper you want it printed on (or ask them what the cheapest option is), whether it's black and white or color, and how you want it bound—folded, stapled, glued, etc. Tell them you're a small group of students doing a project, and maybe they will cut you a deal.

When you get your copies back from the printer, it's time to distribute them. If your school has an area where people leave things out, put your newspaper there, obviously. Otherwise hand them out before or after school, or during lunch period. Don't hand them out during class or during assembly.

If you're worried your school might have some issues with your paper, be clear on your rights before you distribute copies. You have a right to free speech, and a right to express your views at school, as long as you aren't being harmful or disruptive. (This is true in public schools; private schools can usually make their own rules.) The governing case for situations like this is *Hazelwood School District v. Kuhlmeier*, which was decided by the Supreme Court in 1988. The ruling says that if a paper is a public forum for student expression, then school authorities cannot censor its contents or prevent it from being distributed on campus. The only thing the school can do is control the time, place, and manner students are allowed to distribute the paper, in order to minimize disruption of the school day.

You might want to make a Web site for your paper—that way even people who don't attend your school can see it.

Knowing what your rights are is very powerful—exercising your rights is more powerful still. By creating and publishing an alternative school paper, you are demonstrating to everyone that the First Amendment is still alive and important in this country—and at your school.

THE COMMUNITY ACTIVIST

Do an Art Project About Surveillance in Your Community

How many times every day do you have your picture taken? More than you think. It's not just your friends with their camera phones—think of all the video cameras everywhere. With fears of terrorism and with ever-cheaper cameras, more and more private and public spaces are under surveillance. These types of camera systems are called closed-circuit television, or CCTV.

Try going one week and writing down every time a surveillance camera records you. You will be surprised how often you are being observed. Once you start looking, they are pretty easy to spot. Your school might use them. They are probably in your ATM lobby, the post office, elevators, malls, and department stores. Look for cameras at your job. If you go shopping, or even just get gas, look for the camera when you pay—they are often trained on the cash register. Many buildings have them mounted on the outside to catch thieves or vandals. Some parents use them to spy on their housekeepers or children. A lot of times cameras are hidden behind mirrors or in light fixtures, but if you look at them closely, and at the right angle, you will see the lens.

It is not just private entities using video surveillance. CCTV is becoming increasingly popular as a tool for the government to keep an eye on citizens. Washington, D.C., now has hundreds of cameras operating throughout the city, all feeding to a central command room. The system, installed before the September 11 attacks, is used to monitor protests and demonstrations in the nation's capitol—protests and demonstrations that are protected speech under the Constitution. New York City has also installed cameras, as a purported anti-crime measure. There is considerable resistance to this use of surveillance. In 1997 civil rights activists successfully prevented the City of Oakland from installing a CCTV surveillance system. New York City installed cameras in Times Square, then removed them when protests were held (although other cameras in New York City remain). Check the ACLU Web site (www.aclu.org) for the latest information.

Some people think video surveillance fights crime, but that claim has never been proven. One study found that those who are hired to monitor surveillance feeds quickly grow bored and often miss crimes committed on the screen in front of them. The cameras also are often used in conjunction with racial profiling, or to conduct surveillance on groups that the government or the police are suspicious of—even though they have done nothing wrong. While cameras are sometimes useful in catching criminals, they most often aid in the arrest of those who commit petty crimes such as shoplifting. White-collar crime such as embezzlement, stock manipulation, or insider trading will not be caught on videotape.

Surveillance is a civil rights issue for a variety of reasons. Under the First Amendment we have the right to associate with whomever we want. But if that activity is being recorded, some might be intimidated and refuse to attend a meeting. Under the Fourth Amendment we have the right to be free from unreasonable searches. Some civil rights groups have argued that these cameras constitute an unreasonable search—without a warrant. And of course they can be seen as an invasion of privacy.

Try making a surveillance art project. Use a digital camera (if you don't own one, you can sometimes check them out from local libraries, your school's AV room, or the local cable access channel) and take pictures of every camera you can find.

You can do a lot of different things with all of your camera pictures. You could make a big collage. You could go around town and put pictures of the cameras next to the cameras so people notice them. You could make a Web page with all of your pictures and encourage people to upload their own. For inspiration, check out Web site of the Surveillance Camera Players (www.notbored.org/the-scp.html). The group likes to do performance projects in front of surveillance cameras, and the site includes maps of several cities indicating where cameras are placed. The goal for your art piece is to let people know the cameras are out there, and to get them talking about that.

Host a Video Screening About the Fourth Amendment

Under the Fourth Amendment of the Constitution you have the right to be free of unreasonable searches and seizures. The only ways that a police officer can legally search your home or your person are with a warrant issued by a judge, if you consent to the search, if an illegal item is in plain view, if you are being arrested, or if an officer determines that he or she must perform a search because of imminent danger to life or property or in order to prevent the escape of a suspect or the destruction of evidence.

Most people are aware that they have this right, but they have no idea how to act when a police officer attempts to conduct a search. Educating members of your community about their rights will empower them to handle encounters with the police more calmly and successfully.

The civil rights group Flex Your Rights (www.flexyourrights.org) has created a video called *Busted: The Citizen's Guide to Surviving Police Encounters* that is a great explanation of every citizen's rights under the Fourth Amendment. It has demonstrations of how to exercise your rights in a courteous manner, and it also touches on your rights under the Fifth and Sixth Amendments—your right not to incriminate yourself, and your right to an attorney. Flex Your

Rights offers students the video either free or at a large discount—there is a form to fill out on the Web site to see if you qualify.

Make some phone calls to find a place to have your screening, such as a local community center, the rec room of a religious group, or even at your school. Make sure the room you get has chairs for people to sit on and the equipment you need to show the video. Reserve the room, and try to make the screening at a time when as many people as possible can attend. Weekends are ideal because most people have them off from work and school. It's important to promote your screening. On the Flex Your Rights Web site there are promotional flyers and posters for you to download and print out. Put the flyers on bulletin boards around town, in grocery stores, in coffee shops—wherever you think a lot of people will see them.

You might want to invite someone to field questions at a Q and A session after the video is over. This is a great idea because audience members might have specific situations they'd like to talk about, or someone might not have understood something in the program. You could try asking a local public defender or private defense attorney to be your expert. If there is a police oversight committee in your town, that's another option. There is a list of such groups on the National Association for Civilian Oversight of Law Enforcement Web site (www.nacole.org).

On the night of the screening, get there early and get everything set up. Greet people as they come in and ask them to be seated quickly so the screening can start on time. Make sure you have a seat reserved for your expert, if you have invited one. When the audience is seated, briefly introduce yourself and thank everyone for coming. Explain why you decided to host this screening, ask the audience members to be quiet while the video plays, and let them know that there will be a brief Q and A afterward.

When the video is over, introduce your expert. Announce ahead of time how long the Q and A period will be and stick to that. You could get the ball rolling with a question of your own if people seem shy. Try asking something like "What's the most common mistake people make when they are pulled over for a traffic violation?" After the Q and A period is over, thank everyone again for coming.

Whether your community has regular confrontations with the police or not, every citizen benefits from knowing how to act when dealing with a law enforcement officer. Educating people about their Fourth Amendment rights will ensure proper enforcement of the law and help prevent illegal searches and seizures.

THE 5-MINUTE ACTIVIST

The Electronic Frontier Fundraiser

The EFF is dedicated to defending civil rights and civil liberty in the online world. Their action center (registration required) has a "click to e-mail" area that lets you send messages to Congress on selected EFF topics, such as free speech online, preventing intrusions on individual privacy by governemnt and corporate entities, and Internet copyright issues. www.eff.org

RESOURCES

Web Sites

American Civil Liberties Union

Founded in 1920, the American Civil Liberties Union is dedicated to defending and preserving the rights and liberties granted by the Constitution. It has played a major role in nearly every major civil rights case in recent history, arguing for the right to privacy, for the separation of church and state, against segregation, and for free speech and free press. The site has good intros to every civil rights issue you can think of, with historical background and links to current cases. The student's rights section explains the rights of public school students, including information on free speech, dress codes, off-campus conduct, drug testing, and sexuality. www.aclu.org

Civilrights.org

Civilrights.org is a project from the Leadership Conference on Civil Rights, a major civil rights group dating back to the 1950s. It mobilizes major campaigns in response to various issues, using television spots and special Web sites to get the word out. Among Civilrights.org's projects are www.stopashcroft.org, an informational site about the attorney general's civil rights record, and www.fairchance.org, an affirmative action Web site. The site's research center is fantastic, with a civil rights glossary, a key to major civil rights cases, a chronology, and more. The resource section is good too, and includes some organizing manuals. www.civilrights.org

First Amendment Schools

The First Amendment Schools project focuses on the five freedoms listed in the First Amendment—religion, speech, press, assembly, and petition—and provides resources for educators and for students to learn about them and create school projects about them. It's not really an activism site, but there is an "Involve Your School" section where you can get a checklist to see how well your school does at teaching about the First Amendment. www.firstamendmentschools.org

High School Journalism

This site, put together by the American Society of Newspaper Editors, is meant to encourage teen journalists and provide support to them and to their advisors. There's a lot of "how-to" info related to putting out a paper, and encouragement to choose journalism as a career. The resource section lists many sites and publications about scholastic press freedom. www.highschooljournalism.org

Peacefire

Peacefire is a group that works to preserve the online rights of people under eighteen. Its main focus is on Internet filtering programs such as CYBERsitter, which Peacefire refers to as censoring programs. The site has a lot of information on why these programs are both inadequate and possibly harmful, as well as some ways to disable them. www.peacefire.org

PrivacyActivism

The stated goal of this nonprofit is "to enable people to make well-informed decisions about the importance of privacy on both a personal and societal level." The site has a news section that links to current stories connected to privacy issues. The surveillance section is really amazing, with stories about everything from spyware and camera phones to RFI tages, which some retailers are considering using to track their products. There's also "Carabella," an interactive game about college students and privacy. (It's better than it sounds.) www.privacyactivism.org

Restrictions to Free Speech Online

This site has a good overview of the various issues connected to your right to speak your mind on the Internet. It goes through the relevant laws and provides good working definitions for "obscene" and "indecent." www.kwc.org/memorylane/tjhsst/fapage/topics.html

Student Press Law Center

The SPLC provides resources and free legal assistance to student presses. The site is an amazing resource for anyone interested in the rights of student journalists—a good place to start is "The Student Press Law Center's High School Top Ten

List: The ten questions high school student journalists most frequently ask about their rights." Additionally, there are legal guides, research tips, and a news feed of stories related to student presses. www.splc.org

U.S. Commission on Civil Rights

This office exists to investigate complaints from citizens who are being denied the right to vote or being denied equal protection under the law because of race, color, religion, sex, age, disability, or national origin. It also does educational campaigns about discrimination and civil rights, and produces a lot of reports on current civil rights issues. The reports are all collected on the Web site and make for interesting reading—see how the government is grading itself on enforcing its own laws. Of particular interest is the March 2004 report about issues of tolerance and justice since September 11, 2001

www.usccr.gov

The U.S. Constitution Online

Just like the name says, it's the entire text of the U.S. Constitution, plus every amendment, up on a Web page and accessible to anyone. The site also has the Declaration of Independence and clear explanations of things like the electoral college and how a bill becomes a law. Worth bookmarking.

www.usconstitution.net

Books

The Complete Idiot's Guide to Your Civil Liberties
By Michael Levin

The name says it all—this book has everything you could possibly want to know about your civil liberty, including where they come from, why they matter, how you can exercise them, and how you can't. It's all written in that chunky "Idiot" style and completely indexed, so you can just dip in when you want to instead of reading it cover to cover.

Eyes on the Prize: America's Civil Rights Years, 1954–1965
By Juan Williams

A fantastic history of the civil rights movement in the late 1950s and early 1960s. It's filled with lots of pictures, firsthand accounts, and a companionable narration by Williams, a television news correspondent. It's the best book out there on the subject.

Freedom's Children: Young Civil Rights Activists Tell Their Own Stories
By Ellen Levine

The role that many children and teenagers played in the civil rights movement is finally told in this collection of stories. Thirty youth activists who fought segregation facing ignorance, threats, and violence recall what it was like to be on the front lines of the civil rights movement while they were still under eighteen.

The Rights of Students: (ACLU Handbook for Young Americans)

By Eve Cary, Alan H. Levine, and Janet R. Price
The American Civil Liberties Union has been fighting for and protecting our civil rights for more than eighty years. This book details students' rights under the Constitution, with historical information, examples, expert analysis, and cites to relevant court cases. Whether your concern is dress codes, drug tests, locker searches, keeping your records private, or off-campus conduct, the answer is in here.

Promoting Tolerance Toward Lesbian, Gay, Bisexual, Transgender, and Questioning Youth

THE ISSUES

What does "lesbian, gay, bisexual, transgender, and questioning" mean? It's an umbrella term sometimes used to refer to people who don't identify as heterosexual, and it's usually shortened to LGBTQ. You're probably clear on what "lesbian," "gay," and "bisexual" mean, but the other terms may be less familiar. "Transgender" is a term that refers to a variety of identities and behaviors, including transsexuals, intersexuals, and androgynes. "Questioning" is generally used to refer to people who are just that: questioning—not sure where their sexuality lies on a spectrum of possibilities. (And some people never settle on one spot forever; human beings change over time, and many aspects of their identities may as well.)

LGBTQ is a cumbersome term, but it's useful in that it attempts to be inclusive of many different sexual orientations and identities. It's not perfect, and it's very politically correct, but it's in fairly common use. Sometimes people will use "gay" by itself as a kind of shorthand for the spectrum implied in LGBTQ. Another word you'll hear a lot is "queer." "Queer" (also used in this book) has more of a political edge because it's being reclaimed. Instead of a word that is derisive and hostile, it is becoming one that is affirming and proud. Some people also prefer to identify as queer because it's a more open term and allows for possibilities beyond LGBTQ.

It's worth asking why all of these people, or groups of people, are often lumped into one class. The short answer is that they all challenge traditional or restrictive definitions of sexual and gender identity. Their very existence calls many ideologies into question. Additionally, these groups share many of the same civil rights and human rights issues. In America, lesbian, gay, bisexual, transgender, and questioning citizens are not truly equal and accepted. They don't enjoy full civil rights, are subject to discrimination and harassment, and are sometimes victims of violent hate crimes.

For teenagers who identify as LGBTQ, these problems are often compounded by a hostile atmosphere at school. On average, an American high school student hears twenty-five anti-gay remarks every day. A survey of LGBTQ students found that eighty-four percent report being verbally harassed at school. Most LGBTQ students report that they feel unsafe at school and that the faculty and staff are unresponsive when they ask for help. A quarter of them have missed school in the last month because they felt threatened.

The average age of "coming out" in America is sixteen—down from twenty about five years ago.

While this may reflect a cultural trend toward increasing awareness and acceptance of gay identity, it also brings the issues relating to LGBTQ teenagers to a critical level. By identifying as queer while still in high school, teenagers expose themselves to discrimination and harassment at a much younger age, and often have far less access to support groups and resources than those who are over eighteen. Gay and lesbian teenagers may lose the support of their family and friends when they come out. They are sometimes forced into so-called reparative therapy that attempts to "cure" them of their sexual identity or orientation. They are more likely to become depressed and have substance abuse problems, more likely to run away from home, and more likely to attempt suicide than their straight peers. Even students who are straight, but who are perceived as gay by bullies, suffer from homophobia in and out of school.

High schools and middle schools are generally rigid when it comes to gender roles or sexual identities. Anyone who doesn't fit in—a feminine guy, a butch girl, an out bisexual, a drag queen—messes up the system. For these students, being themselves, being visible as themselves, usually means drawing untoward attention and harassment.

Transgender youth are in an especially treacherous situation. Their "otherness" can be more difficult to hide than that of a gay, lesbian, or bisexual student, and that increases their risk. There is very little information available on transgender youth, because their high-risk status means that they often hide their identities, even more than gay youth. It's important that soon all calls for diversity include acceptance of these teens, and that the silence surrounding their lives is broken.

Queer kids can have difficulties getting good health care. Any teenager can find it difficult to discuss his or her sexual activity with a health care provider—for LGBTQ teens it's especially hard. They often don't know if their privacy will be protected, or if they will be treated differently or perceived as "abnormal."

For LGBTQ teenagers who haven't come out to themselves or to friends and family, things can be even more lonely, confusing, and complicated. There are a variety of reasons for not coming out, with fear of repercussions being a common one. Additionally, not everyone has a moment of truth when he or she realizes "I'm gay" or "I'm attracted to girls and to guys." Often there is a period of months or even years of soul searching and questioning. Being in the closet can reinforce a sense of isolation, and it makes reaching out to others who might be in the same situation or who might offer support even more difficult.

Activists are responding to the growing needs of LGBTQ youth in a variety of ways. Established gay rights organizations and support groups are creating youth programs and reaching out to high schoolers and middle schoolers. Civil rights groups are helping teenagers who have been victimized fight back in the courts, calling for anti-discrimination laws in more states, striking down discriminatory laws that are still on the books, and challenging further infringements on the rights of queer youth. Some activists are dedicated to education reform so that sex ed classes will include topics such as homosexuality and transgender issues. Special health initiatives are targeting LGBTQ youth with information on how to get health care that addresses their issues, and ways to reduce risk and practice safer sex. Over two thousand high schools now have gay/straight alliance clubs, which are on-campus groups dedicated to reducing hostility and homophobia at school.

If you choose to become an activist working to promote tolerance toward LGBTQ youth, whether you are lesbian, gay, bisexual, transgender, or straight, you can be proud that you are helping to create awareness and acceptance of others. We all benefit from living in a world with less hate in it.

HIV/AIDS is an important issue in the gay community, and it is discussed in a separate chapter in this book. Major gay rights organizations often work on HIV/AIDS and other communicable disease issues, and many HIV/AIDS groups are primarily gay identified; but HIV/AIDS is not a gay disease. It affects everyone. See Fighting the Spread of HIV/AIDS for more.

"That's so gay."

Many students may be using homophobic language without even realizing it—or they realize it but deny it. Referring to something uncool as "gay" or calling someone you don't like a "fag" or a "dyke" is not okay. This usage is equating homosexuality with something negative. If you've fallen into these habits, it can be difficult to train yourself out of speaking this way, but it's important. The next step is to challenge other people when they use these terms derogatorily. Try saying, "When you say that you think this assignment is gay, do you mean that it's stupid? Why not just say that?" Let people know using these words pejoratively isn't acceptable.

THE AT-HOME ACTIVIST

Talk to Your Parents About an LGBTQ Issue in the News

Even the most open family can consciously or unconsciously exclude LGBTQ issues from its conversation topics. Initiating a discussion on a topic you think will interest them can be a great way to break that taboo and to find out how they feel about things that are important to you.

It's up to you to decide if you want to take the step of launching this conversation. If your parents are extremely homophobic, or if you are just uncomfortable discussing these things with them, there are many other ways you can support the LGBTQ community. If you are gay, or questioning, and you aren't out, raising some of these issues might be something you want to wait on until you have figured out what's going on with you, and how open you want to be about it with your family.

Picking something in the news is a good way to launch the conversation. Gay marriage is a great idea. Other topics could be a new gay/straight alliance club at your school, your local state representative and his boyfriend, or even why tabloids are so obsessed with who is gay and who is not. Whatever topic you choose, make a list of the points you want to make, and be sure to be open to what your parents have to say. Remember that your goal is to have an honest and respectful discussion. Your parents might not see things your way immediately, and perhaps you will never be in complete agreement. But talking to them about one specific topical issue, if you feel comfortable doing it, is a great way to affirm your own beliefs and to learn about theirs.

Let's say you decide to talk about gay marriage. Here's some background information on the issue, though you should do more research on your own. Good sources for up-to-date information on this issue are the American Civil Liberties Union (ACLU) and People for the American Way Web sites (www.aclu.org and www.pfaw.org).

On November 18, 2003, the State of Massachusetts declared that denying gay and lesbian couples the right to marriage violates the state constitution. In February, 2004, the mayor of San Francisco, Gavin Newsom, decreed that his reading of the California state constitution allowed gays and lesbians

SARAH'S STORY

Sarah Alcorn is eighteen, and a senior at Boyd County High School in Ashland, Kentucky. She lives in Catlettsburg, Kentucky.

In the spring of my sophomore year, spring 2002, we decided to form a Gay/Straight Alliance at my school. It grew out of our human rights club. We decided that homophobia was a really big issue in our school and that we couldn't address it through the human rights club because we had so many things going on. We needed a place where we could support kids whether they were LGBTQ or just straight allies.

Our school is pretty small, about a thousand people. It's a very rural community and people are pretty secluded here. It's a traditional community and a very religious region. Kids have been raised here with the idea that prejudice is okay, and they're not used to different lifestyles. They're not used to people being different, or to diverse ethnicities or sexual orientations. It became a big issue when we realized how

to marry, and authorized his local city hall to perform marriages between same-sex couples. Gay and lesbian couples from around the country rushed to the courthouse to be wed. There are now injunctions barring these states from performing more same-sex marriages, while the Massachusetts State legislature and the governor of California fight to prevent gay marriage in their respective states.

On February 24, 2004, President George W. Bush endorsed the Federal Marriage Amendment, which would change the Constitution of the United States to declare that marriage can exist only between a man and a woman. This goes much further than the 1996 Defense of Marriage Act, signed by President Clinton. The earlier law said that the federal government would not recognize or provide benefits to same-sex couples. The proposed constitutional amendment actually bans same-sex marriage in our country. Civil rights and gay rights groups are banding together to fight the Federal Marriage Amendment with petitions, letter-writing campaigns, protests, and demonstrations.

It's easy to see why this is an important issue for same-sex couples. Married people are socially accepted. They sometimes enjoy tax breaks just for getting married. Married people can get on each other's health insurance policies without a hassle, legally adopt children together in every state, and have visitation rights in hospitals, as well as various other benefits.

Many states have what are called domestic partner acts, which provide some of the benefits of marriage to couples (both gay and straight) who choose not to marry. A few states (Vermont and Hawaii among them) allow for "civil unions," which is a legal construct that says that couples who enter into civil unions should enjoy the same benefits as married couples. LGBTQ activists continue to insist that they want full marital rights, while political, religious, and other groups continue to oppose them vehemently.

Pick a time when your parent or parents are able to pay attention to the topic. It might be a good idea to bring a newspaper clipping to jump-start the discussion. You could say something like, "I was just reading about how our senator supports the Federal Marriage Amendment, and I was wondering how you feel about that."

Chances are, the first thing they will say back is, "Why do you ask?" so be prepared. Explain that you are concerned about civil rights for all people, and that you think that LGBTQ couples deserve to have the full suite of rights that everyone else has in our country. It could be good to use an example—something like, "If you got sick and Dad couldn't visit you in the emergency room, that would be awful. I wouldn't want that to happen to anyone."

many people were getting harassed at school on a daily basis because of sexual orientation or perceived sexual orientation. People were being verbally and physically harassed to the point where they felt like they couldn't come to school anymore. A couple of kids dropped out of school because of it and didn't graduate. The administration was looking the other way.

We made out an application to start the club and submitted it to the Site Based Decision Making Council. The council is the governing council of the school, just below the school board. It's two parents, three teachers, and the principal. The application said that we wanted to support the LGBTQ students at our school and create an environment of safety and social awareness. We had about thirty students who said they wanted to be in the club. The SBDMC said that we had submitted our application too late and so we had to wait until the next fall. So we applied again in the fall and we were denied again. They said that the Human Rights club could cover what we wanted to do.

It may be that your parents aren't fully aware of all the issues surrounding gay marriage. Here are some points you could make:

A civil union is not the same as marriage—it does confer some rights, but not the full suite that marriage does. Furthermore, civil unions performed in one state may not be recognized in another state, whereas marriage licenses do cross state lines.

Same-sex marriage doesn't hurt anyone. Two lesbians or two gay men standing up and affirming their relationship doesn't take anything away from families, churches, communities, or America. It in fact contributes to all of these things by creating another stable and happy family unit.

Same-sex marriage doesn't open the door to polygamy or other unconventional marital arrangements. These same fears existed when interracial marriage was first being legalized, and no negative consequences have ensued. Same-sex marriage is merely an extension of this basic right to one more type of couple.

It might be a good idea to connect your feelings on this subject with the values your parents have taught you. If it's appropriate you could say, "You've taught me to respect other people and to always fight injustice, and my support for this issue is in line with those beliefs. I want to thank you for giving me the conviction to have this conversation with you."

If the discussion goes well, and your parents agree with you that same-sex marriage ought to be legal, you might want to ask them to send letters to your state representatives affirming your family's support for same-sex marriage. You could have the letter drafted in advance, or create one together. Here's a sample letter:

Dear elected official:

I am a voter and taxpayer in your [district, state, etc.].

I am writing to tell you of my support for same-sex marriage and my firm belief that it is necessary for our country to extend the right of marriage to everyone, including same-sex couples. I am against the proposed Federal Marriage Amendment, and I hope that you will vote against it. I will be sorely disappointed if you choose to ignore your constituents and support this bill. You will certainly lose my vote and many others.

You may claim that although you don't support same-sex marriage, you do support civil unions. But you must know as well as I do that domestic partnerships do not convey full equal rights in our country. Registered domestic partners cannot file taxes as a couple. They cannot inherit each other's Social Security benefits. They have to

When we were applying the second time, word had gotten out in school that we were doing this. Kids started to wear shirts to school that said "God made Adam and Eve, not Adam and Steve." It didn't seem like it was that big of a deal. It was just some T-shirts and kids who were being rowdy and things like that. And there were other kids, who weren't even part of our group, who had shirts that said "God loves everyone" and "God accepts all people" and things like that and they had rainbows on them and things. It was really surprising.

In October we applied for the third time. The meeting was held in the auditorium because there were so many people there. There were tons of people on the opposing side-ministers and teachers and students and parents and all kinds of people who were in opposition to the GSA. And then on our side there were a few people but there weren't nearly as many, and there were news cameramen, all kinds of journalists and things like that. A newswoman asked me if I was scared, and I said no, but I think we were all pretty scared.

spend countless hours and a great deal of money on complex forms to codify the kinds of rights heterosexual couples get automatically upon marrying: emergency room visits, inheritance of property, medical power of attorney, access to insurance benefits, and the like. This is inherently unfair.

Our history shows that "separate but equal" systems are in fact deeply unequal. Domestic partnership is not an adequate substitute for marriage. Any system short of marriage for all is simply discriminatory.

I realize this is a touchy political issue, but injustice is injustice. Now is the time for courageous, principled leadership. I hope you will speak out in favor of equal rights on this issue, loudly and frequently. This is rapidly becoming a top priority voting issue for me, and for many of the people I know. We will no longer tolerate half-measures that condone injustice. Please join me in taking a stand for equal rights, so that I can be proud to have you as my [senator or representative].

Thank you.

Sincerely,

On the other hand, the conversation might not result in you and your parents finding you have the same views on gay marriage or your topic of choice. Try not to be too discouraged. You've still done something valuable by raising the issue. You've affirmed your own beliefs, you've gotten practice in discussing an LGBTQ issue with someone who has an opposing viewpoint, and you might have nudged your parents just a little way down the road to having a more open mind about your position.

THE CAMPUS ACTIVIST

Start a Gay/Straight Alliance at Your School

The majority of LGBTQ students say that they feel unsafe at school. A gay/straight alliance, or GSA, can help them to have a better environment in which to learn, can promote tolerance throughout your school, and can educate the student body and faculty about LGBTQ issues. It's up to you what your GSA decides to do. Different GSAs have different focuses, and the focus of a group can change over time.

Here are some of the things a GSA might do:

Have social events (bowling, coffee, etc.) that provide a fun and safe time for LGBTQ students and their friends

Have supportive discussion sessions in which students can talk about their emo-

Before the meeting we had gotten in contact with the ACLU. They sent a letter to the SBDMC saying this is the law and this is why you have to approve the Gay/Straight Alliance. If our school was going to have any other clubs, then under the Federal Equal Access Act, the council had to approve the GSA as well. When the council got that letter I think they finally started to get the message that we weren't joking. There was a law and they couldn't break it just because they didn't agree. So at the very end of that meeting they did approve the GSA.

That's when all the hoopla started. It was like parents standing up, saying, "I'm going to take my kid out of school" or "What does GSA stand for? Why do we need this? If this is going to happen then we don't need clubs at all." Then you had students standing up, saying, "Well, we do need clubs to do extra stuff to go to college..." It just turned into a riot. We had to be escorted out.

The meeting when we got approved was on Monday, October 28. The next day more than four hundred students, almost half the

tions, sexuality issues, incidents of harassment, and other personal problems

Organize educational programs within the school, such as leafleting or teach-ins, that will help the student body at large learn more about LGBTQ youth

Lobby the school administration for a sex-ed and health curriculum that includes LGBTQ issues

Work to make the school a more tolerant space by declaring it a "hate free" zone, and urging students and faculty to sign a diversity petition

Protest incidents of harassment and report them to local authorities and the media

Connect with larger LGBTQ groups to attend pride events and gay proms, and get involved in national and state LGBTQ issues

It's up to you if you want to make your GSA a school-sponsored club or not. Being in the system can get you resources and make everything easier, but there are good reasons to go indie, too. If your faculty is hostile to the idea or if you know that the group won't get school sponsorship, you might want to start the group off-campus. That way you can coalesce as a unit, set some goals, and get organized—then your first action can be to lobby for inclusion in your school. (See Sarah's Story, in this chapter, to read how hard some Kentucky students had to fight for their GSA to be accepted by their school).

Having appropriate adults involved is a great idea, though. If you can't find a faculty advisor who is the right fit, try getting a guidance counselor, a social worker, or a local activist to join you occasionally. Depending on your group's goals, such adults can help you to take concrete steps toward them, and to avoid wasting your energy on less productive projects.

Here are some tips for having a vibrant and productive GSA:

Make sure your GSA is inclusive, to gays and straights, of course, but also to all ethnicities, to younger classmates, and to children of gay and lesbian parents. Always be welcoming to anyone who shows up for a meeting or who wants to talk to you about the GSA.

Be responsive to the needs of your group. You may want to go to a pride parade and party, but others might be in crisis and need a safe space to talk or find some counseling resources.

Don't try to do too many things at once. Set reasonable goals, and break those goals up into small, achievable steps. Give everyone something to do.

school, stayed home. Two days later, Wednesday, October 30, was my sixteenth birthday. I got to school and it felt different. I get to school early, and they don't let people stand outside but I noticed a collection of people who had begun to stand outside.

I went inside and I went to our advisor, Ms. King and I said, "I think something is going on; I'm not really sure what it is but I think something is about to happen." Then I went to walk to homeroom, and as I was walking by the door I heard people yelling "If you go in you're supporting the faggots" and "If you go in you're supporting the GSA and we don't want these faggots in our school." Terrible, terrible things. I saw my best friend out there and I thought she was with them, and I was devastated.

It turned out later that my friend had just been trying to get in and got caught and couldn't come inside. I don't think anyone had organized the boycott. I think it just happened. Some kids were like, hey, this would be cool to do. Nothing really bad happened that day. They moved the protestors out to

Set regular meeting times—it's the best way to ensure attendance and keep the group from disintegrating. (Bringing food to a meeting is good too.)

Write a mission statement. It doesn't have to be a step-by-step enumeration of your projects. It should be a broad statement about why you've come together, your desire to promote tolerance and diversity, and your belief that your club can contribute to the campus and the community by promoting these values and educating people about LGBTQ youth.

Hook up with other groups—in school and out. You might want to have a representative from your group on the prom committee, for instance, in order to make sure that all of the prom literature doesn't emphasize heterosexual couples. Local social organizations can offer you support, meeting space, or other resources. You can look on some of the Web sites at the end of this chapter to find listings of groups to approach.

Let the world know about your GSA. Designing a cool patch, button, or sticker will solidify you as a group, and also let other knows that you are proud to be a member of it. Representing for your GSA can spark conversations on campus, at home, and around town, and remember that every conversation is an opportunity to talk about the things that matter to you.

Register your GSA with some of the national networks for gay/straight alliances. They will connect you to like-minded youth all around the country and provide encouragement, guidance, and ideas for campaigns and activities. The two main ones are the Gay-Straight Alliance Network (www.gsanetwork.org) and the Gay, Lesbian, and Straight Education Network (www.glsen.org).

Assess Whether Your School Is Safe for LGBTQ Youth

The group Parents, Friends and Family of Lesbians and Gays, also known as PFLAG, recently launched its Safe Schools Project. It has put up a survey form at www.pflagsafeschoolsassessment.org that you can print and fill out. The survey asks for data on your school and your community, and then goes on to ask questions about whether your school has a nondiscrimination policy, if the library provides LGBTQ resources, and so on.

Once you've filled out the survey, you will be able to see clearly what your school's strengths and weaknesses are in relation to supporting the needs of all its students, not just the straight ones. You can then propose changes to make your school safer for and more tolerant of LGBTQ students.

PFLAG is also collecting filled-out surveys for a national census on school climates, so you should also mail or fax in your results, or take the survey online to submit it electronically.

the parking lot. Some of the kids started to come inside. By the end of the day it seemed like it had blown over and it wasn't such a big deal.

Then, the following Sunday, there was a big community rally against us. There were over a thousand people at the church, which is right across the street from our school. These were ministers and parents and community members who wanted the school to fight us, who wanted the school to not let this happen. They were collecting money to help with legal fees for the school in case a lawsuit happened, which hadn't even been discussed at that point. But if it took a lawsuit, these people were ready to help.

There were people lining the streets, parked up and down the streets, and it was chaotic. I drove by in my car and I just kinda watched people, old and young, walking down the streets to this rally. They brought in a man from California who had written a book about how homosexuals had caused the Holocaust. He was saying if you're going have a Gay/Straight Alliance you might as well have Marlboro club and Nazi club and . . .

THE COMMUNITY ACTIVIST

Make a Voter Guide

Even if you aren't old enough to vote, you can affect elections by educating voters on the issues you care about. Many people go to the polls without being fully aware of the voting records of the people for whom they are voting, or of what the ballot measures really mean. A voter guide is a pamphlet or flyer that provides this kind of information.

Make sure to get started on your voter guide well ahead of the election date. You'll want to be able to gather all the pertinent information and distribute it before people go in to vote. But don't distribute it too early—people might read it and forget it, or put it aside to check out later and then lose it.

A voter guide lists all of the races (local, state, and national) that will be on the ballot, as well as any proposals and measures. Then it recommends to voters how they should vote in each race and on each measure, based on the perspective of the guide's creators. Your voter guide will be built around the issue of LGBTQ rights, but you could make one for any issue or viewpoint.

Call your county clerk's office and ask them to send you a sample ballot so you'll have all the names you need. Next you need to research the candidates to get information on which to base your recommendations. You want to find statements the candidates have made on the subject of gay rights, or their voting records, if they've held office before.

Doing the research on all of the candidates in an election year may prove to be exhausting. You could enlist some friends and split them up, or decide to focus your voter guide on only national offices or only local races.

A great research tool that will help you is Project Vote-Smart (www.vote-smart.org). Project Vote-Smart is a nonpartisan, nonprofit group dedicated to educating voters in order to create a more informed citizenry. On their site you can get detailed information, including biographies, position statements, and voting records for officials at the presidential, congressional, and state levels. You can access all of this information just by entering your zip code. (The site also has information on how to register to vote, and many other cool things.)

Project Vote-Smart only provides information on politicians already in office. It will help you research incumbents who are running for election, or those in office who are running for higher office, but not newcomers to the political races. It also doesn't have a lot of information on local officials or

just all this ridiculous stuff. It was unreal to see all these people rallying against a handful of kids.

In the meantime the club was trying to meet. A lot of the meetings focused on how to document harassment and make sure that everyone was doing okay, because there was so much going on around us. There were so many people yelling and fighting us. We had some speakers. One was one of the kids who dropped out of Boyd County High because he had dealt with so much harassment over the years. He said that if he'd had a GSA it would have helped him a lot. We had a minister come in and speak, and other supportive people came in and helped us. There was usually a big turnout, over thirty people at every meeting.

The other thing that was going on was a lot of back and forth over the status of the club. There were some opponents who tried to say the club wasn't needed because the school had proposed curriculum that taught tolerance. But their curriculum would also teach that homosexuality is wrong. The ACLU fought this. Our

local campaigns. To research the candidates who aren't on this site, call their offices and ask for position statements, copies of speeches, and their biography. Go to the library and look up articles that have been written about them and where they stand on the issues you care about.

Even with all of the research in front of you, it can be hard to decide which candidate to endorse. Let's say the your local state senator is running for reelection, so you check out her record on gay rights.

A search of his or her public statements and voting records brings up that your senator supported the No Child Left Behind act of 2001. Many LGBTQ activists oppose the NCLB act because, among other things, it mandates Internet filtering for schools (which may prevent LGBTQ students from finding needed resources online). It also requires schools to notify parents if they are conducting an anti-bias or anti-harassment seminar, so parents can keep their children from going to the event. So it might seem bad that your senator voted for it.

Then again, you see that your senator spoke out in favor of allowing gays to serve openly in the military. Additionally, your senator has been endorsed by several major gay organizations.

So do you recommend voting to reelect this senator or not? First you have to look at the records of the other candidates in the race.

Your fictitious senator's opponent is a local businesswoman who has never held office before. She's been politically active in the state, and her commercials and posters are all over town, but they provide very little information on her viewpoints. You get all the literature you can from her campaign headquarters and read transcripts of her speeches and interviews. For the sake of this example, let's say that you find that the challenger is against gay marriage, and when a local gay couple tried to adopt a baby, she spoke out against it.

Suddenly your incumbent might start to look better. It's ultimately a judgment call that you have to make based on your research and your best guess as to who, in your opinion, will do the most good and least harm while in office. You can issue a qualified endorsement, such as recommending the reelection of your senator with a call to repeal the NCLB Act.

After you've finished getting all of your endorsements together, it's time to create the actual guide. You can do it on your computer with a word processing program or a fancier page layout program. Use both sides of the paper, and experiment with layouts that allow you to fold up the page into a brochure size. Make it readable, but also try to get as much information as you can into the space you have. Print out your voter guide and then take it to the local copy spot for duplication.

school's administrator kept going back and forth on everything. Finally in December the school board voted to ban all clubs in the district.

We had no idea this was going to happen. It was over winter break. One day I woke up and read the newspaper and all clubs had been banned. Ms. King called me and we were in shock. It was a really bad time.

In January Fred Phelps announced he was planning to come to our town. Fred Phelps is a hate minister. He is based in Topeka, Kansas and he travels the country and preaches hate. Mainly for gays but also for anything in general. He's just a hate minister. He's well known because he was at Matthew Shepard's funeral and he had a sign that said "God hates fags."

Phelps was having a big rally in Ashland about our club. So the Ashland Human Rights Commission decided to have a rally that same night to promote peace and unity and show that Ashland is not a community of hate and things like that. They asked us to come and be ushers. So we went, even though it was kinda scary to be across the street from

Estimate that it will cost about twenty dollars to make four hundred copies.

Distribute your voter guide at the local library, at coffee shops, at the movies, and in supermarkets. Some places will let you leave a stack of pamphlets, but it's always better to hand them out personally if you have the time. Some people will refuse the pamphlet, and some might toss it after a glance. Don't be discouraged. If you educate just one or two voters, you've made a difference.

After the election, check to see if your candidates won. Consider writing to them to tell them about your endorsement and that you hope they will continue to support gay rights. You could also write to candidates you didn't support, and encourage them to be more open minded.

RESOURCES

Web Sites

The National Youth Advocacy Coalition

NYAC is a membership-driven group dedicated to improving the lives of LGBTQ youth. Their site has a legislative update center with interfaces for you to write to the media and your elected officials about issues such as promoting condom use and the rights of transgender youth. The group's other work includes building an activist infrastructure to support a national youth movement, working on various social justice issues, supporting youth leadership, and getting better health care to LGBTQ youth.

www.nyacyouth.org

The Human Rights Campaign

The Human Rights Campaign is America's largest gay and lesbian rights organization. Their Web site's action center has lots of options that are quick and easy. You can make an activist Web page, send letters to the editor, and more. There's also a great tool for finding local media—you just enter your zip code. While you're there, look at the comprehensive and thoughtful guide on coming out. www.hrc.org

American Civil Liberties Union Lesbian and Gay Rights Page

This page has up-to-the-minute news on LGBTQ issues being fought in the courts or the legislature. They've also got good fact sheet pages on things like same-sex marriage, discrimination, and free speech, as well as some action alerts. This site is really good because they explain what things like Lawrence v. Texas mean, not just in legalese, but in terms of what they mean for you. www.aclu.org/LesbianGayRights/LesbianGayRightsMain.cfm

Fred Phelps, who you know just, like, hates you. He just exudes hatred. Even though we were going to be across the street from this man that hated us tremendously we thought we should go.

We were wearing, like we always do, our buttons that say "Ally," and they've got a little rainbow on them. We also had on stickers that said "Gay rights are human rights," and we had all kinds of different stuff all over our shirts. I walked up to the woman who had asked us to usher and said, "We're here, we're ready to do what you need us to do." She looked at me, and she said "You can't usher if you're going to wear that." So I said, "Well I guess we're not ushers." She was like, "This is supposed to be neutral . . . blah blah." I told her, "I think I'm speaking for all of us when I say we're not about to be ushers then. This isn't important enough for us to back down from what we've worked so hard for and the beliefs that we have defended." So that night we weren't ushers. We just got in our seats. Our advisor and some of the students were on the stage, and they got passed over, they weren't introduced.

Association of Gay and Lesbian Psychiatrists

This is basically a professional association for psychiatrists who want to foster understanding about their LGBTQ patients within the psychiatric community, but it does have a referral list if you are looking for a psychiatrist who is gay-friendly.
www.aglp.org

Bisexual Resource Center

This site is a big Web portal for the bisexual community, with an emphasis on the Boston area. It also sells tons of bisexual books, bisexual videos, and bisexual music!
www.biresource.org

The Blackstripe

This site for LGBTQ of African descent (the title is a reference to the gay pride rainbow symbol) is being updated as of June 2004, but you can still browse the archive, which has a huge amount of cultural information. There are great articles, including an amazing one about the lesbian and gay contribution to the American civil rights movement. Check out the Blacklist, an index of LGBTQ blacks and Africans throughout history.
www.blackstripe.com

Children of Lesbians and Gays Everywhere

Better known as COLAGE, Children of Lesbians and Gays Everywhere has been around since 1990. (It was originally known as Just for Us, and still publishes a magazine with that name.) The site has a variety of support options, including joining a COLAGE chapter or getting a pen pal through their network. COLAGE also has resources for children of bisexual and transgender parents, scholarships, queer family lingo, and more. www.colage.org

The Cool Page for Queer Teens

An individual, Scott Bidstrup, who has dedicated a lot of time to making a place that's friendly and really useful for gay teens, created and maintains this site. He's got links everywhere, stories from real kids, and a conversational style that makes the site a bit warmer than some organizational sites or sites that try to use "teenspeak." He also has a whole site just for parents. www.bidstrup.com/cool.htm

The Gay and Lesbian Alliance Against Defamation

GLAAD is dedicated to seeing fair representation of LGBTQ in the media. They call senators on anti-gay statements, organize boycotts of homophobic radio

We were confused because we weren't told that it was going to be neutral toward the GSA until we walked in the door. We were under the impression that this was supposed to be against Fred Phelps, who was against us. So what were they there for? Fred Phelps was across the street making a mockery of our city and our school and holding up vulgar signs—ugh, completely obscene.

After that we had a press conference. People asked us all kinds of questions about what we thought about the rally and what we thought about Fred Phelps. We had to be honest and say we didn't really understand what the rally was for because they were preaching peace and unity yet they weren't supporting us. We were the whole reason that Fred Phelps was in our community. So it was kinda confusing. It was a very confusing time.

When school started again, it turned out that some clubs were still meeting. The school district was letting some clubs get around it because of some loophole. The Future Farmers of America were still meeting, Beta (which is an honors club) was still

DJs, and meet with network representatives to help them incorporate more positive images of gays in entertainment media. It may seem like a losing battle, but download one of their accomplishment sheets and you'll see how much of a difference they've actually made.
www.glaad.org

Human Rights Campaign
The front page makes it look like it's another site focused on legislative stuff (important, but not so interesting all the time), but drill down and you'll find lots more. There's a comprehensive and thoughtful guide on coming out and a great action center where you can make a Web page, send letters to the editor, and more. There's also a great tool for finding local media—you just enter your zip code.
www.hrc.org

International Gay and Lesbian Human Rights Commission
The mission of this U.S.-based nonprofit is to document and respond to human rights violations made on the basis of sexual orientation. The organization works with communities to end abusive practices and laws, build coalitions, and effect positive change. Reading its news page provides a sobering look at the status of LGBTQ and HIV-positive people worldwide.
www.iglhrc.org

National Gay and Lesbian Task Force
The Task Force is a thirty-year-old progressive

organization operating on several fronts. Among other things, it supports grassroots organizing and coalition building, it has a think tank, it trains activists, and it promotes legislative solutions to discrimination on both the national and local levels. The issues section is really strong—you can click to the youth page to see information about youth and campus organizing, or look up what you are interested in by topic.
www.ngltf.org

The New York City Gay and Lesbian Anti-Violence Project

Just like the name says, the organization is dedicated to preventing anti-gay violence, helping the victims of anti-gay violence, and prosecuting those who commit hate crimes. There's a twenty-four-hour bilingual hotline (212-714-1141) and good safe-dating guides that cover online and offline relationships.
www.avp.org

meeting, and Drama. We said this is not right. If they're still letting the other clubs meet and we can't meet, then they're breaking the law because they've established this rule and they're not abiding by it. So that's when we decided to file the lawsuit. The ACLU filed the suit in federal court in January, saying that the decision to ban clubs violated our rights under the federal Equal Access Act and the First Amendment. The lawsuit also asked the court to issue a preliminary injunction so we could meet until the lawsuit was settled.

In March there were two days of hearings for the injunction. Our witnesses were ourselves and their witnesses were everyone they could find. They took teachers and administrators and all kinds of people who sat on the stand and made us look like we had done something wrong. Teachers that we trusted, people that we had trusted with things that we had said. . . . It was bad.

They were claiming that we caused disruption so they had the right to keep us out of school. We had to watch all these teachers that we knew really well get up there and say, "Well I really loved

The P.E.R.S.O.N. Project

This is a grassroots network of people who want their communities to provide unbiased education that acknowledges and supports diversity in sexual orientation. (P.E.R.S.O.N. stands for Public Education Regarding Sexual Orientation Nationally.) There's a great handbook about organizing to reform K–12 public education and a comprehensive resource list.

www.personproject.org

Parents, Family and Friends of Lesbians and Gays

PFLAG is a support and advocacy group for family members and friends of LGBTQ. The site has a great introduction to gay issues and information on how to come out, as well as how to deal when someone comes out to you. PFLAG also supports documentaries about LGBTQ families and does community education projects.

www.pflag.org

Queer Resources Directory

The directory is an electronic library dedicated to information and publications about sexual minorities. It's all organized by subject, but within each subject you could come across anything from an Oprah transcript to a flyer in PDF format. Be warned that it also stores some anti-gay literature—its position is that it helps to give a complete picture. The site does not have erotica, though. You can also submit your own stuff for listing.

www.qrd.org

Transgender Forum's Support Group Database

This is a free page within the TGForum, which is subscription-based and costs money to access. Among the free offerings, though, is the support group list, where you can enter your zip code and find a group near you.

www.tgfmall.com/info/search.html

The Trevor Project: Saving Young Lives

The Trevor Project is dedicated to preventing suicides among LGBTQ youth. It has information on the signs of a possible suicide, advice for those in crisis or trying to help a friend, and a twenty-four-hour suicide hotline (866-4-U-TREVOR). The group also created the Trevor Educational Package, a learning tool available to schools who want to create awareness and provide support to students of every sexual orientation.

www.thetrevorproject.org

YouthResource

YouthResource is an offshoot of

so and so but . . . this is what they did wrong."

We learned a great lesson while we were in court about honesty, dignity, integrity, and maturity. And that just because you're an adult, it doesn't mean that you're grown up. We learned a lot from court. It was one of those things where not many people have had that experience, especially when you're so young. For us to have to go through that-it was really hard. All of us, it's been really hard for us to go through. But we've learned a lot and we especially learned a lot from court and now I know a lot about the law.

In April the judge announced that we got the injunction and we could meet, but the school board wanted to continue with the lawsuit. We were like, oh no. For a long time we thought we would have to go to court. We were scared because we didn't want to go to court again and we were tired. It had been exhausting and emotionally we were just drained, and we didn't know how much more we could take. We really wanted a settlement, and we finally got one in February 2004.

We got pretty much

Advocates for Youth, a group that works to ensure that young people get the information they need to make informed choices about their sexual health. This site is specifically aimed at LGBTQ youth and those who want to support them. There's a peer education section, tons of health info with everything from safer sex to what to do if you or a friend is cutting, and online communities for lesbian, gay, and bi youth, including a community for young gays of color and deaf LGBTQ youth.
www.youthresource.com

Books

Families Like Mine: Children of Gay Parents Tell It Like It Is
By Abigail Garner

Garner's parents divorced when she was five years old, and her father came out soon after that. The book tells her story and the stories of many others who were raised by one or more gay parents. She resists portraying the experience as wholly positive or wholly negative, and instead goes into the challenges, joys, irritations, and epiphanies of life as a "culturally queer" heterosexual.

Free Your Mind
By Ellen Bass and Kate Kaufman

Free Your Mind is the book a lot of gay youths cite as their "gay Bible." It's an excellent sourcebook, with advice from experts and peers on topics from coming out to spirituality and how to connect with the gay community. It also has practical information for friends and family of gay youth on how to talk with and support their loved ones.

Growing Up Gay/Growing Up Lesbian: A Literary Anthology

Edited by Bennett L. Singer
This is a cool collection of more than fifty stories, poems, and excerpts from longer pieces about growing up gay. Some are by contemporary youth, and others are by famous authors such as Jeanette Winterson, James Baldwin, and Audre Lorde. It's good reading that may inspire you to write yourself, or to seek out other works by these writers.

Is It a Choice? Answers to 300 of the Most Frequently Asked Questions About Gays and Lesbian People

By Eric Marcus
If you've got questions about homosexuality, they're probably answered here. Marcus is informative, easy to read, and expansive on topics ranging

everything we wanted in the settlement. There are trainings now that are going to be held every year at school. It's anti-prejudice training in general with an emphasis on sexual orientation. We have the right to meet and we have the name Boyd County High School Gay/Straight Alliance. The only thing they got is that we have to meet after school, not during school or before.

I think things have changed. I know that not only the school but also the people in the community are more aware of the environment that our school had, the amount of tension and homophobia. Not even just homophobia-racism and just prejudice in general that circulates through our school. But I can honestly say that this past year, while I've been a senior, the environment in the school hasn't been anything like it was in the past. You used to walk down the hallway and people would scream "faggot" at you if you were gay or if they just thought you were. People still use slurs and homophobic remarks like "that's so gay"—that's one of the worst—but it's definitely died down. I haven't heard any more direct blows at

from gays in the military to how to tell if you're gay. This is a great book to have and a necessity for your school library. There's a newly revised edition, so try to get that one if you can.

Telling Tales Out of School: Gays, Lesbians, and Bisexuals Revisit Their School Days

Edited by Kevin Jennings

This anthology of essays by LGBTQ adults talks about their experiences as students. Some of them were out in school and some weren't—they look back and talk about how their high school and middle school lives are affecting them now. The stories are painful but offer a lot of insight into why it's so important to reach out to gay youth now.

Two Teenagers in Twenty: Writings by Gay and Lesbian Youth

Edited by Ann Heron

This is an update of a book that came out about twenty years ago called *One Teenager in Ten*. Both books are collections of autobiographical narratives by young gays and lesbians across the country. These heartfelt stories document struggles with homophobia, unresponsive parents, and broken hearts, but overall the book is emotionally affirming as each writer comes to self-acceptance and sometimes even joy. Heron includes advice on contacting social service organizations, as well as a list of books that deal with gay and lesbian issues.

When Someone You Know Is Gay

By Susan and Daniel Cohen

This book is aimed at straight teenagers. It's got lots of answers to questions about LGBTQ issues, plus historical and social information about homosexuality. The authors promote tolerance and respect without being preachy.

people of different sexual orientations or perceived different sexual orientations. I haven't known of any really extreme cases of harassment that have been based on sexual orientation.

I think the best thing that we've gotten out of this is awareness. Even if tolerance hasn't really come about that prominently yet, we've definitely got awareness. Hopefully we can just keep teaching tolerance and more things will come in the future. I think that people in this community—it's so based on tradition. For such a long time they've taught generation after generation to just think the same things and believe that it's okay to make fun of someone who isn't like you. Hopefully we can break that mold. I think that's what we've tried to do, is just break the mold, and even if we can just crack it a little bit, it would be great.

To read more about the legal decision the Boyd County High School GSA won, and what it means for their school, visit www.aclu-ky.org/news.html

STACEY'S STORY

Stacey Jensen is nineteen and recently graduated from Castro Valley High School in Castro Valley, California.

When I was sixteen and a sophomore, I got caught smoking pot. They sent me to a drug assessment program to see if I needed to go to rehab or anything. The program was at a place called Project Eden, in Hayward, California. It's a youth counseling center. In the drug assessment the counselor asked if I was gay, and I said, "Actually, yeah, I think I am."

She was the first person I really talked to about it, and then I came out to my best friend a couple of weeks later. The counselor told me that Project Eden has a thing called Lambda and that it was a group for gay kids to kind of get together and express themselves. They could be totally open or whatever without being afraid of any judgement. I started going to the meetings every week.

At first I was nervous and scared. There were about twenty kids there, from all over. Some kids would even come from San Francisco, forty-five minutes away. There was this one girl who would always talk a lot so it made me not want to talk a lot because she was the bigshot and stuff. But then I got to know people and it was fine.

There's a check in at the beginning and you go around the circle and everybody says their name, their age, where they are from and just how their week had gone. Sometimes we would have a topic or an issue, like when a transgender youth from our area went into a party and got shot and killed. But most of the time it was just how your week went. After that part people would start to mingle outside and that was how I got to meet everybody. You kind of just got to kick it there and hang out and really see who people were. It was a lot of fun.

During my junior year they asked if anyone wanted to join their speaker's bureau. I was interested, because I love to speak, and I thought if my being out is going to help somebody, I might as well help somebody. I went to one training session at GLSEN (The Gay Straight and Lesbian Alliance Network) and then we had another one back at Lambda. They told us about the California law AB 537 which says that you can't judge any students or staff on the basis of their sexual orientation or their sexual identity.

Back at Lambda we had a meeting with Christine. She had each of us partner up and we had to practice saying our story to somebody. They said to decide which are the important parts and don't say too many extra details. You don't want to take up too much time because you want to let the kids ask questions at the end.

The first time that I spoke was at my own high school, to the teachers. I was extremely nervous, especially because they all knew me. It was just weird. But they wanted parents of gay kids to talk to, so I got my best friend's mom to speak with me. She told her experience and her side of the story so I had her there to help me through it all to and that was pretty cool.

The teachers were open to what I had to say. They said, "I understand what you went through now and how you act and why the way you are." They asked different questions, like anything I'd left out of my story. One teacher actually told us his own story about his son coming out to him. He said that he was really upset at first and then eventually he opened his mind, he had to because it was his son. I explained about AB537 too.

I'm glad I did it, because our school had a lot of homophobia and ignorance. The year before there was a boy in the boy's locker room and somebody went on his locker and wrote "You Faggot" and stuff and they pissed on his locker. It was never reported or anything and no one ever said anything about it. It was just put under the carpet and nobody knew about it. That was the type of school it was.

I also spoke a few times at Bishop O'Dowd, a big Catholic high school. The first time I went I was nervous because it was in front of students so I didn't know what to expect, not to mention it was a Catholic school. It was actually good. I just told my story about my coming out to my family and my mom and my dad and everybody and their reactions and everything. At first they didn't know how to respond, but then they started raising their hands and stuff. They were like "So what happened after your dad said that?" They want to know more of the story. They get interested, and they learn, and once you learn about something you're not afraid of it.

At Lambda we also work on the Gay Prom. It's a prom for all the gay students in the area who want to come, so they have a prom if they couldn't go to theirs as a gay person. Maybe they had to go with somebody of the opposite sex just to hide their identity. This is an opportunity for them to be who they are, and it's a big party. Because of AB 537, schools are not allowed to discriminate against gay couples, but I have heard of high schools who try to hide it and who try to say no don't do it.

I actually went to my regular prom too. It was the first time that any same sex couples went. I went with my girlfriend, my best friend went with someone from another school, and there was a guy couple, too. It was weird at first because everybody started when we first walked in but eventually they got used to it and had to deal with it. There was nothing they could do about it.

Gay prom was almost twice as much fun though, because they had a game room. I loved it. It's basically to educate you about your health, and STDs and stuff. They have like a beanbag toss and you toss a beanbag on something and you've got to answer a question. Or they've got a fishing one with a magnet and it picks up a question and you've got to answer it and then you get a prize. They also have all the things like a regular prom: dancing, a photographer, refreshments, and prom royalty, except it's like Queen and Queen and King and King, all this different stuff. I got best-dressed last year, I was like the Emperor and my friend got Empress. It was an awesome night.

Being out and not being afraid to be out, it makes you more self-aware. It allows you to see yourself and understand yourself better as a person. I'm happy that I did work that helped people to accept themselves and to help people be more accepting of others.

To learn more about AB537, visit www.gsanetwork.org/ab537; to learn more about LAMBDA visit tk; to learn more about gay prom, visit www.gayprom.org

Acknowledgments

I love teenagers. There is no other time in life when we are so passionate, so open to new ideas, and so willing to stand up for what we believe in. Teens wield great economic power—their tastes have enormous influence over fashion, music, and even the cars we drive. But what about their political power? Too often their political ideas and desires are treated with derision or put on hold until they are of voting age. That's stupid. Teenagers have a right to speak out and to have access to the marketplace of ideas just like anyone else. I hope that this book will help and inspire some of them to step up and fight for what they believe in.

There is no way I could possibly thank all the people and organizations who have helped with this book, but I will try to name a few. Jennifer Klonsky, my editor at Simon & Schuster, kept the various aspects of the project in line throughout the process and patiently waited for copy; 17th Street Productions helped me sell the book; Neal Hoffman, Marjorie Ingall, Jack King, Lucas Shapiro, and Farai Chideya read various chapters and provided invaluable feedback. Amy Richards, Marcelle Karp, Gina Magid, Annemarie Iverson, Jennifer Dalton, Johnny Temple, Ingrid Eberly, Elizabeth Wallace, Wendy Shanker, Dakota Smith, Jody Berger, Jennifer Baumgardner, Jill McManus, Sia Michel, Tanya Selveratnam, Jennifer Braunschweiger, and Gloria Fisk all helped just by being themselves—

my amazing friends never cease to inspire me and to support me in every endeavor.

Some specific thanks go to Judith Newman, Casey Ellis, Kate Schram, and Katherine Hardy for their help with fund-raising. Sharon Heilbrun worked tirelessly to help locate and interview the many wonderful teenagers in the book and helped with the resource listings. Pat Delaney and Crystal Bahamie transcribed, and Matthew Caws provided key emergency technical services.

In writing the book, I had make some hard choices. There were so many teenagers doing so many fantastic things that I could not possibly have gotten them all into one book. Here are some of the activists I spoke with but unfortunately could not include: Aaron McGee, Anna Jakimuk-Chu, Linh Dao, Mercedes White, Molly Birnbaum, Nick Ellenberger, Mark Sandford, Shannell Walker, Lizz Petroff, John Wood, Sara Trunzo, Igor Volsky, Jasmine Chauca, Kate Amos, Lucas Hartstone Rose, Jeff Konen, Antonia Dublin, Jamaal Thomas, Jessica Santiana, Naomi Gordon-Loebl, and Lee Huber.

The activists who do appear in the book are describing their lives and their experiences in their own words. I interviewed them on the phone, transcribed the interviews, and then sent them the final copy for approval. Special thanks to all the parents of activists under eighteen who agreed to let their kids appear in the book.

Many organizations helped with time and resources: The Tony Hawk Foundation, NARAL, Kitty Kind, Choice USA, the Lambda Youth Project,

YouthBloc of New York, the National Youth and Student Peace Coalition, the Young Democratic Socialists of America, the AWID Young Women and Leadership Email List, the Marin AIDS Project, Students Against Violence Everywhere, the Teen Pregnancy Coalition of San Mateo County, Kids First, the Student Peace Action Network, FIERCE!, Youth United for Community Action, and Tolerance.org, among others.

And there's more! Many thanks to Marty O'Shea at Longmeadow High School, Carleen Wray, C. C. Sapp, Aziza Ahmed, Elizabeth Kolodny, Tamar Rothenberg, Christina Cappelletti, Kris Popplewell, Jaishri Abichandani, Steve Hawk, Hector Ibarra (the most amazing science teacher in the country), Nora Gelperin, Sam Grabelle, Denisse Andrade at the Urban Visionaries Film Festival, Garrett Wright, Jill Davidson, Eliot Levine, Misty Moysse at MADD, Sabrina Smith, Michelle Ferrer, Laura Flaxman, Alexandra Ringe, Tamara Rothenberg, Pauline DeMairo, George Wood, Paul Shapiro, Lee-Li at YUCA, Barbara Battle at amfAR, Sue Treiman, Kristy Evans, La Fawnda Williams, Lisa Provence at The Hook, Amanda Guma, Gin Ferrara at Wide Angle Media, Emily Bieber from the NYC Gay and Lesbian Anti-Violence Project, and Brian Willoughby for taking time to answer my questions and help me track down elusive leads.

While I was writing this book, Sarah Jacobson died. Sarah was a filmmaker, a writer, an activist, and my friend. I miss her more than I can really explain, and I only hope that I can live up to the standard she set for honesty, enthusiasm, and truly believing that the world is on the verge of being a better place.

Finally, I have to thank my mother. Even though I was mortified when she put an "ERA Yes" sticker on our station wagon when I was in elementary school, she has always been my activist role model—and I wouldn't be who I am today without her. Thanks, Mom, for the *Ms. Magazine*s and the marches.

General Activism Resources

Web Sites

ACT UP New York

You can read more about this radical AIDS activist group in the chapter "Educating Others About HIV/AIDS"—it's listed here because of all the information they provide about civil disobedience and how to plan a demonstration. The Demonstrator's Manual has great advice on how to plan a protest (like when you need a permit and when you don't), plus info on what to do if you do get arrested. The Civil Disobedience Manual has a history of nonviolent action, tips on how to organize a campaign, an explanation of consensus decision making, and more.
www.actupny.org

Creative Action

This site is a project of a group called Facing the Future—they work on global issues like poverty, governance, and hunger. If you are interested in any of the topics they work on, the site has great resources: quick sixty-second tours, in-depth analyses, and bibliographies to learn more. Of use to any activist: their Action Toolbox, which has lots of fund-raising ideas and media tips, including things like a press release template.
www.creativeaction.org

Institute for Global Communications

IGC used to be a group that provided technology services for many different grassroots organizations—now they've scaled things back a bit and run four major Web sites: PeaceNet, EcoNet, AntiRacismNet, and WomensNet. Each of these sites has articles, a newsfeed, and links to other related sites. The really good thing on the IGC site is their Advocacy Tips section. It has links to organizations that support activist work via online training, how-to publications, and advice for nonprofits. www.igc.org

The Just Cause Law Collective

Hopefully you will never need a lawyer or ever do anything against the law, but many innocent people still end up having interactions with law enforcement officials. It's really important to know your rights so that you can protect yourself from any abuses or misunderstandings. The Just Cause Law Collective has a good section on the rights of minors on their site. (Did you know that a parent, teacher, or police officer has no right to compel a minor to answer questions? Only a judge can.) They used to have a good activist's handbook on this site also, but it's gone now. www.lawcollective.org

NetAction

Founded in 1996, NetAction was one of the first Web sites launched in order to take advantage of the Internet's political potential. They have an online publication called *The Virtual Activist* that goes over some ways to do organizing and outreach online—but be aware it's aimed at non-techy people, so you might skip over a lot. They used to have a newsletter about technology-based social and political issues that seems to have ceased publication in 2003, but the archives are up on the site and worth reading. www.netaction.org

Organizers' Collaborative

The Organizers' Collaborative is a group of activists and technology experts who work to help other activists get the technological tools they need to create social change. Their site has a great tech-tips section with everything from how to set up a listserve or research a foundation, to how to buy a good cheap computer. The site also has a comprehensive resource section that relates to technology and social change. www.organizenow.net

Protest.Net

Protest.Net is a clearinghouse for activists to list their marches, demonstrations, and other events. Of course it's useful for finding details about something you plan to attend, but it's also inspiring to browse and see what's going on all over the world. You can search by topic, date, and geographical location. A recent search found a youth activism training camp in Yellow Springs, Ohio, and a demonstration about tuition hikes in Stuttgart, Germany. Protest.Net also has a great section called the Activist's Handbook, a collection of previously published articles about why we become activists, why activism is important, and tips on being a better and more effective activist.

www.protest.net

SERVEnet

This site has a huge database of what they call "service opportunities"—anything from joining an organic gardening collective in Germany to working at a county fair fundraiser for an AIDS organization in Colorado—for those aged fifteen to twenty-five. You can plug in your personal info and get suggestions, or browse through the whole thing to see what appeals and is doable. They use a lot of language about "service" and "volunteerism," but the options here really are activism.

www.servenet.org

www.SoundOut.org

www.SoundOut.org is specifically dedicated to promoting student-initiated change within schools. They don't tell you what to do, but they will help you do it, with resources and connections to other youth with the same goals. Whether you want to help more minorities in your high school go to college, get childcare on campus, or fight against high-stakes testing, the site is a great place to see how others have met similar challenges and defeated them. There isn't a lot of actual how-to advice, but some good links.

www.soundout.org

YES!

This is a group dedicated to supporting young activists. The two people who started it do a lot of speaking tours to talk about activism, but the main thing at YES! is the Jams. A Jam is like a big convention of young advocates—they get together and exchange stories, develop strategies, and form networks and friendships. You can get information on upcoming Jams on the site. The site also has a good resource section with articles about social justice, why we become activists, and links to some student-run organizations.

www.yesworld.org

YouthNOISE

YouthNOISE is the teen site of the Save the Children Federation, and it's one of the best known teen-oriented political sites out there. They've got a lot of issue-oriented stuff—opinion pieces, polls, background info, and easy-to-do action alerts— and some stuff that's useful no matter what your cause, such as a fund-raising section and a place where you can enter your zip code to find volunteer opportunities in your area. The best resource is the tool kits, which have tons of tips and how-tos on everything from how to write a good letter to a politician to how to conduct a sit-in. The tool kits are kind of hard to find (try clicking "Take Action" and then look on the left under "Change the Rules") and to navigate, but it's worth all the poking around.

www.youthnoise.org

Youth Venture

Got an idea for a project that will help your community? Hook up with Youth Venture and they might give you a thousand bucks to get started. They are a nonprofit that supports teenagers who have civic-minded ideas—and that means anything from a bike store to a juvenile diabetes support group—with tools, resources, a great community, and cold hard cash. This is a great place to go if you know exactly what you want to do and are ready to launch it now.

www.youthventure.org

Books

The Activist's Handbook: A Primer Updated Edition with a New Preface

By Randy Shaw

Every activist, experienced or novice, will benefit from Shaw's book. He discusses the origins and history of grassroots organizing, with examples from across the country, and then goes on to give insightful, practical, and strategic how-tos for you to create your own political movement—global or local. The chapter on dealing with the media is especially strong.

Fundraising for Social Change

By Kim Klein

If you want to go beyond the bake sale or the car wash to get the money you need for your project, Klein's book is a useful introduction to the world of fund-raising. She covers everything from cold-calling phone solicitations to direct mail, pointing out the pros and cons of every strategy and giving good instructions on how to launch your own fund-raising effort.

Future Active: Media Activism and the Internet
By Graham Meikle
Meikle is a university professor, but he has written an accessible and interesting book about online activism. The book's strength is in his inclusive view of activist work: The book includes profiles of hackers, Czechoslovakian Net radio producers, and the organizers of a virtual sit-in. Meikle provides a balanced take, avoiding both rah-rah futurism and anti-technology cynicism.

The Global Activist's Manual: Local Ways to Change the World
By Mike Prokosch and Laura Raymond
Although this books is nominally about anti-globalization activism (it grew out of the 1999 Seattle protests), it's really useful for anyone interested in local activism. There are forty-five stories of various activist projects, both successful and unsuccessful, including several youth-led actions. The book also has a great tips and strategies section and a glossary.